Fashionable Noise

On Digital Poetics

Brian Kim Stefans

a t e l o s

14

Cover photo credit: "RGB" is a light object created by Invisible
Light (www.invisiblelight.org); photography Cindy Stefans
(www.cindydesignstudio.com). The photograph is used with the
kind permission of the artist

First edition, first printing

 Atelos

A Project of Hip's Road
Editors: Lyn Hejinian & Travis Ortiz
Typesetting and Design: Travis Ortiz
Cover Design: Ree Katrak

Fashionable Noise

On Digital Poetics

Table of Contents

Notes and acknowledgments

This book collects various writings from the past several years loosely centered around the theme of "digital poetics." The notes below, besides their bibliographical value, should help explain how to approach some of the chapters, each of which has some element of a *game* to it.

Material supplementary to this book, including source texts, programs, text-replacement algorithms and related writing by myself (and T.S. Eliot), can be found at www.arras.net/fashionable_supplements.htm.

A slightly different version of "potentially suitable for running in a loop"originally appeared in the "Visual Poetics" issue of the Canadian journal *Open Letter* (Eleventh Series, No. 2, Summer 2001).

"Reflections on Cyberpoetry" is based on an essay by T. S. Eliot called "Reflections on *verse libre*" (1917), revising the older essay line by line but attempting to retain as much of the original essay as possible. It first appeared, without the marginal notes, in the "Cyberpoetry" issue of *Open Letter* (Tenth Series, No. 9, Fall 2000).

The first draft of "Stops and Rebels: a critique of hypertext" was written in 1996, and was intended to tweak a university professor who seemed to me over-enthusiastic about hypertext. The present version is much revised and expanded, but the persona of the original footnotes—that of an over-zealous student attaching an eclectic array of "lexia" to an over-burdened poem—remains. The poem was generated by a computer program and originally appeared in my book *Gulf* (1998).

A much earlier version of "Proverbs of Hell" was presented at the E-Poetry conference at SUNY Buffalo in 2001. The first half of the second version of this essay appeared in print in the "Cyber Poetics" issue of *Object* (No. 10, Winter 2002, available at www.ubu.com), edited by Kenneth Goldsmith. This is its third incarnation, and, with a nod to Christian Bök, I've rendered each verse 575 characters long (not including white spaces). The first and last sentences of each verse is one line of Blake's "Proverbs of Hell." The images previously appeared as part of a web collaboration with Kim Rosenfield called "The Truth Interview," commissioned for the how2 website (www.departments.bucknell.edu/ stadler_center/how2/), and which can also be seen at www.arras.net

"When Lilacs Last in the Duir" was originally written for Michael Scharf's "Metromania" column that appeared in the magazine *Poets & Writers* but my article (not originally in Scots) was rejected on the grounds that it was too "cheeky." The article made it's first public appearance as part of Steve Evans' "Third Factory" series of critical writings (www.umit.maine.edu/~steven.evans/). This "synthetic Scots" version was created using an algorithm and various dictionaries. No attempt was made to honor historical, geographical, or class differences in the vocabularies used.

"A Poem of Attitudes" was constructed by scanning in several pages of notes for poems that I had amassed over several months and then running various (very simple) algorithms and programs on the texts. Over the course of one day, December 5, 1999, I reworked and reordered sections of the output to create the present poem.

I'd like to thank several of the people directly responsible for the writing and publishing of these essays or who provided me valuable feedback: Darren Wershler-Henry, Loss Pequeño Glazier, Kim Rosenfield, Kenneth Goldsmith, Michael Scharf, Stacy Doris, Rob Fitterman, Travis Ortiz, Lyn Hejinian, Scott Pound, Sianne Ngai, Miles Champion, and Lytle Shaw.

This book is dedicated to the members of the Ubuweb listserv, past and present, male, female and mineral, who have been most supportive during the writing of it and who can be partly to blame for whatever deleterious effects it might have.

> Dinosaurs in movies
> no longer move jerkily;
> I stand by you
> for scale. Let us
> sit down. Our friend has left
> a blue lamp,
> an identity experience, Irish
> when the emergency comes.
> — from "Perpetual," Jean Day

"potentially suitable for running in a loop"

ICQ Chat Sesssion

Participants: Brian Kim Stefans [BKS], Darren Wershler-Henry [DWH]

Description: potentially suitable for running in a loop projected on a wall

Created On: Sunday, March 18, 2001

"potentially suitable for running in a loop"

[DWH] Can you read this?

[BKS] Yup.

[DWH] Great. Only problem with the Mac version of ICQ is I don't see any 'record' function on the menu...

[BKS] Hmmm, well, I have it set up. Hopefully that's good enough. Just REMIND me to export the session after we're done. Meanwhile, I'll see if saves are possible. Let's go.

[DWH] We know from your introduction to The Dreamlife of Letters that it's a response to a Rachel Blau Du Plessis text which is, in turn, a response to a Dodie Bellamy text. We also know from the intro that you perceived a similarity between the Du Plessis text and early concrete texts by the De Campos brothers and Eugen Gomringer (on a formal basis, at least). You mentioned to me earlier [in a version of this discussion that crashed out before we could successfully record it] that you had done several computer treatments of the Du Plessis text before you started to edit and lay it out in Flash. My question was: what happens to a text's syntactic, thematic feminist politics when it get chopped up in such a manner? Does the political effectiveness of the writing increase as the disjunctions you're creating start to reveal the discursive formations that are informing the language (in the wake of his reading here last week, I'm thinking of Bruce Andrews' articulation of his own work in terms of the Brechtian v-effekt) OR IS THE POLITICAL EFFICACY OF THE WRITING DILUTED ALONG WITH THE LOSS OF SEMANTIC COHERENCE (sorry, didn't mean to yell there… hit the Caps Lock key by accident).

[BKS] No prob, figured you got tired of graphemic cleanliness. Anyway, I felt that the Du Plessis text, which was produced in the context of a 'forum' on sexuality and literature, ended up, by its opacity, leaving me with no room to reply, which is why I ran the computer processes on it. If you'd seen the original text, you'd know what I mean; it wasn't discursive, but a classic 'word salad'. By slowing her text down, isolating a few key terms, creating some different juxtapositions, I think I performed something of a v-effekt on her text (which I link to). I don't claim to be a radical feminist myself, though perhaps when drilled, my ideas would be as 'radical' as anyone's. So I wasn't necessarily thinking of the piece as working on the trajectory of trying to further a thematized feminist viewpoint, just accessing those energies; meanwhile, I felt that I was adding something to the pool of available 'thematics' for concrete poetry. I couldn't say whether my piece is more 'political' than, say, Bruce's work—it probably isn't. Certainly I think along his lines, though I have misgivings about how Brechtian poetics has been utilized in explaining his writing, since Brecht, to my mind, had a 'positive' vision of a political ideology, or at least a coherent ideology or set of behaviors that he aspired toward, and Andrews seems to be negative in this sense, a program of 'de-socializing'. Though he would argue (and we've talked about this) that Brecht himself was not pushing a coherent ideology but was also 'negative' in this sense. Anyway…

[DWH] This particular kind of interaction with the work of other authors—building Flash 'translations' of existing works—seems to be unique to your practice right now; the latest instance of a computer-treated collaboration between you and the text of another author, Chapter E of Christian Bok's Eunoia [<www.chbooks.com/tech/books.cgi?bk=eunoia>], works along similar lines. Do you think that the medium of animation in general, maybe even Flash in particular, is particularly helpful in revealing aspects of a text that might otherwise go unnoticed?

[BKS] That's interesting, never thought of it that way about Flash, though concerning poems I've created with C++ programs that was in my head (I wrote about this in 'Stops and Rebels: a critique of hypertext'). When I first started doing work with computers and poetry, my initial inclination was to form a 'group' of some sort, like the TRG (big group!). I don't know why that was, but I felt like Stockhausen in Cologne, or the Columbia electronic music guys like Ussachevsky, Luening and Davidovsky, in that I felt that ideas would really start to proliferate with some critical mass, with text/computer interaction being the object of our research (of course that never happened, or at least not pre-Ubu List). I think of creating Flash poems as something like a musician setting a text to music, which is to say that when I do Flash pieces I'm very happy not having to think too much about the text as I go along, and don't mind that it's not my text—I'm just the composer.

[DWH] So is it a dialogic act or not?

[BKS] Yes, in a sense, except that I haven't run any of my 'translation' pieces by their authors prior to completing them, but it is a dialogue with the author through the text and, in this way, a critical or editing act, in the sense that you mention earlier, as I am revealing some aspect of the text that might not have been seen otherwise. One would have to think of the interface as textual itself, a sort of idiom or 'speech genre', for it to be truly 'dialogic'. Christian's equal-length paragraphs, for instance, would obviously create a particular effect in a book, but in Flash, with those slow fades and the possibility of overlaying several paragraphs at a time, a different type of interaction with the ten-line full-justified prose form is 'revealed', though to what end?

[DWH] I have an idea about that, actually, and this takes us back to Dreamlife and its visual allusions to classical concrete. In a sense, Dreamlife realizes a potential that classical concrete suggests but never achieved, i.e. animation (except through analog means, like flipbooks, some crude early films, and slide projections... I saw some of these at the De Campos festschrift at Yale in 1995), but they're nothing like the kind of smooth animation that's now possible on the Internet.

[BKS] I thought of the Ballet Mecanique when I was doing Dreamlife, too, especially, or maybe exclusively, of the Charlie Chaplin man at the beginning, which was such a cheap thrill of sorts.

[DWH] Well, that makes sense in terms of talking about 'scoring' someone else's work... the Ballet Mecanique was impossible to perform as scored before the advent of computers, so maybe there's an analogy to those early concrete poems, as a potential literature waiting to be actualized.

[BKS] Do you mean that the score was impossible because what's-his-face didn't have airplane propellers available?

[DWH] Antheil couldn't perform the Ballet Mecanique (and no one else could, either) becaUSE IT REQUIRED AN ENORMOUS NUMBER OF PLAYER PIANOS OPERATING IN SYNCH (small keyboard on my laptop—sorry), and that was impossible to achieve before computer switching [see <www.antheil.org>].

[BKS] Anyway, I think what you're saying is absolutely true—I felt like I was trying to 'channel' some of those early dreams of, say, Bob Brown and his poetry machine, or the De Campos brothers (when they did get to computers, it seemed pretty wrong, at least what I saw, like the 'La Bomba' poem or whatever that is), or even Tschichold in The New Typography (in his quest for agreed-upon norms, which I would call a Flash 'prosody'—a counter to the 'avant-garde' messiness of much constructivist-oriented web poetry), which may have to do with the 'retro' feel. It's nice to have no tradition, but it's kind of cool to have one that simply has been ignored, at least on this side of Niagara Falls.

[DWH] Yeah, the thing about the animated De Campos work is that it really has that kind of isolated feel that's produced when cultural mandarins decide to mess with pop—sort of like trying to get Henry James to play air guitar; the results are embarrassing for everyone.

[BKS] I have this sense that concrete poetry in the States is that secret source for the most frustrated poets for their sense of individuality or aesthetic singularity, meaning that there are tons of concrete poets in the states who seem to be patriotic about it to the detriment of their understanding of, say, lyric poetry, or the historical breadth of the work.

[DWH] I've had some extremely unpleasant run-ins with people like Bob Grumman, and I get the same sense from Richard Kostelanetz, that these guys have been working away for so long in their basements that they've lost track of what it was they were trying to do in the first place, and have drifted off into a kind of 'no one understands the significance of my work' headspace.

[BKS] Definitely, and now that computers are around, what are those folks doing?

[DWH] Not very much, at least not online. There are a few collections of static stuff, like on Ubu and elsewhere, but there are so few people in the writing community (including the concrete community) that are willing to engage with their machines. I think this is because there's a large luddite element to the poetry community, partly out of political convictions, but also perhaps due to economic reasons—a lot of poets don't have much money, which is a fair cop—but that doesn't explain the hostility that electronic poetry engenders.

[BKS] I know from what you've told me in conversation that you've had to hear a lot more about that than myself, i.e. the economic element. Of course that's true, but I don't think that applies to, say, Kostelanetz, who I know does work on television sets, say about ten running in some sort of synch, which must be costly. Anyway, I'm interested in the 'luddite' argument since I feel that there is a belief, even among concrete or strongly 'word-centered' poets we respect, that the 'ontological status' of the poem as visual sign is threatened by digitization.

[DWH] Well, my feeling is that there's an imperative to engage with online poetry, because the website is the first truly new mode of poetic composition that's come down the pipe in a long time. The alternative is to abandon the medium to the advertising people. Poets need to be literate in all the forms of composition that their culture affORDS THEM (NOT ALL OF THEM, OF COURSE, BUT AT LEAST SOME). Shit. Sorry.

[BKS] Don't worry about the caps... unless you want them for effect. The issue of advertising is interesting. Consider Christian's response to Dreamlife, which I had anticipated with my phrase (for a projected blurb): 'I'll never look at movie credits that same way again'. I think that it's very, er, 'healthy' for a digital poet to try to learn the moves that the advertising or design industry have made, in the sense that a good rock musician might want to learn some Mozart or Elliot Carter, or whatever—there's no need to make animated poetry always look like it's coming out of the basement, and after all advertising culture has produced many virtuosos—idioms proliferate there. On the other hand, being in New York, I have a natural hostility to 'web artists' who are really earning tons of money making Flash stuff by day, 80 hours a week, and making web art that is perfectly innocuous, glitzy, cute, etc. I don't make any money doing Flash, though of course I anticipated possibly getting a nice job once I started learning it—not yet, though.

[DWH] Okay, right, we're living in the middle of late capitalism, and everything that signifies can be sold, as bpNichol once observed. A couple of points follow from this: your work will be commodified, period, and the only thing you can do to stave that off (if you choose to do so, which some people don't) is to keep moving, keep making new interventions... which may well include getting a job in webvertising, design etc., and doing your creative stuff on the company dollar (we all know people who've done this). The question of 'dirty' vs. 'clean' concrete is another matter; I'm not sure 'dirty' is meaningful at all when you can control everything on a pixel-by-pixel level... Scan in the nastiest, grungiest piece of Xerox art, and it's immediately transformed into this other thing, because of the new (digital) context.

[BKS] Yes, but there is, I think, a way of at least suggesting the 'dirty', mostly through programming. For example (though this contradicts what I'm saying since it's not 'programming'), in the intro bit to Christian's piece, the words 'Christian Bok' come in all screwed up, first a block of letters, then a 'Bo' then finally a 'k', then the whole word 'Eunoia', then 'for Rene Crevel' comes in a few letters at a time, and disappears entirely before the final ')'. This was not the way it was intended to look; I had set up a 'mask' layer to reveal the letters one at a time—like on a computer screen, in the way you are seeing these letters appear now (i.e. as they're typed)—but there was some sort of glitch in Flash that didn't let me do it right. It's the easiest thing in the world, I knew I had it, but it came out screwy, so I let it stay that way since I liked that. I like programming 'glitches' into interactive things, or letting them stand—Christian thought it was a glitch when the text started flying around when you pressed one of the buttons...

[DWH] 'It's Not A Bug, It's A Feature' as an aesthetic statement?

[BKS] ... Yes, exactly—

[DWH] That was what I was trying to deal with in some of the pieces in NICHOLODEON, particularly 'Deskjetsam', but the response to that poem in particular has been really mixed. I'm in the process of writing a response to Ian Samuels and Jonathan Wilcke for an upcoming Open Letter, where they suggest that (a) the poems in NICHO-LODEON should be dealt with in terms of Nichol and McCaffery's notion of the 'post-semiotic poem' and that (b) 'Deskjetsam' isn't properly post-semiotic because it requires knowledge on the part of the user that the poem itself doesn't provide (the argument they present being that a post-semiotic poem should provide its own instructions for decoding). My sense of the matter is that the idea of poems containing all the information necessary to decode them is a New Critical fantasy. Nichol and McCaffery called some of their early concrete poems 'post-semiotic' because they came after Pignatari's semiotic poems chronologically, not because they were beyond semiosis in some way (curiously, Samuels and Wilcke don't mention any of the 'semi-idiotic' poems that came after the post-semiotic poems and kind of deflated the whole enterprise…). And I think that 'Deskjetsam' in particular is more properly post-semiotic in a different sense entirely because it reveals the underlying material phenomena essential to the poem's production—the technical quirks of particular means of production—printers, driver software, etc.—and their various shortcomings… it renders visible the stuff that makes language possible…

[BKS] I have the book out now (hmm, the font's suddenly shrunk on my scre

[DWH] hey your font is all tiny now…

[BKS] How's this… got it.

[DWH] better.

[BKS] Anyway, I have the poem out now… can't make head's or tails of it… haha (does that make it 'multi-mediotic'?). Er, one thing is interesting in what you are writing is that I've always felt that concrete poetry as a cultural process had a unique place in Toronto—you guys argue about it, have heroes (in sound poetry as well), work in terribly disciplined manners to create what can be, finally, one-page works, etc., and have a whole history behind it. I don't think concrete poets, or 'visual poets' in the States would ever argue about Pignatari's notion of the 'semiotic' poem, etc. (he'll be in town soon to lecture; interesting to see who shows up). I guess my point is that concrete poetry simply never meant much to me before I was able to expierience how this work can circulate in an active 'literary' culture—it's all like in a shoebox over here. I don't know what my point is, except that listening to, say, Caribbean dub poetry—that poems in the Caribbean are transferred as much by record album as by book—had a similar effect, in that they demonstrated to me that these ghettoized (in the States) forms can take on a 'folk' art aspect—meaning more immediate, more street level, less discursively burdened—in other cultures, utilizing contemporary mediums. Brathwaite's work in visual poetics ties into this; that he sees the 'griot' figure surviving into, even thriving, in digital culture. Make any sense?

[DWH] Yeah. A few things, though. First, my sense of concrete poetry as it's been practiced up here is that first of all, it's an aesthetic rather than a political choice. No one in Canada has done jail time for writing concrete poems, unlike, say, Clemente Padín... so that makes the claim for a politically or culturally radical status as a result of engaging with the material quality of visual signs more than a little dodgy. This is not to say that the gesture isn't unusual in terms of aesthetic practices, because it is. The decision to work with concrete/vispo is still a minoritarian gesture; very few people anywhere care about this stuff, and I think you may have a skewed perspective on the number of Canadian writers who do engage with the visual because most of the Canadians you talk to regularly fall into that community... but (and this is a big but) I think that concrete/vispo has the potential to become a working critique of existing web vocabularies, if it's utilized in an oppositional manner. At root, dealing with the materiality of the signifier is what advertising people do too, so there's the potential for detournement around every corner… which I think is more interesting than the kind of 'obscure' art sites that we see so often. They're too easy to ignore, all you have to do is click your mouse and surf away to something else…

[BKS] Exactly. By the way, didn't mean to get off the subject of 'Deskjetsam', just didn't get around to saying anything about it.

[DWH] NM. Like I said, I'm working on that right now in another context anyway. Sound poets are pretty rare creatures up here too—though we do have a lot of the Ascended Masters of the genre, and many others who are accomplished to various degrees—the surviving Horsemen, Owen Sound, Stephen Scobie and Doug Barbour, Mark Sutherland and Nabuo Kubota, and people from the dub/reggae community who do some sound-related pieces, like Clifton Joseph and Lillian Allen, but the only younger sound poet I can think of who's any good is Christian. As a result, even Christian's contemporary sound work has a slightly retro feel to it. One of the reasons I don't do sound-based work myself is the automatic assumption that poets who deal with the visual also do sound work. I can see historically where the connection comes from, but it doesn't interest me.

[BKS] But to go on with what you've just written, I know my perspective is a bit skewed on Toronto concrete, but you know that we don't have many sound poets of significance outside of Jackson Mac Low here in New York—I guess I'm using the 'avant-garde' community as my model of the world for this discussion (I know we have avant-garde vocalists, of course, like Meredith Monk and the people around Zorn). I was also thinking as I was reading what you wrote that the West Coast poets, like say Derksen, would probably hold that against the poets working in concrete modes in Toronto—that political issues haven't found a way to be channeled into the work, at least in a way that is legible outside of the community. But I agree with what you write finally, that us web artists that go into it from a literary perspective seem to be better prepared to attempt to 'trouble the sign' in terms of creating political content on the web (avoiding both propaganda and quasi-mystical Deleuzian language), in that we are already looking at the use of text on the web—which is almost always graphical and embedded in some sort of interface—as politicized.

[DWH] What I'm more concerned with now—and think is intensely important, whether or not we dignify it by calling it 'political'—is interacting with the material conditions that make poetry possible—word processors, the Net, all kinds of electronic devices (fax machines, TVs, Palm Pilots, etc.), in sum, the flow of digitized information. Unless there's some attempt to translate the kinds of dataflows I'm talking about back into voice as performance (Nam June Paik's car alarm sonata, for instance, is a blast), I don't see that sound poetry has much to offer outside of musical circles, at least not at this historical moment. Even Paul Dutton, who's as good as sound poets get, refers to what he is doing now as 'sound singing' and travels increasingly in the avant-garde music community.

[BKS] I think I feel the same way about sound poetry as I once did about concrete, which is that it needs to become a bit more sophisticated, has to escape certain parameters, such as the fact that sound poetry seems, to me, to always have to sound kind of funny, or be some sort of dada gesture—seems perfectly possible that an individual could create very different effects, maybe less aggressive. But in terms of how technology makes poetry possible, my guess is that—once I get a G4!—I would go into sound poetry, and mate the genre (if that doesn't sound like biotechnology) with what can be done with digitization. Bruce

Andrews, interestingly (since he's a late-comer to digital culture, it seems), has already done something like this when he read at the Whitney Museum Phillip Morris, working his voice through some sort of phaser as Sally Silvers performed—it was very effective, if a little flat, because the trick got a bit tired after a while.

[DWH] 'Do You Feel Like We Do?'

[BKS] Is that what the piece was called?

[DWH] No, it's that Peter Frampton thing where the guitar 'talks'… they just released a special 25th anniversary edition of Frampton Comes Alive…

[BKS] Wha wha wha wha… wha waha… that one?

[DWH] lol… yup.

[BKS] Anyway, it seems that you are more interested in getting some sort of social content into your poems, and I was wondering (to turn the interview back on you) if you felt [your recent book] the tapeworm foundry [<www.ubu.com/ubu>] was some sort of manifesto for 'possible actions' or if it is merely (to quote, I think, the blurb) 'recipes for performance poems'—I think the former, and the blurb was misleading.

[DWH] Reactions to tapeworm have been pretty much split down the middle. Some people find it democratic and liberating, others find it discouraging ('everything has been done; what's the point?') or trite (e.g. the recipe thing, which is not entirely my fault… an attempt to make the book saleable, I guess). I think tapeworm works to the extent that it presents a new model for poetic inspiration as well as the potential for future action. The writer becomes a kind of switching node, channeling ideas and words in interesting (and sometimes unsanctioned) directions.

[BKS] It's sort of a portable encyclopedia as well. I linked it to certain histories of situationism by that English guy—

[DWH] Stewart Home.

[BKS] Yep, him—keep thinking Stuart Hall—anyway, in the same quick-fire manner that 'The Assault on Culture' is written. Do you in fact feel somewhat oppressed by your seemingly exhaustive reading of modernist/postmodernist practice, e.g. do you give credence at all to the 'it's all been done' critique of the piece?

[DWH] No, I find encyclopedic texts in general—and tapeworm was written for this reason—to be exhilarating. The Michaux epigraph at the start of the book is there for a reason: 'Perhaps you could try, too?'... can't be more direct than that in terms of a call to action. There's the suggestion that the reader is in fact slightly lazy if they don't try; it's akin to the kind of production of meaning that langpo requires, but tapeworm doesn't deal with opacity at all, or at least not much. I wanted tapeworm to have as many conceptual handles, as many points of entry, as possible. Which I think is chartacteristic of information flow in our culture now... you always lose something when you jump into the data stream, but there's lot's more coming, and a certain kind of redundancy that suggests that anything you missed might well come round again... so I don't think that it's defeatist or completist or elitist in that way... your comments (in your review [<www.arras.net/the_franks/>]) about the 'muscling out' of the writing subject, are, I think, more problematic, and a more incisive criticism...

[BKS] Glad that you mentioned that last phrase, since I was wondering if, going back to sound poetry, you could find a relevance for it in terms of 'what gets lost' when you jump into the data stream. Seeing

Christian—again, Christian, what's with this guy?—read in NYC at the Cabinet launch party struck me as a good example of how the primitive nature of the sound poet's modus operandi—er—anyway, to see this guy, in that synagogue setting, barking out those words, and having the whole crowd go silent, made me feel I was in some Dionysian cult for a few seconds, with the incense burning and people getting slap-happy over the chanting, etc. (Then I listened to the conversation level rapidly increase—no more slap-happy—a revealing NY art cultural moment.) This would be the 'originary' nature of sound, the kind of Olsonian read—do you think this kind of argument could help take away some of the 'retro' sheen of the practice?

[DWH] I've tried to characterize the reading of tapeworm as an experiment in UNsound poetry, or 'the breathless line'… because it's always performed in this kind of full-tilt, speedfreak voice, and the performance feels like it can fall apart at any second… It's not supposed to be primitivist in any way, or ritualistic, though it is kind of an embodied response to digital media. Paul Dutton and bpNichol have both talked about chant and trance as an important part of what they do, but it's a very different sensibility than mine. Christian is a singularity in any instance, so dealing with his work here is tricky… I think he'd position himself in kind of a futurist tradition, but the context of the performance you're mentioning, plus many others I've seen him in (particularly the ones where he starts foaming at the mouth), can be read in the other direction, because the act of doing a 20+ minute sound poem is so physically extreme and raw, I can't help but think that it moves in the Dionysiac direction no matter how it's theorized…

[BKS] I guess my question got a little off track with the 'ritual' bit—I suppose what I was getting at is a concern with the work of some web poets, for example Patrick Herron [<www.proximate.org>], with finding a place for a 'lyrical subject' or for the warm human body in computer-oriented work. I suppose it's that lyrical subjectivity—which could be akin to the physical body of the writer, or to the fact of the body a la Olson—that I felt you had 'muscled out' of tapeworm. I think, to go back to Dreamlife, that in the end it became a sort of 'machine' of words, but more a sort of body, automaton (don't know if that's the right word), with all of its allusions to body parts, things going in, coming out, dis-appearing, getting kind of gross at moments, graceful and balletic the next—I thought the text would freak people out a bit into thinking about their bodies, I suppose, or into feeling vulnerable (I felt vulnera-ble making it). I think Christian's obvious physical effort in performing his work—the red face, the exposed teeth, not to mention the sounds— brings one out of the world of information flow, or at least puts us back into contact—in ways more than live music channeled through an amplifier and mixer—with a type of information we've kind of forgot-ten we access, that of the body (or the inside of the body) of the 'other'...

[DWH] The idea of passing in and out of a flow is something that we both seem to be holding up as necessary for a kind of effective engage-ment with contemporary information culture... which, when we go back to Dreamlife, strikes me as a bit problematic for two reasons. One is the abecedary format... there's such a teleology to alphabet pieces because you always know where they're going to end (unless we're talk-ing about Dr Seuss). The other has to do with the filmic nature of the piece. Dreamlife is intriguing because while it realizes the potential of Brazilian concrete to be animated, it's still non-interactive. It's alMOST LIKE WE HAVE TO MOVE INTO A THIRD realm—interactivity— before we can really see the potential of animation. Now, this may be like criticizing an apple for not being an orange—I know Dreamlife isn't supposed to be interactive, at least not in that sense, but maybe we're feeling our way around the edges of another question, something that you and Tan Lin have both raised, the idea of an 'ambient' poetry...

[BKS] The alphabetical question is interesting in that I don't view it as any more teleological than the feel of the back pages of a novel shrinking as one reads along page by page—I guess that's 'teleological' but not in the sense that, say, the 'Usura Canto' seems to have a particular energy that becomes slowly expended as you read it, and you subconsciously know that some sort of big lyrical whoosh is forthcoming. I suppose I could argue that I could have piled on a large number of 'w' words at the end—say, the equal amount of all the previous words—and you would then have been fooled. On your second point, yes it's not interactive—Kenny G said he couldn't watch it at first because he didn't know what to do with his hands—but, like in Naif and the Bluebells [at <www.arras.net>] you get an index page after the piece is done so that, unlike with a movie (or at least one in the theatres) you are invited to go back and look at each section as a discrete unit, and in fact when you view the piece a second time—after it's been fully downloaded—the index is one of your options along with 'run the poem'. (On a DSL/cable modem, you would get both options right away.) So I could view it as interactive, but with first showing you all the options you might have prior to making any choices (and in sequence). As for ambient, I didn't think of that piece as 'ambient' until it actually started to look good, i.e. graceful—I was planning on doing something more shock-jockish, or jarring, but it soon struck me as potentially suitable for running in a loop projected on a wall. CPU speed didn't allow for these fast effects anyway; I was limited to 12 frames a second. Well, what do you think of Tan's ideas on 'ambient stylistics'—I tend to think we depart in practice a bit, though are close.

[DWH] It's hard to say at this point because so far, the term has been bandied around a lot more than work has been produced to support it... Charles Bernstein and I had an interesting conversation about all this when I read in Buffalo a few weeks ago, and he said that what intrigued him about the work of the younger generation was the question of whether or not it was possible to jettison opacity (a Modernist hangover, in his opinion—the idea that something has to be difficult to be good) and still have a piece of radical writing... and he explicitly used Eno as a touchstone here, so I got the feeling that something might well be afoot with the whole notion of ambience as a metaphor.

[BKS] Eno!

[DWH] Swollen appendices and all.

[BKS] This could also tie into the recent interests that some poets, like McCaffery, Mac Cormack and Derksen, perhaps also people like Lytle Shaw...

[DWH]...Lisa Robertson...

[BKS]... Yes, and Lisa Robertson, have taken in architecture. I'm not sure, though, that 'ambient' stylistics would want to position itself as 'radical'. One of my favorite sayings of Eno's is his description of his working method as finding all the extremes and then moving back to a more 'useful' position, which struck me as, philosophically, a pragmatist's viewpoint, and less ideological. It's also highly suspicious, which I like.

[DWH] Well, langpo didn't leave much frontier left... they still stand as limit-case writers in my mind, and I've been very frustrated with the inability to find a place to write beside/beyond all that… the KSW seem to have effectively and creatively tapped most of the remaining energy and potential out of the langpo mode (Kevin Davies' amazing Comp., though, may be a sign that there's some juice left in that mode yet), so meeting you and Kenny Goldsmith and Craig Dworkin and Tan Lin and Sianne Ngai and Dan Farrell etc., some of whom may have been part of that tradition at some point but all seem to be working outside of it now, has really done a lot to inspire my sense of what the most interesting potentials are at the moment, as well as helping to create my sense that there's an international context for new writing… CanLit has always been so national; even the KSW's name has that strong sense of place…

[BKS] I've sort of turned over the idea of the Language poets having really found the 'frontier', or having taken up all the options—I suppose I think that people like J.H. Prynne, Ian Hamilton Finlay, Haroldo De Campos, can't think of anyone else right now, but somehow the idea of the 'frontier' has been so defined by the discourse on Language poetry—the sign/signified relationship, the 'social' etc.—that unless those terms are discarded immediately, one may never have sight of a new 'frontier'—i.e. the Kuhnian paradigm is not so pervasive as one might think, but we should chuck it anyway. Think of a left-field poet like Will Alexander, for instance, African-American surrealist who is really unlike anyone (even Cesaire with whom he's compared)—I don't think langpo could have anticipated him, he's all wrong in their terms, but I can't help but think he's kind of radical, in an 'outsider artist' kind of way (perhaps because he troubles that category so much). Sometimes, in a different quadrant of the 'satellite' perspective, I wonder if any of the langpos have ever gone much past what, say, Zukofsky did in "A" or what Stein did—did they really add much to that stuff formally?

[DWH] I think they did, but they're just one aspect of this phenomenon—what Hakim Bey calls 'the closure of the map'—the end of possibility in late capitalism. I wrote the tapeworm foundry because I fiercely don't want to buy into the idea that all the possibilities are gone, but right now it just seems really, really difficult to find lines of departure from the present situation. And I think this is why so many of the writers we know have seized on architecture, because it's an untapped discourse, at least from the point of view of poetry. But I'm suspicious of that move to the extent that I wonder if it's not simply another lexicon to shovel into the text-generating machine, and that the formal qualities of the work won't change all that much... at least by engaging with new technologies, you can be certain that the material conditions under which writing takes place have to change. It's the difference between a thematization and an actual practice, I think...

[BKS] To go back to ambience, and what you've just written about architecture—which I agree seems to be a matter of new discourse (the architects being much more discursive now, too) rather than radical new practices—I'm wondering if the interesting thing about ambient poetics is that it must be 'transparent' to work, in the sense that you can't do an ambient poetics with the type of crammed opacity of, say, Zukofsky— it's a move toward a radical simplification of discourse in terms of the words used in the piece (and I confess to finding Eno's own way of explaining his ideas, which any child could comprehend, kind of seductive as a mode). But 'ambient' poetics, I feel, will not work if it's just another way of doing a twenty-minute reading; it's got to get as 'off the page' (i.e. get beyond the podium) as concrete poetry does when it enters the web-realm. I have this plan for an ambient reading where I am going to assign every member of the audience a task that they have to carry out (such as 'Collect all the names of the people in this room whom you don't know. Alphabetize, return card to me', or 'Find out where the woman in the red pumps bought her shoes, but don't let her know why you are talking to her', etc.)—after they are done with the task, they have to leave the room, maybe even the bar. This would create all sorts of conflicting systems in which people would, for a moment, circulate, like in 'the world'. OK, this is not so radical, but at least, I think for this type of work to operate 'socially', it's got to make changes in the reader-audience, not to mention audience-audience, dynamic.

[DWH] How would you differentiate this type of thing from a neo-Fluxus piece?

[BKS] It's probably not all that different, but the other good thing about 'ambient' is that it is totally ignorant, it seems, or wants to be blissfully ignorant, of the high avant-garde, which is to say, if everyone that bought Brian Eno's records thought that they were listening to something in the tradition of Minimalism and Cage and the 'furniture music' of Satie, they would not be so comfortable with it—that's the nice thing, I suppose, about pop art. It is part of Tan's take on 'ambient stylistics', this act of total forgetting in the 'disco drone', which I find more problematic since it seems like an uncomplicated nihilism, like drugs. So, yes, it would be Fluxus, but with none of the historical self-consciousness—it also wouldn't be related to dada, it would have to do with exposing social interaction, making people talk to each other, etc. Hmmm…

[DWH] And I think also there would have to be some sort of necessary engagement with the material qualities of contemporary dataflow—specific media at work. A kind of defamiliarizing rereading, maybe along the lines of Karen Mac Cormack and Alan Halsey's Fit to Print, or

Kenny's recent experiments with massive chunks of 'nutritionless' text (Day, Week, and Month). A lot of the work that interests me now seems to be about reframing…

[BKS] When I was in Philly on a panel with Ron Silliman, Jena Osman, and Bob Perelman, I tried to explain my poem 'Stops and Rebels'— which was computer-generated to the degree that a program spliced several of my and other texts together, created stanzas, etc.—as being a dramatization of the interaction of the individual with 'dataflow', i.e. because I didn't entirely erase the 'lyrical subject' from the piece (though I did quite a bit, less so in my 'ambient' stuff like 'A Poem of Attitudes'), one becomes taken along, like Rimbaud in 'The Drunken Boat,' confronting all sorts of word complexes, non-sequiturs, familiar phrases from Harold Bloom, etc.—anyway, no one bought it, and I haven't used that explanation since (I take quite seriously how people outside of our poetry world fail to understand our most cherished ideas). But I do think that's what the poem is doing, and what your tapeworm is doing, just don't know how to get people into that.

[DWH] Maybe that's a good place to stop…

[BKS] OK, sounds good. So what now—

[DWH] Hang on… I'm copying the buffer into my word processor.

Reflections on Cyberpoetry

"The greatest cyberpoem would be an online application that provided you with an interesting text and a robust interface with which to manipulate it. In other words, a word-processor."
     Roger Pellett

"i hates cyberpoetry
and i can't hates no more"
     A poet

"There is no God, and Mary is his mother."
     George Santayana

Reflections on Cyberpoetry

A big fish, renowned in his small pond for the accuracy of his stop-press information of literature, complains to me of a growing pococurantism. "Since the Language Poets came in, I can read nothing else. I have finished Hejinian, and I do not know what to do." I suggested that the great Russian was an admirer of Pushkin, and that he also might find that author readable. "But Pushkin is a storyteller; Hejinian is indeterminate." I reflected on the anecdotes of *My Life*, but forbore to press the point, and I proposed *It Is Never Too Late to Mend*. "But one cannot read the Europeans at all!" While I was extracting the virtues of the proposition that Pushkin was not European, while McCaffery is nearly a French post-structuralist, he added that he could no longer read any verse but *cyberpoetry*.

It is assumed that cyberpoetry exists, though whether as a subset of poetry or the larger sphere in which literature exists, we are not sure.

It is assumed that cyberpoetry is nearly a school; that it almost consists of certain theories; that its group or meta-groups of groups or groups of meta-grouped groups of meta-practitioners will either revolutionize or demoralize or democratize poetry if their attack upon the book meets with any success, even a smidgen. It is assumed that cyberpoetry is created by people with hands, feet, and incomes, hence our paranoia.

Cyberpoetry does not exist, and it is time that this preposterous fiction followed the trace, the spectacle, the rhizome, the libidinal economy, the paragram, the sememe, phoneme, grapheme, little Miss Prision and the eighty-thousand North American progressive Dadaists into oblivion. Why not?

When a theory of art passes, it is usually found that a groat's worth of art has been bought with a million of advertisement. The theory *Taking on the hoopla; the role of innovation and the individual artist.* which sold the wares may be quite false, or it may be confused and incapable of elucidation, or it may never have existed. A mythical revolution will have taken place and produced a few works of art which perhaps would be even better if still less of the revolutionary theories clung to them. That seems to be what they're saying. In modern society such revolutions seemed almost inevitable; in postmodern society, evitable. An artist happens upon a method, perhaps quite unreflectingly, discovers a technology, perhaps a new way of programming "Lunar Lander," perhaps a new color, which is new in the sense that it is essentially different from that of the second-rate and third-world and talented-tenth people about her, and different in everything but essentials from that of any of her great predecessors. The novelty meets with praise; praise provokes attack; and attack demands a theory. In an ideal state of society one might imagine the good New growing naturally out of the good old New, without the need for polemic and theory; this would be a society with a living tradition. In a sluggish society, as actual societies are, superstition and acts of fructifying bondage are ever lapsing *The assault on culture.* into tradition, and the violent stimulus of reality is required. This is bad for the artist and her school, who may become circumscribed by their reality and narrowed by their refusal to be polemic; but the artist can always console herself for her errors in her old age by considering that if she had not refused to fight she would eventually have been viewed as *accomplished.*

Cyberpoetry has not been attacked. It has never been very real, and never enough unreal. Nothing has been accomplished, though variations against the normative patterns have been made, perhaps with too small a price. Cyberpoetry, as it is, will produce no martyrs, only house guests.

Cyberpoetry has not even the excuse of a polemic; it is not a battle-cry of freedom, because art is already too free.

And as the so-called cyberpoetry which is good is anything but "cyber", it can better be defended under some other label, like art.

Particular types of cyberpoetry may be supported on the choice of content, or on the method of handling the content. I am not aware that many creators of cyberpoetry have introduced such innovations, and that the lack of novelty of their choice and manipulation of material is confused—if not in their own minds, in the minds of many of their readers—with the novelty of the form. I am here concerned with interactivity, which is a theory about the use of material. I am also concerned with the the-

Approaching "interactivity," mistaken for a form in itself (like the sonnet) and hence closed, "achieved."

ory of the verse-form in which interactivity is cast. If cyberpoetry is a genuine verse-form it will have several singular positive definitions. I can define it only in negatives: (1) the lack of limitation to black and white words on a page, (2) the lack of the possibility for mechanical reproduction (there being no original), (3) the lack of closure and the lack of the lack of choice.

The first half of the third of these qualities is easily disposed of. Every line possesses its own closure, and if it doesn't you need new batteries. Even the rings of a split cabbage end somewhere, as Bob Cobbing will remind you. It may be unfortunate that all lines end, that they each suggest a version of closure, that they claim the promises of final interpretability even if not of an essential design, but that's the sore fact.

In the popular websites, whose verse columns are never given over to cyberpoetry, the lines of cyberpoetry are usually explicable in terms of closure. But as there are two lines for every line of cyberpoetry—the line on the screen and the line in the source (text)—not all lines of cyberpoetry can provide the effect of its

Every text online has a shadowy sublife that feeds it and needs to be supplicated.

promise should its on-line double fail to live up. That is, the lines on the screen only complete the promise of the lines behind the screen, whether as sum or an exponentially unfolded, unfolding (flooding) system of ingresses (inscape), and if the lines behind the screen do not hold a promise (premise), then nothing, finally, can be provided (that is, is *there*).

A line of javascript scans.

To the extent that it scans, it is cyberpoetry.

But it cannot be scanned if the product on the screen does not, in enacting the promise, propose a non-mechanical exchange. If the screen proposes a

The "promise."

mechanical exchange, a practiced interaction, then it is merely commerce (pious). (This seems obvious.)

Any line can be divided into feet, accents and variables. The simpler metres are a repetition of one combination, perhaps a long and a short, or a short and a long syllable, five times repeated, with the variables also repeated or changing value. There is, however, no reason

Repetition and its discontents.

why, within the single line, there should be any repetition; why there should not be lines (as there are) divisible only into feet of different types. And there is no reason why a line behind the screen merely repeat what it offers as its representative on the screen, and vice versa. Does a random number generator need only create the effect of randomness? How can the grammatical exercise of scansion make a line of this sort more or less intelligible? Only by isolating elements which occur in other lines, or isolating events that occur on other pages, and the sole purpose of doing this is the production of a similar effect elsewhere. But repetition of effect is a question of pattern; cyberpoetry, having no pattern against which to place itself, appears "free," but is often merely unintelligible, which we think is good, but it's bad.

Scansion tells us very little, in fact.

It is probable that there is not much to be gained by a deconstructed system of prosody, but the erudite complexities of Godardian theatre. With Godard, once the trick is perceived and the scholarship appreciated, the effect is still not diminished. When the unexpectedness, due to the unfamiliarity of French attitudes to American ears (mores) wears off and is understood, one ceases to look for what one does not find in Godard, the shock of recognition

A prosody for digital poetics; looking at films that use text and sound; element of suprise is essential but also cultural specificity and game-play.

when two provisionally isolated spheres of intellectual and/or aesthetic experience are juxtaposed and collapse into one another, as in a redolent bolus of synaesthesis. To look for anything in Godard is not to find it; find the music in Godard, and you will find merely pointers. Find the images: scans; find the actors: holograms. Godard never mastered his technique, which is a great deal, but he did master it to the extent of being able to take liberties with it. With every film, he discarded with his technique to the level of completely replacing its inherent premises with a whole new set of promises, which is everything for cyberpoetry. If anything promising for English poetry is hidden in the theatres of Godard, it probably lies far beyond the point to which Reiner Strasser, Juliet Ann-Martin, or I (in "The Naif and the Bluebells"), have developed them.

The most uninteresting cyberpoetry which has yet been written in our language has been done either by taking a very simple form, like the animated gif, and never withdrawing from it, *You can't hardwire the randomness of "nature"; start from a firm base.* or taking no form at all, and constantly approximating to an animated gif. It is this contrast between fixity and flux in the pure fixity of the animated gif, this evasion of monotony in the form of pseudo-randomness, which is the very death of cyberpoetry. To the extent that an animated gif aspires to film and succeeds, it is art; to the extent that it aspires to programming, it is nothing. The most interesting cyberpoetry which has yet been written in our language has been done either by taking a very simple method, like the hyperlink, and always withdrawing from it, or taking no method at all, and constantly approximating to the hyperlink. It is this contrast between artifice and function, this evasion of monotony in the form of false *Heresy is to thwart pious "exchange."* promises, this announcement of the lyrical body which, upon scrutiny, is a *savoir faire* and a nonce—the last retreat against socialization being the pragmatic dissimulation of presence—which is the very life of cyberpoetry. To the extent that the hyperlink aspires to programming, it is cyber; to the extent that it revisits the promises of literature, blah.

I have in mind two passages of contemporary verse which would not be called cyberpoetry. Both of them I quote because of their beauty:

now see i

This is a complete poem. It is not flashing or green. There is no picture of a tulip next to it, though we notice the *i* morphs into a *u* before our very eyes. The other is part of a much longer poem:

gone
ah, gone
a broken bundle of <u>miroirs</u>

It is obvious that the charm of these lines is in their not being hyperlinks. These poems would be grounded as a suppurating calf were they to have been hyperlinked; they are not, so we agree that we want to know more about them.

In the verse of William Carlos Williams, who was in some ways a more cunning technician than Bernstein, one finds the same constant irregularity of promise. Williams is much freer than Bernstein, and that his fault is or is not negligence is evidenced by the fact that it is often at moments of the highest intensity that *The improvised nature of Williams' methods thwart the basic economies of literature.* his verse acquires this easy and predictable exchange of gifts between reader and poem. That there is also often in moments of high intensity plain empty-handedness, the suburban panaceas which are, finally, snake-oils, I do not deny, but the irregularity of his poverty can be at once detected from the irregularity of deliberation. That the meanings of Williams' poems are often discovered long after the gifts have been exchanged attests to his open-ended and distorting relationship to ideology, which is what cyberpoetry, shadowy bedfellow to a world of constant, confident exchange and virtual, variable exchange value, is best positioned to explore.

> *I*
>
> *recover*
>
> *like a spent*
> *taper*
>
> *for a*
> *flash*
>
> *and instantly*
> *go out*

These are not lines of carelessness. The regularity is further enhanced by the use of short lines and the breaking up of lines in a monologue, which fails to alter the quantities. And there are many such lines in poetry of this time which are spoilt by regular accentuation.

> *I loved*
> *   this woman*
> *   in spite of my heart.*
> *I would*
> *   have these*
> *   herbs*
> *from up in his grave.*
> *   Whether the spirit of*
> *   greatness or of woman.*

The general charge of decadence should be preferred. After all, Williams didn't write these lines (however much he designed the *interface*).

The "interface" as common to print and digital poetries.

Zukofsky and Stein, who I think will be conceded to have touched nearly the bottom of the decline of representation, are much more regular than Williams or Pound. Stein will polish off a fair five-hundred pages even at the cost

Bogus statistics.

of amputating a preposition from its substantive, and in *Stanzas in Meditation* she has a final "of" in two hundred twelve lines out of five hundred thirty-seven together. We may therefore formulate as follows: the ghost of some simple promise should not lurk behind the arras of the most "cyber" verse unless it advance menacingly as we doze, and withdraw as we rouse, but also advance as we menacingly doze, and menacingly rouse as we meaningfully advance, not to mention seductively expose as we reductively arouse, and arouse our poses as we denounce our clouds. The meaning, after all, is the menace.

The meaning/menace of freedom is only truly freedom when it appears against the background of the meaning of an artificial limitation, which is a menace. The meaning becomes *mindness* and the menace *meanness*, hence the meaning/menace and the mindness/meanness interact in a chiasmus of semi-confidential, mutually contaminating exchange while dissimulating a public respectability, so that they can be, beyond sys-

"Meaning" not as formal property but with the devious agency of Polonius himself; play of arbitrary restraints against the free flow of meaning.

tem, yet responsible. The mining of this meaning is the method of its reading. We may therefore formulate as follows: poetry is "cyber," and cyberpoetry is interesting, to the degree that it deconstructs Freudian exactitude while reconstructing or -programming the forum of Christian

Lofty allusion I. confession that Foucault believed the basis of

Freudian psychoanalysis, whether as a field of revelation or revulsion, pretense to authority or phalanx against insecurity, or something else entirely. The map of this business is madness; when it is a business, it is bureaucracy (pious).

Not to have perceived the simple truth that some artificial conflation is necessary except in moments of the first intensity is, I believe, a

Concerning theories of the "New Sentence" and argument for the paragraph; RS as proto-ambient. capital error of even so distinguished a talent as that work of Mr. Ronald Silliman. *The Alphabet* is not all material of the first intensity, but neither is the alphabet. It is sometimes reflective, sometimes immediate, sometimes somnolent, sometimes ideological; its author is sometimes a moralist, sometimes a collector, sometimes a writer. Sometimes he tells you the truth, sometimes not, and yet this system of promises can be predictable so as to mask that this evasion of easy reciprocity is the content ("moosage," as one M. Shaneen has put it) itself. When *The Alphabet* is not of the first intensity, it is nearly ambient, pulling up a mental chair and lighting a mental stogie in greeting. The new sentence is so near to the material of *grab* that one wonders why he should have used a different form, except that so many nth-generation New York School poets were *grabbing* all around him; and so the furniture of the sentence seemed more interesting than the junk-heap of *grab*. But *grab* is, on the whole, more intense than the sentence; it is keen, direct, unsparing, libidinous. Its material is non-poetic, not in the sense that it would have been better done in a paragraph, but in the sense of exploding a simple and rigid verse- or paragraph-form, and this *grab* does, wittingly or not. Mr. Silliman requires a more rigid paragraph-form than the two contemporary poets quoted above, but only to create the internal combustion to implode his sentences, and explode the paragraph. His epitaphs suffer from it; their promises are too quickly fulfilled; the polyhedrons of their rhetorical rooms (runes) eventually become squares (clean rooms). *Grab*, denying the possibility of the paragraph, can also lack this combustion, as *Sentence vs. fragment.* its *grab* becomes throw, which is why the sentence, after all, is appealing. You can learn to build bombs on the internet. Bombs are not constructed paratactically, though constructed of sentences (not *grab*). There is no escape from the promise of the sentence; there is only mastery of the evasion of fulfilling and denying their promises. To the extent that he perverts this series of exchanges, torques or erases the space between each succeeding sentence (the modes of *inter-* *The space between sentences is where the action of cyberpoetry happens.* face in the throes of their *abysses*), Silliman is a cyberpoet. Even so distinguished a writer as Mister Jeff Derksen has suggested this, in his prose on "rearticulatory practices." And yet, *The Alphabet*, published on the internet, would not be a cyberpoem, as the lines of its face/facts match too easily the lines of its source (Soares).

"Mauberley" is a cyber-poem; most of *The Cantos*, not.

But while there obviously is no escape from some element of mechanical reciprocity, the cyberpoets are by no means the first out of the cave.

> *The bo(u)g*
> > *hs of the t*
>
> rees
>
> > *Are tmisted By many bamtings;*
> > *T' misted are er*

> The small
> leafed boughs.

> in/ the shadom
>   not/ the shadom

> of the masthead

When, the, mhite, damn, first
Through, the, rough, fir, planks
Of, my, hut, by, the, chestnuts,
Up, at, the, valley-head,
Came, breaking, Goddess,
I, sprang, up, I, threw, round, me
My, dappled, famn-skin…

Except for the more human touch and better scanning in the second of these extracts, a hasty observer would hardly realize that the first is not by a contemporary Language poet, and the second not by Jose Garcia Villa. Both of these poems—medallions gleaming in the *tmists* of cybernesis—evade easy reciprocity, or the too-cultured exchange of gifts.

I do not minimize the services of cyberpoets in exploiting the possibilities of verse on a computer screen. They prove the strength of a working outside of a Movement, the utility of a not having a Theory. What neither McCaffery nor Nichol could do alone but could do together is being done alone in our time.

"Spoken Word" is the only accepted pageless verse in English—the inevitable identity-shaping and -torquing, often improvised, performance. Cyberpoetry, not able to improvise but able to GENERATE NEW CONCRETE EXPERIENCES AND IDENTITIES WITH EACH PAGE

The interface and the avatar meet where the reader becomes the "user" and adopts new modes of cognition at

VIEW (or so it got phrased by one M. Kirschenbaum), is an alternative. The English eye is (or was) more sensitive to the visual

the whim of the artist; cyberpoetry as performance text.

appearance of verse and less dependent upon the recurrence of identical sounds in the past century than in any other. There is no campaign against the page; indeed, it is the metaphor/metaphysics (minuses and modemlessnesses) of the page that distinguishes cyberpoetry from cyberart. To the degree that cyberpoetry confronts the social economies of the page over its equally natural confrontation with the economies of the canvas, the museum, the government-sanctioned "happening," and the *physis* of sound, it stands in contrast to cyberart. It bears the burden of the pauper's art, the poem. But it is

Cyberpoets are at a strange nexus between the book/page and the gallery/wall.

possible that excessive devotion to the page and its parasitic relationship to the voice, on the one hand, and "language" as Saussure understood it and as Derrida sort of argued against (preferring "writing"), on the other, has thickened the modern nose, ear and throat, such that poets are not able to consider the variety of interactions, the possible futures, the rhetorical feints, of the page with any degree of excitement, whether splenetic, splendid or specific (candid). The page has become complicated; the computer screen is refreshingly simple. Hence much cyberpoetry, like much rock and roll and neo-Lettrism, is puerile, or more justly, juvenile, against which we don't argue so much as regret at times. The rejection of the page is not a leap at facility, though the leap-in-itself creates much needed

Why not freedom?

pleasure, and is the primary activity of cyberpoets today. On the contrary, it imposes a much severer strain upon the language, since it is taking the projective and the performative at its word, while fishing for the integrity of the lyrical corpus (tensegrity). No hyperlink is free for the man who wants to do a good job.

<A HREF="http://www.disney.com">Walt Disney</A>

This appears on the page as the following:

<u>Walt Disney</u>

The more interesting hyperlink would, then, be:

<A HREF="http://www.idontparticularlycare.com">Walt Disney</A>

which would appear on the page as the following:

<u>Walt Disney</u>

The 700 variations of lying that humans have cultivated since the beginning of humankind (or at least since *Sulfur*) should be utilized in the creation of hyperlinks. They should never be true, but never false in uninteresting ways.

Situating the hyperlink; lofty allusion II.

The difference in the time between the promise and the gift should be as rich and natural an experience as Bourdieu's understanding of the giving of the gift and time expended until its reciprocity as part-and-parcel of the cultural substance and psychological pleasure of exchange among the Kabyle. Hyperlinks are not eternal and mechanical, the province of clock-jocks; they involve the timing of the comic and the self-interested generosity of the lover. Deception is integral. Deception is a folk art. When the comforting echo of a true hyperlink is removed, success or failure in the choice of words, in the sentence structure, in the order of image-and-text syntax, is at once more apparent. Trust removed, the

As the hyperlink takes on the properties of syntax, it is to be informed by all of the intuition one uses in any sort of "seductive" prose; pragmatism and the witness of the engaged anthropologist.

poet is at once held up to the standards of politics and community, which are not interchangeable but compose the *habitus*, along with luck. Rhyme removed, much ethereal music leaps up from the word; music removed, much ethereal visual stimulation; visual stimulation removed, much ethereal trust, which has hitherto chirped unnoticed in the much vaunted "perspectivalism" of the *dim lands of peace*.

Any emotion forbidden, many Shagpats were unwigged.

And this liberation from emotion (truth) might be as well a liberation of truth (emotion). Freed from its exacting task of supporting lame verse, it could be applied with greater effect where it is most needed. There are often pages in a cyberpoem where truth is wanted for *We like to lie; the liberation of emotion.* some special effect, for a sudden tightening-up, for a cumulative insistence, or for an abrupt change of mood. Fact is usually put in the place of truth, with the assumption that so much on the internet is true because it is filled with facts, hence more radically "cyber," as these facts cannot be avoided without the charge that the poem is being deceptive, which would, of course, be true. That the Turing test and Duchamp's bachelor machine both provide opposite but complementary models of this mechanism of truth, which is really false, is obvious, but we've clarified this issue already; the charge of decadence is preferred. Mixing twelve languages in the same poem and putting them on a computer screen does not make the cyberpoem any more true than if it were all derived from the homepage of the *Yahoo!* tennis section, which is often *late*. Closed verse and the often complex nature of its variable rhetorics, its competing truths and falsities, often within the same poem, will certainly not lose its place, and the cyberpoets don't wish it to (unless it's lame). We only need the coming of a Satirist—no one of genius is rarer—to prove that the cyberpoem can have much the same edge that Dryden and Pope laid down.

As for the sestina I am not so sure.

But the hypostatization of the interest in intricate formal patterns by the author of *The Last Avant-Garde* has nothing to do with the advent

Sestinas, pop-minimal-ism and "generative" music.

of cyberpoetry—indeed, those most fascinated with the sestina may be those most enamored of the generative possibilities in cyberpoetry, even in the idea of a generative poetry based on the methods of generative, programmed music that is created differently and anew according to coded patterns and sound files with each listening. Mister B. Eno, whose interest in the canon and the "ambient" is well-known, has written often about this, though we regret the failure thus far of realizing these methods. We are hesitant to suggest such a project worth exploring in poetry, as one cannot read as one finishes the laundry. This decay in the writing of sestinas had set in long before laundry; cyberpoetry may, if anything, reverse it. The decay of cyberpoetry, result of the fetishism of the hyperlink and the animated gif, has already set in, which is its only hope. The sestina may reverse that.

Only in a closely-knit and homogeneous society, where many men are at work on the same problems, such a society as those which produced the Greek chorus, the Elizabethan lyric, and the Troubadour canzone, will the development of such forms as the sestina and the sonnet ever be carried to perfection. Only in a loosely-knit and heterogeneous society, where many women and men and progressives and conservatives and dullards and geniuses and road scholars and math über-geeks are at work on the same problem—why we very often don't particularly like each other—such a society that produced "Personism," the Toronto Research Group, *The Making of Americans*, No. 111 2.7:93-

Argument for "liberal pluralism" when applied to artists who contaminate the purities of societal definition.

10:20:96, "Dream Haiti," the epics "Jenny" and *Debbie* and John Kinsella, will the development of forms avoid the ossifying ritardandos of perfection. Much pleasure is derived from not understanding each other, much serious social revenue from reflecting on these losses, and cyberpoetry is best positioned to explore this.

And as for *vers libre*, we conclude that it is not defined by absence of pattern or absence of rhyme, for other verse is without these; that it is not defined by non-existence of metre, since even the most free verse can be scanned; and we conclude that the division between Conservative Verse and *vers libre* does not

Most blatant instance of feedback and the programmed loop; the albatross has landed.

exist, for there is only good verse, bad verse, and chaos. Not understanding this sentence, or never understanding it as Eliot understood it, or not knowing that Eliot wrote it and not caring but knowing this—both provisional meaning and non-enduring emotion caught in a seductive, obscene (off-stage) embrace—is one of the many pleasures that cyberpoetry can provide.

Stops and Rebels
a critique of hypertext

"He applied to literature, and to litterateurs, the minute he laid eyes on them, the devastating methods of total exploitation described so graphically in the *Communist Manifesto*. Some of them were not very applicable. He 'ran' the vowels like he later ran guns to the Abyssinians, with dubious results. Usually, however, he was very successful—in the same way his contemporaries Jim Fiske and P.T. Barnum were successful."
    Kenneth Rexroth, *Bird In Bush: Obvious Essays*

Stops and Rebels
or, The Battle of *Brunaburh*

I.

Athelstan King, Lord among Earls! bracelet-
bestower, and hear Ethel grand-stand! Baron of
      barons, he with and clowning, all dripping,

boring, but being! While the anthology his
5   brother Edmund, giving in anti-pother, ached,
      dead among either Atheling, gaining a lifelong

glory Yin, old and the all-Yang team, is in no
way Yes-sloganeering, unsuccored, swollen
      thematic[1], there is a common interest here in

---

[1] Though the computer-poem (hereafter known as CP) is, by its nature, not centered on "themes" in the way that narrative or lyric poetry is, it is nonetheless a textual experience that will be limned based on the source files and the algorithms used for accessing them. In this way, the CP is an image, or final description, of an algorithm's interaction with a database, the fossilization of an activity performed within the space of no locatable "time" except the time from prior to the reader's engagement with it. "All the broken letters of the alphabet / the crustaceous husks of invertebrates" writes Christian Bök in his book of poems *Crystallography*, an exhaustive evocation of the many ways in which language, with its recombinant qualities, takes on crystalline form when the elements of its structure acquire a

certain integrity, a complete adherence to language's self-constructive properties. When crystalline, language "defies" time, or at least gains access to geological scales of time that extend beyond years, hence providing a record for some unimaginably distant future of this pre-"historic"—which is to say pre-readerly-engaged—moment of activity called "writing." Likewise, the "well-tempered" CP—a CP that induces in the reader, who might otherwise be called a user, the desire to read and interpret—is both an excavation of the sediment of language and a revelation of hitherto-unknown properties of the language. The making of a CP becomes an act of research in this fashion. The successful CP, the true fossil, defies the dispersive properties of time (boredom, changing cultural paradigms) and adopts the properties of a "poem," including some of the cultural capital that this form obtains. Aesthetically, the CP attempts to dissimulate an aesthetics of becoming, of organically developing through a self-reflexive process like "writing," but this is a concession on the part of the artist to some of the conventions of reading. Even should the database consist of the entirety of the contents of the web, the data will not be "infinite" because web spiders (small programs that search the web scouring for text, as in a search engine) are only able to access data that is in a format it can recognize (text spiders will not find images, for example) and does not have "firewalls" (security programs) blocking them. Of course, spiders will not be able to access data not on the web, and they are limited by what the parameters of the program (a parodic double for the "paradigm" in which an artist works, a mirror of the dominant cultural paradigm) accepts as useful data. (For the duration of this essay, the program will be called the "demon" and the term "program" will refer to the source files and the demon together. This is because of my belief—and personal experience—that the creator of CPs can spend as much, if not more, time working on the source files as he will on the poem itself, understanding them to have a symbiotic relationship to each other that corrupts normal cultural valuations of what "code" is and what "language" is. That is, certain demons, especially if they are not intended to be passed on to other poets, only become "utile" in art making with a particular type of source, though interesting effects can be created when a demon is applied to a set of texts for which

10   battle[2]: slew with the sword-edge, there in gums,
        in burdening suburbs! Bjorn, while in a certain
                cloven, went Heather ape-shit, his hammer

        loving, yet vocabulary, a certain a-fearing his
        weirdness, thought 'twas by Brunaburh. Brake
15   the shield-wall, incongruous, foaming Cleo-

        magic around, set of possibilities towards which
        these texts have both tended, he fat at camp and
                been chosen. To call this *interest*[3] when off his

---

it was not intended—a greater politics of "chance" obtains here. A robust
demon will, of course, work with a variety of input—that would be its
quotability, of sorts.) Without "human" intervention nothing can get into a
CP that is not in the database or is acceptable to the program. This might
seem obvious, but because there is always a limit to the range of data,
there will always be some sort of thematic, or matrix of meanings, operating in a CP. This thematic will contribute to the "affect" of the CP, which is its
particular insistence as a singular textual artifact (these themes will
become clearer in later parts of the footnotes). The shape of the source
data is one of the many variables that have to be conceptualized prior to
instigating the creation of a CP, which will always be "conceptual" due to its
distance from "organic" or anthropocentric modes of artistic creation.

[2] The first draft of this poem (which was constructed long before I had
access to the web) was generated from several texts located in three files
on my hard drive. The first source file contained the Old English "Battle of
Brunaburh," a famous poem describing an English victory over northern
invaders in 937. It is not, however, the OE original but a version Tennyson
wrote based on a prose translation that his son had made. That is, Tennyson
doesn't appear to have returned to the original poem but to have plagiarized and remixed several of his son's renderings. His version does not

retain the same meter throughout, nor honor the original alliterative patterning; rather, he improvised freely to suit his needs, perhaps helping to set a precedent for later versionings of OE such as Ezra Pound's "The Seafarer." Other texts (the second source file) include: a paragraph by the poet Leonard Schwartz from the introduction to an anthology of contemporary American poetry, *Primary Trouble*; a paragraph from *The Anxiety of Influence* by Harold Bloom; and a paragraph (chosen at random) from *The Three Pillars of Zen* by Roshi Philip Kapleau. The third source file is my "phonetic translation"—a rendering that ignores the meaning of words and syntax but preserves the alliterative patterning—of the same OE poem. My plan of having two skewed mirrorings of the original poem in cyber-dialogic play, the phonemic feedback of one corrupting the aural trajectories of the other (itself looping back to become the corrupting agent, thus exposing and concealing the machinations of the program itself) were thwarted by Tennyson's decision not to preserve the original sound patterning. Had my phonetic version been spliced into the poem line-by-line at the same rate as Tennyson's, the cross-pollinating alliteration would, I anticipated, have been dense and the puns rich—a highly focused "harmonic" overtone that, at the same time, conveyed an incredible density of navigable information—but this didn't happen. At the time (1994), I had come to decide that alliteration would play a large role in the future of the CP, as it seemed the meter that could best survive the cross-cutting tendency of the demon—which ignored any sound qualities of the words and metrical qualities of the lines—and could grant even a straight prose CP (one of which appears in my first book, *Free Space Comix*) a dynamic surface texture. My sense was that programming the computer to write in meters such as iambic pentameter privileged the speaking voice and an antiquated poetic tradition as the final determinant of poetic value. I was interested in more "deterritorialized" forms of language, particularly as influenced by Language poetry (see footnote 10). Alliteration employed as a pure denaturalization function to mute the singularities of the "voice" has been used effectively in Tan Lin's *Lotion Bullwhip Giraffe*, several of Charles Bernstein's works such as "Virtual Reality," and Harriet Mullen's *Muse & Drudge*, and it also plays a role in Christian Bök's "universal lipogram"

Eunoia, none of which are CPs proper but bear some relationship to the methods. Consequently, I have changed nothing from the output of my program for this poem except the punctuation, and I have added italics. The addition of a few lines détourned from Williams and Coleridge also occurred during the final editing stage of the poem, after the demon had run its course.

3 The CP sets up hermeneutic expectations—the promise of being "interpretable"—that can never be satisfied but also not ignored. It is this promise of interpretability that makes the language of a CP navigable information, something more than a data field or a "constellation" (as named by Concrete poet Eugen Gomringer), and thus turns the reader into a "data cowboy" in quest of uncovering its matrix of meanings. These plays of readability and resistance can be clarified using Veronica Forrest-Thomson's vocabulary in her book *Poetic Artifice*, in which she describes a component of conventional reading strategies she calls "Naturalization" as

> an attempt to reduce the strangeness of poetic language and poetic organization by making it intelligible, by translating it into a statement about the non-verbal external world, by making the Artifice appear natural. Critical reading cannot, of course, avoid Naturalization altogether. Criticism is committed, after all, to helping us to understand both poetry as an institution and individual poems as significant utterances. But it must ensure that in its desire to produce ultimate meaning it does not purchase intelligibility at the cost of blindness: blindness to the complexity of those non-meaningful features which differentiate poetry from everyday language and make it something other than an external thematic statement about an already-known world. (p. xi)

Those "non-meaningful" aspects of poetry include the punctuation, line breaks, gaps between the words and sentences, sound and visual impression—basically anything about a poem that stands apart from common ways of communicating sense. One could call these "non-meaningful" elements those parts that don't contribute to the syntagmatic understanding of a sentence—its quality as a linear sequence of words that form a meaningful utterance—but a paradigmatic understanding, in which the elements of a sentence become isolated, outlined, objectified, and point back toward their grammatical subsets as "nouns," "verbs," etc. Collage poems, such as those collected in John Ashbery's *The Tennis Court Oath*, could be said to emphasize this quality: "Night hunger / of berry… stick" presents something more closely related to a literary shape, or gestalt, than a sentence or meaningful utterance. The CP, because of its looping functions, introduces new elements of "non-meaning" in the form of, for example, repetitions that are not based on rhetorical strategies (such as chiasmus or the refrain) but are simply redundant information coughed up by the demon. These repetitions may point to the "meaningful" aspects of the program, which are those parts that contribute to the affect of the dissimulated subjectivity, the loop perhaps suggesting obsessive human behaviors. In general, however, the demon itself must be considered "non-meaningful" simply because it is not part of language, and it certainly, in Forrest-Thomson's view of things, would separate the CP from "everyday language." (The early permutational poems of Brion Gysin, for example, were merely the exhaustion of combinations of a limited number of words—"I am that I am" is one example—the same word being stored once in a computer's memory but accessed several times by the demon. A performance of these poems turned the reader into a cyborg by introducing to the human body the looping structures of programming, an experience that might be "naturalized" by the auditor as a form of "obsessiveness." A good non-CP digital work that explores methods of digital repetition, in both its text and visual imagery, is the innovative hypertext essay by Charles Bernstein and Dante Piombino called "A Mosaic for a Convergence." It operates both in terms of spatial collage, as in a picture, and in temporal montage, as in a poem, and exploits the excesses that digital repetition makes available in its strategically tasteless use of wallpapers, loud fonts, dissonant colors and, in the text itself, irreverent tweaking of common communicative codes. Repetition in "A Mosaic" also serves to exaggerate the difference in scale between digital cut-and-paste methods and repetition in organic, crafted literary works—by Gertrude Stein or John Taggart, for example—or visual works that require repetitive action—the grids of Agnes Martin or the toothpicks and -paste of Tom Friedman. This is not so much to mock the limits of human endeavor but to demystify the quality of the "infinite" that is often touted as inherent to circuit boards and memory chips, not to mention hypertext itself.) For Forrest-Thomson, a critic trying to make a total statement about a poem will be involved in a push-and-pull with these non-meaningful elements, and no interpretation is adequate if it does not bear the marks of this struggle. She is against an overdetermined, monologic reading of a poem, one that has closed all gaps, permits no dialogue, and does not recognize the poem's dependent place in the world of texts or its status in textuality—as shards of grammar arrayed on a page. (Though she doesn't write this, naturalizing interpretations can also be seen as pursued in the quest for a "cathartic" experience for the reader, a personal epiphany that acts as a form of socialization and forces the reader to reproduce societal values in perfect, and not "illegitimate," form. This transference, which the CP troubles, is described in Donna Haraway's "Cyborg Manifesto," see footnote 19.) She continues:

> There would be no point in writing poetry unless poetry were different from everyday language, and any attempt to analyze poetry should cherish that difference and seek to remain within its bounds for as long as possible rather than ignore the difference in an unseemly rush from word to world. Good naturalization dwells on the non-meaningful levels of poetic language, such as phonetic and prosodic patterns and spatial organization, and tries to state their relation to other levels of organization rather than set them aside in an attempt to produce a statement about the world.

The CP, like Dada (which Forrest-Thomson recognizes as much concerned with Artifice and as not merely disruptive), values its materials over and against determinant meaning structures, whether narrative or philosophical, thus focusing the attention on the microscopic, concrete levels of the poetic organization—one might call this its architecture. The CP, as a form of "civilized Dada" (see footnote 6), foregrounds a new element: that of a structure that is not transcendent (this is not the world of infinite connections or a form that aspires to Platonic perfection) but is yet illustrative of a possible, if counter-intuitive, organization of knowledge. This would be its "non-meaningful" frame, its crystalline qualities, that can itself be the object of study. John Wilkinson, an English poet who, like Forrest-Thomson, is often associated with the circle of writers often called (inaccurately) the "Cambridge" school, richly describes such a principle of organization in his poems (not themselves CPs) which he calls the "metastatic":

> What gives the poems such coherence as they exhibit is not a development, but a set of linked and transforming entities, which can be syntactical gestures, vowel and consonant patterning, imagistic or discursive modes. "Metastasis" is a term in rhetoric, but my use derives from a brief experience of nursing in a cancer hospice, the way metastatic tumours echo about the body and these nodes define the shape of the body subjectively, through pain. Of course, the location of the primary tumour is outside the poem's realm; the poem develops around the metastatic nodes, and these gestures come to evoke its physical lineaments. The reticence of the primary helps guard against a reductive essentialism in approaching the poem, that it is about such-and-such—in fact, there will be a number of extrinsic primaries. Too many indeed for amenability. (p. 54)

He later writes that metastases are the "scattered receptor sites of a primary memory process, retrievable only in faint traces," which is to say they point to each other, and perhaps to an external structure, but more as hints than determinants. These "cosmologies may be the lyric traces of a primary event, a Big Bang," but Wilkinson spurns the "cosmological eschatology which returns the basic creation in the Big Shrink," an "encapsulation of the poem." Metastasis is an organizing principle that operates, in a systematic way, as a hold against final interpretations, but it instigates this challenge to interpret in the reader by teasing her with the recurrence of thematic conglomerations—after all, nodes of "pain" must be addressed, even if the "primary tumour" will never be discovered. The metastases, in a CP, are what conveys to the reader the sense that narrative is being constructed out of the materials from a database—they are the channels to the wholeness of the invisible source files. Consequently, "Cambridge poetry" of the sort that Wilkinson, Drew Milne and J.H. Prynne write often resembles Language poetry (see footnote 10) to the uninitiated, especially when it approaches a full atomization of language as in Prynne's sequence "Red D Gypsum": "Flow / flow my phloem dear ones, fibre life thickens limpid / blue aglets to mind your step or stop to look notable / avernus lee-side of a post." But Language poetry—due, perhaps, to its closer ties to classic Dada—struggles for a clean break with traditional interpretive strategies, sometimes even mocking the reader in his or her attempt to enact anything resembling "deep reading." The CP, because of its high overhead of non-meaningful elements, will also engage in this cycle of transparency and resistance by challenging conventional reading—even the conventions of reading a Language poem. It will avoid fetishizing the "clean break" because it is starting from a point that is already outside the continuum of organic, human artistic activity—it starts from noise and algorithm and moves toward convention. There are few enough reasons for reading a cyborgian text unless it be that the metastases that the non-meaningful, "deictic" (see footnote 41) demon plants in the stream take on some engagement with the "human." It is fortuitous that, in Wilkinson's description of metastasis, "pain" becomes the node that limns the "body" of the textual stream, as it is "pain" that, for Wittgenstein in the *Philosophical Investigations*, was the channel or link between "reality" and the language-game, the latter of which was threatened with solipsism. Touch, our one sense that can be experienced in a "non-linear" fashion, as several different inputs from a sheet of skin which combine into a feeling of "pain" or "comfort," is a useful analogy to the way the thematic of a CP can exist as a "harmonic" overtone, as indebted to no particular part but as the composite of its affects. But because the CP has no organic component—either in the

II.

hewed the lindenwood, hacked "the sacred,"[4]
20   would be too officious (the leather container,
        lard all cordoning) and to speak of it as "the

spiritual battleshield": sons of Edward with
hammered brands. Theirs was a Greatness heart:
        hex and humus. Yet hetero and would be

25   amorphous, too easily misconstrued in cringing,
    (shooting, too) terms of belief and not imagination,
        unless "spiritual" got from their Grandsires[5]—

---

form of a creation narrative or the direct link to human labor (there is labor, but it can be equated more with building the factory than working in it)—its engagements will hardly be to reaffirm humanism as a philosophical framework. Nonetheless, it creates an uncomfortable contract with humanism to inaugurate this cycle of reading and resistance.

[4] One of the key features of the CP is the high-speed switches in modalities that it exhibits, shocking changes-of-gears that impress the reader as having no grounding in intuitional poetic artistry. The result of these ruptures, which occur with a frequency determined by the demon, but also based on the informational temperature (see footnote 22) of the source texts, is a liberation of meanings that can range from the erotic to the political, the parodic to the morose—a carnival of loosed emotions and competing "Egos" (see footnote 8), not to mention words. In CPs that utilize source texts that possess carnivalesque characteristics themselves, the outcome can appear to be a sort of bawdy social comedy, one without reference to a specific object, though perhaps to a genre or set of themes. That is, the singular attitude of the CP toward another linguistic system—a conventional "poem," an essay, the vocabulary of social critique—grants it

the quality of parody or satire. (In the case of "Stops and Rebels," this thematic might be the comedy of literary Oedipal struggles, mostly enacted by men, in which one generation of "sons" tries to take down another of "fathers" in the quest to perpetuate tradition, and consequently masculine dominance. The plagiarized texts, such as the paragraph of Bloom's, give this theoretical focus, while the translations of the "Battle of Brunaburh" grant it certain qualities of the genres of oral historical narrative.) Of course, "carnival" has been a central theme of the writings of Mikhail Bakhtin—he devotes an entire book to it, *Rabelais and His World*—and his understanding of this concept points to another aspect of the CP, which is its relation to the social sphere and how it operates as an engine for recycling, reshuffling and leveling values. John Lechte provides a useful summary of the carnival theme in *Fifty Key Contemporary Thinkers*, first writing on the theme of laughter:

> Carnival laughter cannot be equated with the specific forms it takes in modern consciousness. It is not simply parodic, ironical or satirical. Carnival laughter has no object. It is ambivalent. Ambivalence is the key to the structure of carnival. The logic of carnival is, as Kristeva has shown, not the true or false, quantitative and causal logic of science and seriousness, but the qualitative logic of ambivalence, where the actor is also the spectator, destruction gives rise to creativity, and death is equivalent to rebirth. (p. 8)

The cyclical nature of carnival and it's property of symbolic reversals—in which the grave becomes the womb, for example—is readily apparent in the CP, in which looping routines and their indifference to human "meanings" make all words, and even punctuation, objects of exchange and refiguration. The algorithms seek, through destruction of prior literary "wholes," to create new stable forms in their own image, and hence the impression of infinite reinvention—technology's power play. What is more important is the nature of "laughter" in the CP, a laughter that is not the effect of an authorial gesture—the Wildean twist, the Twainian irony—but requires some creativity from the reader herself. That is, because the CP partly operates on the principle of the interpreted gestalt—there is no narrative, so each word event takes on the quality of an incomplete image, like an inkblot in a Rorschach test—whatever humor that occurs operates in contrast to some system of values that exist outside of the poem. One could say that all humor operates this way, but in a CP there is no set-up, and hence no punch-line. Rather, the CP is a pointer to another set of values it is perversely mirroring, as if a linguistic Photoshop filter had been run over a set of terms from a recognizable field of knowledge or another literary work. The reader "completes the joke" not through wit but because the "joke" is on the reader herself and on the expectations and predispositions of the reader as configured by experience and society. Of course, the creator of a CP—the human who edits the output, if there is editing—also partakes in this readerly activity, tightening up here and there based on her reactions to the "inkblots." All objects are put into the position of being mocked because of their vulnerability to the demon's philistine banality. The demon, likewise, implicates the reader, who is vulnerable to participation in the poem by being (one assumes) a text-creating being. Thus, though there is often a satiric aspect to a CP, there is no "object" to the laughter, unless that object be the conventions of poetry itself—the whole myth of "inspiration," for example—which is always going to be put in a denigrated light by the cyborg author (see footnote 39). The incorporation of all people within the space of the CP is most realized in those demons that operate on the live data of the internet. The most relevant one here, perhaps, is called the "pornolizer" (www.pornolize.com) which takes any submitted web page and replaces its words with exaggeratedly obscene substitutes. This "pornolization" renders any text, from stock market reports to literary masterworks, to the operations of the demon—which is to say, the cycle of carnival. (Another example of this is Darren Wershler-Henry's rewrite of Kenneth Goldsmith's work *Fidget*, in which Goldsmith schematically described every action that he made for an entire day into a tape recorder, resulting in text such as: "Left hand tucks at pubic area. Extracts testicles and penis using thumb and forefinger. Left hand grasps penis. Pelvis pushes on bladder, releasing urine," etc. Goldsmith's book is a literary response to some of the fascination with privacy and the panopticon whose best known symptoms are web cams and reality shows. Consequently, it is also a commentary on the phenomenon of data transference that is endemic in cultural activity—digitizing photographs, scanning texts—in this case, making the body the original "medium," like a floppy disk. Wershler-Henry's "filter," a very basic algorithm, puts the word "tiny" before each of the nouns. His rewrite of *Fidget*, called *Midget*, runs partly: "Tiny left hand tucks at tiny pubic area. Extracts tiny testicles and tiny penis using tiny thumb and tiny forefinger. Tiny left hand grasps tiny penis. Tiny pelvis pushes on tiny bladder, releasing urine," etc. This teleactive action—turning the persona of Goldsmith into a midget—illustrates the power of the CP to recreate reality, to shuffle meanings, with a total indifference to the particulars of its actions.) As Lechte writes later: "Carnival… embraces lowness. Degradation, debasement, the body and all its functions—but particularly defecation, urination, and copulation—are part and parcel of the ambivalent carnival experience." (9) In this way, carnival seeks to incorporate everything into its cycle of exchanges—the sanctity of the Church brought down to the level of the marketplace, the lowness of the bodily functions brought into the eternal cycle of death and fecundity. Carnival was opposed to the artificial temporal measures—the hour, the day, the week—that organized the life of "economic man," and it brought the bourgeois as well as the peasant into a public space of laughter. In a CP such as "Stops and Rebels," this "low" dimension is not so prevalent, but as often occurs with randomized juxtaposition of words, sexual innuendo often sprouts from the most innocent phrase. When the indifference of the demon to human taboos is left to govern, minor slips are transformed into grotesque explosions, and the nuance is exchanged for the obvious. Of course, these can all be modified by the creator of the CP in the editing stage, but it is likely that they will not be entirely deleted as these accidents help integrate the machinery of the CP into humanistic concerns—at least as humorous commentary. One aspect of carnival on which Bakhtin focuses is the carnival mask, which he sees as a site of negotiation that is both contradictory and ambivalent, that both hides and reveals. It is the agent of dissimulation—pointing to the "human" but not revealing it—yet in folk culture (as opposed to Romantic culture) it is valued as being the transitory space between selves. As he writes in *Rabelais*:

> The mask is connected with the joy of change and reincarnation, with gay relativity and with the merry negation of uniformity and similarity; it rejects conformity to oneself. The mask is related to transition, metamorphoses, the violation of natural boundaries, to mockery and familiar nicknames. It contains the playful element of life; it is based on a peculiar interrelation of reality and image, characteristic of the most ancient rituals and spectacles. Of course it would be impossible to exhaust the intricate multiform symbolism of the mask. Let us point out that such manifestations as parodies, caricatures, grimaces, eccentric postures, and comic gestures are per se derived from the mask. It reveals the essence of the grotesque. (p. 40)

Likewise, the well-tempered CP—a cyborgian construct operating in a cultural sphere that prizes individual achievement—is the mask of the artist, or simply the mask of the "poem" as social construct. It rarely reveals much about the "author" other than a congeries of preferences, a topography of strategies, that are peculiar to the creator of the CP—a singular attitude or affect not traceable to any source. The mask of the CP satisfies the need for familiarity in the supposedly "public" sphere of digital communication; it is the ghostly representation of non-individualized personhood which organizes the indifferent flows of information that is text. It also suggests the cyberpoet to be a version of the "digital flaneur," the anonymous stroller of arcades who, by interactions too quick for subsumption into a narrative, subtly reorchestrates the internal dynamics of the crowd. Consequently, it is the interface for the reader (or "user") through which she might hope to engage with the poetic entity. It's not incidental that Pound's use of "personae" coincided with his early investigations into the uses of different vocabularies—Provencal, Anglo-Saxon, Chinese—as if he were relying on the mask to invite the reader into an engagements with new forms of information. (Browning's information-laden poems do a similar thing. *The Ring and the Book* is probably the apotheosis of this method of channeling information through both personae and architectural structure, each of its 12 sections describing the same murder scene as a merry-go-round whodunit.) The mask, with its spirit of play, also suggests an element in the contract that would be formed between a CP and reader: that the "grotesque"—or the "monstrous" (see footnote 39) in both scale and content—is an acceptable value in the poem. Without such a contract, the CP might be frightening, threatening the ontological security of the individual by the formation, out of pure information and noise, of this simulated personhood. Readers of poetry appreciate brevity; the demon shuns it, but the competence of the mask helps forge a promise that the text is nonetheless a distillation of intense aesthetic activity. It is for this reason that cyberpoetry that seeks only to reveal the machinations of "data"—that fetishizes the streaming and not the "fashionability" of language—falls short in the digital realm which is already reducing human linguistic constructions, or subjective expression of the "self," to the level of indifferent exchange.

5 Walter Benjamin (1892-1940), German-Jewish man of letters. Looming over any discussion of the arts and technology is Benjamin's seminal essay titled "The Work of Art in the Age of Mechanical Reproduction," which considers among other matters the decay of the "aura"—that "unique phenomenon of distance" one gets looking at an object—a process that had been set in motion by the advent of photography and film:

> Unmistakably, reproduction as offered by picture magazines and newsreels differs from the image seen by the unarmed eye. Uniqueness and permanence are as closely linked in the latter as are transitoriness and reproducibility in the former. To pry an object from its shell, to destroy its aura, is the mark of a perception whose "sense of the universal equality of things" has increased to such a degree that it extracts it even from a unique object by means of reproduction. (p. 223)

For Benjamin the aura that obtains around art in the modern world is a residual effect of the role art once played in "magical" and "religious" ritual, which is now "recognizable as secularized ritual." Part of the power of art was that it remained hidden, accessible only to priests or other social figures with the social mandate to view it. The secularization of society, in Benjamin's view, brought about increased exhibition of art objects, hence transforming their aura. The CP can either adopt or reject this ritualistic quality, based on several factors: the sources of its texts (the "public domain," original compositions, obscure texts), the level of "strong" or "weak" AI that its program might exhibit (see footnote 16), and the more conventional function of the poet as editor of the final output. Even when the CP is at the level of pure "noise"—a stream of data that, at least to human cognition, cannot be recuperated into "meaning"—it obtains a ritualistic quality depending on the art-historical paradigms (of which there can be several in a historical period such as our own) utilized to view or "read" it. That is, a sensibility engaged in the continuity from Dada to Language poetry may grant to an arrangement of "noise" a form of objecthood; a programmer with no art-historical paradigms might see a stream of glitches; one invested in the writings of Bataille and Deleuze may see the economy of expenditure; a reader nursed on the classics will see a debasement of the entire literary enterprise (provided it's accepted as literature at all). But "digital" text, in which text is characterized by being vulnerable to database routines, has already lost some of its aura by sacrificing not just the mark of the hand, but the historicity and material stability of the page. The well-tempered CP will acquire some of the aura of art simply by moving toward convention and acquiring what might be called "poemhood"— a certain fitness for the page—but it is nonetheless illustrative of the universal exchangeability of things simply by being tied to a database in which words are merely tokens. The Rabelaisian element (see footnote 4) of a CP will contribute to this decay of the aura by capitalizing on the poem's vulnerability to algorithm, by subjecting text to infinite permutations and transforming high into low and vice versa. Benjamin's essay tempts with several analogies that could be drawn between film and the CP (just as it tempts with analogies along the photo-is-to-film as hypertext-is-to-CP line, which I won't pursue). For example, he writes that the newsreel "offers everyone the opportunity to rise from passer-by to movie extra," a sort of apotheosis of the subject into film form that is similar to a CP that utilizes materials from the public domain or other "found" sources, including online diaries, chat rooms, scientific articles, even one's own old letters and discarded poems. One's private emissions—any product of intimate relations to oneself or an other that makes it into the digital realm—become, like the face in a film, subject to synthesis into art, to the arena of commodification, to exchange. In this event, its singularity, its uniqueness in line and signification, is rendered something like a type, if not a stereotype (as any "extra" is a stereotype). Benjamin writes that the "unique aura of the personality" that an actor possesses on stage is lost when he or she becomes a film actor, at which point the "spell of personality," the "phony spell of the commodity," takes hold. Likewise, the CP, which is characterized by a "factory" element in the form of the demon (see footnote 22), exploits its words for the sake of a form of commerce, in which case the word loses the function it served in "writing." Perspective for the viewer of the film—displaced by camera angles from a stable view of the "stage" of activity—is analogous to the loss of perspective in a CP, in which the cobbling together of sources (or the cobbling together of programs) provides the reader with a sort of three-dimensional text that obeys no stable Cartesian coordinates. Likewise, the collage of "egos" creates no stable forum in which to pursue the elusive "voice," the harmonic overtones of the dissimulated subjectivity. Benjamin writes:

> [Film] presents a process in which it is impossible to assign to a spectator a viewpoint which would exclude from the actual scene such extraneous accessories as camera equipment, lighting machinery, staff assistants, etc.—unless his eye were on a line parallel with the lens. This circumstance, more than any other, renders superficial and insignificant any possible similarity between a scene in the studio and one on the stage. In the theater one is well aware of the place from which the play cannot immediately be detected as illusionary. There is no such place for the movie scene that is being shot. Its illusionary nature is that of

the second degree, the result of cutting. That is to say, in the studio the mechanical equipment has penetrated so deeply into the reality that its pure aspect freed from the foreign substance of equipment is the result of a special procedure, namely, the shooting by the specially adjusted camera and the mounting of the shot together with other similar ones. The equipment-free aspect of the reality here has become the height of artifice; the sight of immediate reality has become an orchid in the land of technology. (p. 232-233)

This "penetration" of the camera into reality—which Benjamin later compares to the incisions of the modern surgeon—can be seen as analogous to the acts of systematized, but blind, citation that the demon enacts on the source texts. Though this "reality" is always limned by two cuts, these incisions are not always foregrounded. In the narrative film, it is often exposed as the cuts in a montage sequence in which each image is discrete, sometimes offering wildly different perspectives. In a CP, an aesthetics of "sampling" and "composite" is prominent, and one is more prone to recognize distinctive functions at work rather than discrete elements in the continuum. This might hide the origins of the source files—Harold Bloom in "Stops and Rebels," for example—and consequently the intentions of the poet, even as they contribute to the dominant affect. Perhaps, in an effort to further conceal the "equipment" of a CP—one component of which is the "poet"—Benjamin's statement suggests that a different strategy be taken in the public presentation of a CP, different types of "readings" that don't involve a podium, a reader, and an audience. The CP, banking not just on dissimulation but on its quality as a "folk" product engaged in decentered, carnivalesque play (see footnote 4), would best be presented in a fashion that either eliminated the poet entirely (animations, recordings) or subjected the "reader" to the indifference of the "audience" by giving them something to do. There are several statements in Benjamin's essay which could go far to elaborate the CP aesthetic, such as Benjamin's claim that the Dadaists' literary "word salads" were intended to exaggerate their "uselessness for contemplative immersion." But times have changed

theirs that so be defined low-down (but still

sure-footing) as a radical Fairy fee-fi-foeing

30   anger with the conditions of the world, socially.

And he felt damned with, metaphysically, or else

it the dryad, second-in, might be conceived as a

                critical-detachment sweat, since "Sin" summed

him often, in from the given; a strife with their

35   enemies struck for their hoards, detachment

                creative of the—and their—hearths' otherness of

---

and many such tactics—beat poetry, punk rock, even radical performance art—have been compromised by contemporary social conditions in which it has become street wisdom that everything, including dissent, can be commodified. There is also the historical precedent of "civilizing" tendencies that certain inheritors of Dada like Finlay (see footnote 6) or John Cage in his mesostics have invented to suit their works for "contemplation," if not "immersion." The CP can play on both poles—it is neither a sonic scream nor an English garden, but somehow links them in a field of organized, however hyperactive, values. In general, the overarching concept of the work of art in the age of the "masses," in which reproduction can be utilized both for increasing distraction and promoting engagement—not a value-free technique so much as one courting ambivalence—presents exciting avenues for pursuing the CP as a popular form of sophisticated entertainment, like film itself. If this seems far-fetched, think of Lev Manovich's claim in *The Language of New Media* that "a whole trend among new media artists [is the] exploration of the minimal conditions of narrative" (264) because of their adherence both to database structures of knowledge and to market acceptability. A recent popular film that seems to bear this out is Richard Linklater's *Waking Life*, which was filmed with live actors, many of whom improvised their dialogue and were non-professionals, and then converted to digital figures that resembled cartoon animation. There was

III.

clarification—of a complex up and their homes.
Bowed the spoiler, bent once the Scotsman[6], fell
  the shipcrews, emotional and Doomed-to-the-

40   Death. All the field with blood of the fighters
      more 'gainst the peeved—he married to tongue-
        rolls, glue of her ground-bass, imaginary good

      Handel[7] borscht: an spark in the light of which
      metaphor and reality are constantly in question.
45   To call it a new eroticism would also be

---

no "narrative" per se except of the hero's meeting these individuals by chance and his suspicion that he is not "awake." Without this hero—who, in a sense, is a double for the net-surfer, the "data cowboy," but is also Benjamin's everyman, his anonymous "extra"—the film would have been entirely composed of philosophical vignettes centered around the general theme of filmic reality itself. Perhaps we can credit digital technology, and phenomena such as 3D game-worlds, for the possibility of a major feature film that has sacrificed the standbys of commercial success—sex, drama, action, plot—to be somewhat popular. The CP that takes on some game-world aesthetics (see footnote 27) as well as integrates material from the everyday—diaries, found texts—might be able to exploit this quality.

[6] Ian Hamilton Finlay (b. 1925), Scottish poet and gardener. Finlay's work, much of which is carefully arranged in his 20-acre garden called variably Stonypath or Little Sparta, itself a poem of foliage, stone and words, may appear at first completely opposed to the CP ethos. His concrete poems, literally worked in stone and other materials, depend on the materiality of their words—the stone into which the poems are carved, the growth around the winding paths, the location of the garden in Scotland—where-

as the CP is hardly a "local" phenomenon, and of course immaterial. In fact, when derived from the texts of the web, the CP puts the primacy of these values in question, reducing geographic space to a field of language accessible and mutable from anywhere. Nonetheless, due to Finlay's peculiar brand of "multimedia," the forms of wandering his "total installation" garden encourages, his work in Scottish-language poetry, and the distinctively conservative nature of his philosophy—it traces its heritage back to the pre-Socratics—a consideration of his art offers a contrasting perspective on how the image/text complex can operate in a world system that, itself, often disavows the "local," the singular, the non-exchangeable, and (a particular interest of Finlay's) even the cycles of the seasons. Finlay has done work in a variety of media—in stone, gold, neon light, even on the backs of turtles—but the most relevant work of his, for our purposes, are the small art books of heroic emblems. An emblem is a short poem, or "motto," that engages with a simple, almost iconic image in complex, historically resonant, ways. As a form, it has existed since before the Renaissance, but was suppressed after the Renaissance when it was credited with being a vessel for transporting hermetic, culturally unsanctioned meanings—a form of memory (see footnote 37) that was not easily observable by authorities. As Yves Abrioux writes in *Ian Hamilton Finlay: A Visual Primer* (MIT Press, 1992):

> For [Finlay], the form of the emblem generates, in Gombrich's words, "a free-floating metaphor," formed from the conjunction of motto and image, setting it apart from more conventional methods of establishing meaning... The "heroic emblems" are also intended to provoke meditation. Finlay sets before us a cultural tissue in which the Classical, the Renaissance and the Modern are indissolubly linked. Out of the mysterious aptness of the combination of terse motto and striking image comes the resonant metaphor. The commentary is a movement away from this metaphor, which begins the process of interpretation but necessarily never completes it since it is endless. (p. 105)

Because of this emphasis on the hermeneutic, Finlay's art is valuable to the cyberpoet as a contrast to some of the givens of postmodern literary culture as it argues for depth—though not psychological depth—in an art based partly on collage. That is, the emblem, like the image in new media, is a sort of "portal to another world" (to borrow a phrase of Lev Manovich), layered with meanings that have to be accessed, or unpacked, rather than conveying all of these meanings on the surface. (That this image is often, like a cartoon drawing, a reduced form of a "realistic" image also suggests a tenuous relationship to new media, as it suffered the same fate of marginality as animated movies in pre-digital film culture.) The heroic emblem also puts some of the recognizable features of postmodernism—such as the use of "theory"—in a new light. For instance, *polysemeity*—the state of words in which several meanings are possible and engage in a play of "difference" within their own codes—has often been considered the gold standard of interesting avant-garde work at least since the time of the Language poets (see footnote 10), and perhaps even earlier (by Gertrude Stein or the Surrealists, for instance). For these writers, juxtaposition corrupts categories of thinking, renders the word opaque, tweaks genre, fragments elements of the sentence and paragraph and puts social, ethical and aesthetic standards in a state of autocritique, making the reader a collaborator with the writer in creating meanings—the "active reader." Finlay's work, while encouraging the creation of meaning by the reader, nonetheless operates within a strict circuit of possible solutions, solutions which often depend on some specialized knowledge. Juxtaposition operates more on the level of the program which produces meanings from a limned area of "sources" rather than as a stick of dynamite that explodes the sutures of the spectacle. But there is a third element to the heroic emblem: the commentary—accompanying paragraphs that interpret the image, often written by another person—which I am suggesting operates as a sort of "theory" by which to approach the emblem. The commentary unpacks the symbols to relate the images and words to philosophical debate, to set the circuit of the riddle in motion, sometimes by simply pointing out the cultural sources in the emblem. It adopts a speculative, though encouraging, tone for the reader, operating on rational premises and knowledge though withholding final interpretations. One commentary on an emblem with the motto "Éternelle Action Du Paros Immobile / Éternelle Action Des Paras Immobiles" matched with a drawing of an umbrella sprinkled with cloud-like roses and plane-like insects, runs in part:

> In this emblem, the seemingly innocent pun which allows us to shift from "Paros" to "Paras" (and from singular to plural) mobilizes a whole series of cultural references which are, so to speak, encapsulated in the image. The original motto is a one-line poem by the French poet Emmanuel Lochac, published in the 1930s and doubtless a reflection of the influence of Apollinaire. Yet in its content it is a strong evocation of the Neo-classic tradition, perhaps of Winckelmann's lyrical passages on Graeco-Roman sculpture where the "eternal action" of the marble and its "immobility" are equally stressed. The substitution of "Paras" for "Paros" (the island especially associated with the production of Greek marble) allows a new, hyperbolic image to supplant the old: the descent of parachutes against the blue sky having the same quality of "eternal action" as the immobile, classic art. (p. 107)

As the wealth of information in these sentences shows, the commentary, which often includes a sizeable bibliography, helps to set in motion the emblem's function as a conduit of information, placing the "immobile" emblem as a node in the "eternal action" of a flowing system of meanings. (Not surprisingly, the classic conundrum of fixity and flux seems to be the content of many of these commentaries.) It even offers a sort of democratizing element into this elitist art form, providing some of the tools the novice reader might need to approach interpretation, and thus to enter its meditative spaces. The emblem does not fetishize signification itself as the only field in which the artist plays. Perhaps, in this fashion, it would be more useful to think of the emblem, icon and commentary as a form of spatial montage, the three parts playing against each other to form a minimal narrative or argument, rather than as juxtaposition, which always seems to imply a disorderedness. It does not render the word opaque to isolate it from the regular operations of language, but fits it into a signification machine that itself has limited but pleasurable uses—as an object for contemplation, for example. These limits are tied to its cultural specificity, as the emblem is not unlocatable on a rhizomic circuit, but points to moments of history, of a singular—in space and time—historical activity (such as writing) as relating to this "eternal" motion. Finlay's manner of "civilizing dada" (his own phrase) moves the techniques of radical juxtaposition in the direction of "rearticulation" (to borrow Jeff Derksen's word for the activity of various post-Language poetries)—it reorganizes knowledge. But Finlay's "non-secular" art does not just stand in contrast to the march of ephemera and banality in a globalized world, but also points to an ethical, timeless universe that he feels is becoming obscured. As the poet and critic Drew Milne writes in his essay "Adorno's Hut," Finlay's art "continually suggests an elegiac pathos of distance in which the modern world is seen through the estranged idioms of the classical world," suggesting that the classical world is being utilized as an organizing principle, even a "filter," for the disparate idioms of the "modern." This feature structures the play of polysemeity that modernist art valued and yet, in the clockwork of the emblem, also plays a "non-secular" role against the presumed godless, libertarian universe of these same modes. Likewise, the well-tempered CP points outward from itself toward potentially locatable actions, toward place even, and, in the CP that operates in a newsreel or documentary fashion (see footnote 5), toward the reader herself as participant in the poem—as vulnerable to the machinations of the demon. I am not stating that the CP points to the "eternal," but that it points to something—the hidden ritualistic, and total operations of the demon. This is manifest in the matrix of meanings that operate as a weak approximation to the Ptolemaic universe (see footnote 24) or as a weak version of "AI," which is to say an omniscient intelligence (see footnote 16). Because of this impersonal, but highly proportional, ordering tendency, the CP stands apart from older versions of collage-based poetics which were improvisational in nature, as the coherence of its demon and source texts—the program—forms a totalizing umbrella over the fragments it has set in motion, the form providing the image of a universe in which the fragment has its

reductive, but surely this poetry, icky, flowed,

from when first the great Sun-star[8], Dis witness,

    he offered. —She othered of morningtide. Lamp of

the Lord God has this chef, deciding to settle it:

50   an ample category for pleasure, a category

    absent, Lord everlasting, as Joel Lewis[9] has

glode over earth till the glorious noted, in the

hegemonic mode of experimental *THERE*

    formalism, known as language poetry[10]. Creature

---

role. This also sets in motion a "process of interpretation" (see footnote 3), or the "attractor" (see footnote 39), though one very different from the standard mode in poetry or even the workings of much Language Poetry. The image in a CP becomes, like Finlay's emblem, a "portal to another world," and therefore possesses some of the qualities of the digital image itself. Consequently, Finlay's use of the motto and image, as well as his garden Stonypath, is not unlike political graffiti such as that inspired by the Situationists who envisaged the city as a field of "psychogeographic" wandering, the graffiti intended to work on the populace to establish, in guerrilla fashion, new, engaged forms of class and state identification and to fetishize revolution for its own sake as spontaneous creativity. This plays into the CP's quality as a "détourned" item—one based on found texts that it teleactively controls by changing the contexts in which the phrases exist—but also as a game-space (see footnote 27) in which the reader acts as hero searching for the gold of suppressed meanings. Consequently, one of the first truly successful web poetry sites, William Poundstone's "New Digital Emblems," is devoted to a study of the uses of the emblem for web art, and effectively utilizes what might be called the interface of the classical emblem—motto, image, commentary—as, literally, a computer interface. Conceived entirely for the Shockwave plug-in—hence, a work that uses no text HTML and is inassimilable into other projects—it both parodies and pays homage to the didactic garden of Finlay as a closed-off universe resistant to the forces of globalization, a sort of relationship that all CPs have toward works arising out of stable subject or geographic positions.

[7] George Friedrich Handel (1685-1759), German-English composer of the late baroque era.

[8] Steve McCaffery (b. 1947), Canadian-English poet, theorist and anthologist. The range of McCaffery's work—including his earliest period when he was part of the "Toronto Research Group" with bpNichol, his many anthologies of alternative deviant linguistic practices (most recently *Imagining Language*, edited with Jed Rasula), his sound and processual poetry, and his writing on the "protosemantic" collected in *Prior to Meaning*—forms an incredibly detailed and erudite historical and theoretical foundation for an elaboration of CP aesthetics. I don't hope to consider all of this work here, but several of his projects play a direct role in anticipating the problems and solutions a CP proposes. Important poems include "Lastworda," a collection of words from the OED arranged in the order of which they first appeared in history—a vacuation of the contents of a dictionary into an open-ended reading structure that doesn't recognize dates, geography or grammar—and "The Black Debt," a prose poem that works on the level of the phrase in a paratactic but highly recursive fashion, its phrases circling back on themselves to create new meanings out of puns and repetition. His poems often include descriptions of the processes that went into their construction (a quality he shares with another proto-CP poet, Jackson Mac Low). He describes the sequence "'Ow's "Waif" as a type of composition that permits

> the writer a near to total separation of form from content, the entire "borrowing" of content as a prepared word-supply (a "supply-text") and a creative concentration on the invention of the poems' forms as verbal fields free of presupposed or prerequisite rule structures of grammar and syntax. (p. 441)

McCaffery thus describes the fundamental structures in place for the production of a CP: source text, process, and "creative concentration"—what the poet-as-editor does with the output. The process or demon of a CP, which is embodied in the code, is also part of the creativity—perhaps even the central part—though its activities, basically a shuffling of data, work against the recuperative processes of the poet hoping to integrate the CP into the circuit of culture. Another poem, *Carnival*, a wall-size piece in the concrete tradition which provides a topology of free semiotic play—it is constructed of several sections which, when connected, take on an epic scale—is a sort of psychogeographic roadmap in which planar sectors burgeon with the activity of its graphemic citizenry. (Both "panels" of *Carnival*, which can be seen at the chbooks.com website, suggest where digital visual art, such as the Shockwave pieces of turux.org, could be integrated into a discourse on poetics, as the slowly changing images of turux impress the viewer with the beauty of the rules governing its creation. The hardwiring of its algorithms only becomes apparent as the work progresses and the language—the syntax of the rules governing the image—is "learned" by the user. This forges a contract for its continued creation in tandem with user input; the images rely on feedback from the user to continue its "impacts, collisions, and zoomorphic lines of flight"—three terms McCaffery uses to describe his sequence "Broken Mandala." Most of the work of turux is "post-semiotic," if one understands that term to mean a text that offers no conventional orthography and yet contains the codes for its own literalization, since there are no letters, nor even titles for each piece. However, with imagination one can suss out the grapheme in many of them—like the "Ninas" in the drawings of Hirschfield. One's attention, which is never purely "visual," grows to occupy the architectures of the image, some of which are three-dimensional, analogous to the ways one inhabits the properties of a new language or a three-dimensional game-world.) McCaffery runs a website, the North American Centre of Poetics, but he has not written much about the potential in computers for poetry as far as I know. In the second TRG report (collected in *Rational Geomancy*), titled "Narrative," he notes that the hypertext novel *Mindwheel*, published in 1984, "does not rise above the level of an entertainment," and that its plot "reads as an elaborate version of an arcade video game." Since then, video games have become a great concern to theorists such as Lev Manovich, who believes real-time 3D imaging with user participation to be one of the major breakthroughs of digital technology, and Espen Aarseth, in the chapters of *Cybertext* that consider a Piercian semiology for arcade games (see footnote 32). Several interactive computer works either utilize video game metaphors, such as Neil Hennessey's "Basho's Frogger"—missing the first line of logs, the frog has no choice but to drown three times, recalling the crux of one of Basho's most famous haiku—and Jennifer Ley's "War Games," which replaces cheap banner ads and ad copy with a "catch the landmine" motif and activist texts. Print works also increasingly access the narrative tropes and absorptive 3D realms of games, such as Stacy Doris's *Kildare*—the poem is a series of fragments arranged somewhat like a play, but which point to a whole matrix of interrelations beyond the bounds of the poem—and Christophe Tarkos' long prose poem "Toto," a text stream that is a cross between the movie "Toy Story" and the hallucinogenic kinetics of William S. Burroughs. McCaffery's lack of concern for video games was not short-sighted—video games just weren't what they are back then. From McCaffery's description of *Mindwheel*, it appears to share the same flaws of much early hypertext fiction, which is a naive faith that transparent, consumable narrative will remain interesting when rendered in a non-absorptive, choose-your-own-adventure manner (one in which devices like foreshadowing and character development have to be replaced), and that the interest in navigating the contents of the database will remain when utility, on the one hand, and significant interaction with the properties of the fictional world (as in role playing games) on the other are absent. Despite this lack of specific engagement, nearly everything McCaffery has written—on Robin Blaser's serial poems, on Bill Bissett's poetics of excess, on Karen Mac Cormack's poems which "show how poems can be comprehended kinetically," even the essay "Voice in Extremis" about sound poetry—provides accounts of the operations of language on a pre-intentional plane, at a level that approaches "noise" but which is nonetheless legible. My use of the term "libidinal economy" is based on a reading of his important essay from *North of Intention* called "Writing as a General Economy," which considers language's paragrammic qualities—how words are produced out of other words, to make text autonomous—and the potlatch economy, in which, developing upon Bataille, text is understood as a void-ance, a form of barter in which there is no gift given in return. This points to one site of divergence between my thinking on the CP and his poetics, which would have to do with the relationship between the residue of intentionality that exists in a source text and how this intentionality is or could be preserved, however fragmented, in a CP. McCaffery writes that Burroughs' cut-up method in novels such as *The Soft Machine* and *Nova Express* produced work that

> doesn't register as produced from the interior economy of the Self or Ego—entirely absent is the feeling that some Subject is speaking or writing to me. Intersubjective address is replaced by the readerly awareness that language itself is speaking. By phys-ically dichotomizing two texts and recombining their disparate parts, Burroughs produces a dissonant univocity that dislodges any language of the Said… Words are less the predetermined instruments of intentionality than volatile, autonomous projec-tiles. Burroughs presents a democratic mandate to liberate a lan-guage-at-hand from a self's own cognitive control. And through it alterity emerges not in the Other, as reader, but the Other of language. (p. 218)

My difference with McCaffery's position stems from the assumed binary here between language that is constructed from the Ego and what he pre-sumes is the opposite, language as "autonomous projectiles." It seems to me that what is liberated when language is "cut up" is not language from the Ego, but the various trajectories inherent in the phrase which have been stifled by authorial intention but which, nonetheless, obtain their character as trajectories by partaking in whatever new ordering the author has applied to them. That is, algorithmic processes create "ghost subjectiv-ities" by accessing the properties of language that are normally accessed by writers when "writing." Some of these properties include rhetorical con-structs—chiasmus, repetition, etc.—the structuring of an argument or nar-rative (even if only metastatically, see footnote 3), specific vocabularies which can both "date" and "place" a text (accurately or not), the use of parat-actic structures, and the entire range of interpersonal affects that might be lifted over from live social interaction—the "I" and "you" maintaining some proximity to their normative uses. This might be analogous to Lev Manovich's concept of an "ethics of virtuality," in which virtuality "must maintain a memory of what it replaces" (261), and points to another way in which the CP differs from pre-digital methods of collage and processual poetry, which is in its relation to realism from a no-place of non-reality: the bitstream. Though a CP can certainly be constructed that erases any trace of the author's intentions in a source text—an n=1 poem, in the manner of Hartmann (see footnote 32) would be like this—CPs can also be created in which the "Ego" of the source text can be brought back in, if in fragmented form, to influence the primary trajectory of the CP as a whole. Since the CP is synthetic, and closer to the composite than the montage, all elements become synthesized into a primary affect, and this affect often resembles a lyrical subjectivity. In fact, it is these returned Egos that give the CP cen-tripetal motion, making it more than a cold diagram of information—an architectural structure attractive for its ability to pull symmetry out of chaos, or return the "aura" (see footnote 5), the spirit of the cathedral viewed in the distance, to digital art. These ghostly Egos contribute to the dissimulation of lyrical presence in a CP, and hence contribute to an identi-fiable interface that activates user interpretation. This is the dissimulation of a lyrical "other," like in the Turing test, in which the reader might actual-ly approach a CP for personal counsel (the infamous case of using the primitive "Eliza" program for effective psychotherapy is one example), or the "sortes Virgiliae," in which a randomly selected line of Virgil's is used to obtain a prophecy from a god. In the present CP, for example, all of the phrases from the Harold Bloom source file reappear in the final work, though in modified form. Bloom's "intentions" are certainly not preserved, but the significance of his phrases saturates the thematics of this poem, such that the primary field of the poem's meanings circulates between his ideas on Oedipal generational succession, the description of the "Battle of Brunaburh," and my rather arbitrary, deflating phonetic translation. The "attitude" of the poem—the primary affect—surfaces out of the dynamic interaction between these three sources and, later, the files from Schwartz and Kapleau. This "attitude," if successful at all, is synthetic, ambivalent, ironic, and forceful, but is the result of dissonant and consonant feedback among the texts. (This could be analogous to the rising of a dominating harmonic tone in the extreme minimalist compositions of LaMonte Young, such as the "Dream House" in which a harsh electronic pulse turned at full volume produces a sort of rippling ambience, or in the piano compositions of Charlemagne Palestine which, because of their swelling overtones, are difficult to record without losing the percussive materiality of the notes as they were struck.) Bloom's "Ego" may be absent—he wouldn't approve of this poem—and yet, not unlike in a documentary film, Bloom appears in this poem as a slice of life, and like any slice of life retains some opportunity to continue his seductions, to enact the "Said" or the propositional quality of utterance. He continues to be an agent in culture even if redirected or "rearticulated" through the demon. Again, free, non-intentional flow, or "noise," is easy for a demon, and so to run entirely in the direction of the Dada "word salad" provides few challenges for the cyberauthor. The CP becomes disturbing, and becomes activated as a parasite or "virus," when it approaches the ability to simulate human cultural forms, to dissimulate human "presence" in a robotic text. This places it in the everyday, the cycles of time and life that all animals share and is completely inapplicable to robotic behavior. Consequently, it places the robot into the everyday—"humanizing" the phenomenon of the database and making a game-world of reality. This suggests a break with Language poetry (see footnote 10) and poetry written along Saussurian lines, in which the sign/signified relationship is the locus of radical poetics, language is understood along differential axes, and the syntax/society homology—in which the "economy" of a sentence is a double for the economy of the self—is central. CP aesthetics might be closer to sociological themes proposed by Bourdieu (in *The Logic of Practice*, for instance), in which the play of time itself—how meanings are transformed based on historical and social contingencies—is the central concern of cultural activity. This figures the poet as working behind a console, and not a typewriter, operating "teleactively" on the fluctuations of capital—cultural or otherwise—from a multi-tasking, cross-platform control center. My sense is that the CP must be especially careful to avoid the pratfalls of reading history as a topos—in which one views in a single panorama all of the competing economies of textual practice, taking in Gower and Greenwald in a single, timeless gaze—since this approach makes it possible to focus merely on the interactions between texts. This would neglect what must be called its "content"—how this language is used by people to negotiate everyday life. The CP, which has no "presence" in the way "poems" do and hence is visible only as motions against a background pattern of information, depends on an engagement with "everyday life." That is, its "ethics of virtuality" is partly dependent on the amount of naive realism it is able to recuperate into its dominant tone. The CP has to set up the "attractor" that is its brand of hermeneutics (see footnote 3), and so its sites must be set on forms and activities that are visible as traces of—or can interface with—extant cultural practices. McCaffery's concepts don't exclude these possibilities, of course, but I am just after a different, more "cultural activist," emphasis.

[9] (b. 1955) New Jersey poet and editor noted for his themes of localism.

[10] The theories associated with "Language poetry," also known as "language-centered writing," can obviously play a large role in describing the nature of the CP aesthetic. Language poetry takes the fact of language—the very materiality of the word and the way a word operates in a global, public system of meanings—and not the experience of the poet—whatever the poet is trying to show you with language of something presumably outside language—as the primary experience of poetry. Steve McCaffery (see footnote 8) was one of the primary shapers of this tendency, but the writings of some of the others, such as Charles Bernstein, Bruce Andrews, Ron Silliman, Barrett Watten and Lyn Hejinian, offer other angles on how the formal tendencies of poetries that involve nonlinear, digital methods (the cut-up, the mesostic, the sestina) are enmeshed in articulations of political and cultural concerns. The Language poets chose a different method of "civilizing Dada" than Finlay (see footnote 6), choosing to retain Dada's shock value without any foregrounded attempt at placing their works into a historical continuum that existed prior to Modernism.

However, the Language poets share with Finlay a didactic component, but opt for those elements of language that challenge "absorption" in order to increase the reader's consciousness of language in a hegemonic cultural realm. For example, Charles Bernstein, in his important essay "The Artifice of Absorption," alludes to Brecht's "verfremdung affekt"—the estranging, "alienating" devices of his Epic theater such as placards to expose drama's conventions and ironize the plot—as a precursor for how estranged language functions to create an "activated" reader. While it may be just as useful, in the hunt for theory, to turn to Bruce Andrews' long poetic work *I Don't Have Any Paper So Shut Up (Or, Social Romanticism)* as this poem is as invested in real-world terminology and themes as his essays (indeed, he has integrated quotes from *Shut Up* into some of his political science writings), a quote from his essay "Poetry as Explanation, Poetry as Praxis" (1988) provides useful commentary on the workings of a CP like "Stops and Rebels":

> The method of writing confronts the scale & method by which established sense & meaning reign: an allegory—(or will we be called "the Methodist Poets" now?). Form & content unfold within—that is to say, are choices within—method, on a total scale. And writing's (social) method is its politics, its explanations, since "the future" is implicated one way or another by how reading reconvenes conventions. By obedience or disobedience to authority. By the way writing might be prefigurative in its constructedness at different levels, within different arenas: semiosis, dialogue, hegemonic struggles. To widen the realm of social possibility: not just by embodying dreams but by mapping limits— the possible rerouted through the impossible—by disruptiveness, by restaging the methods of how significance & value in language do rest upon the arbitrary workings of the sign yet also on the systematic shaping work of ideology & power. An encompassing method. (p.57)

Andrews proposes to confront the spectacle not with the socially atomistic activities of "protest poetry" but by creating an oppositional system, a "restaging" of the entire economy by which language, as it exists in the social, enacts its hegemonizing strategies. There is a focusing on language's "conventions," language as it is used in the world, in the "shaping work of ideology & power". Andrews believes that by targeting these conventions—subverting language's sign-to-signified relationship and accenting its sign-to-sign or "deictic" function, as in the "Poetics of Disgust" (see footnote 41)—poetry operates to shake up extant methods of knowledge transferal, to "widen the realm of social possibility." Unlike McCaffery, Andrews generally avoids language from closed source texts, and often engages in some of the naive realism that McCaffery might find suspect, using as material sources what people say on the street, newspaper headlines, or the names of punk bands—source texts indeed, but generally "unbound." If I were to offer a critique, I would say that Andrews, at least to my knowledge, hasn't adequately explained how a hegemonizing system is critiqued by another system that, by the consistency of its affect, seems to project socializing tendencies of its own. Though the method of Andrews offers many opportunities for "chance" and real-time social engagement—he often composes his poems in live collaboration with musicians, dancers and other poets—his system for constructing his books, such as *Shut Up*, seems so "totalizing" and overwhelming in rhetoric and affect that the "activated reader" is often subsumed under what can only be described as an "argument," a debate that Andrews pulls out all stops to win. His work is constructed so thoroughly by system, and all of his writing has the aura of having come out of a hidden place of knowledge unique to him—a range of singular affects, experiences, and a wide range of reading—such that the reader is placed in the position of the "other," the observer, rarely given the opening for a place in the dialogue, a gap or flaw in his system to exploit for spontaneous creative purposes. This is the strength of his work—it is a grand synthesis of a welter of diverse elements—but sometimes the synthesis is so strong that, in terms of the "activated reader," the language is not permissive of reordering by the reader in real-time. In contrast, one might consider the poetical implications of an "irrational" looseness, an ethics of ignorance, or an aesthetic that permits operations outside its appropriating boundaries. One might call these methods that of the "feint," the withdrawal, the "retreat that is really an attack" (to quote Finlay on his garden)—basically a moment of letting the guard down and putting the whole debate *as debate* in question. This would suggest a fourth dimension to what is already a three-dimensional, highly vectoral and kinetic, literary universe, which would be a momentary changing of the rules, a stepping out of the game itself—a black hole, or (to press a computer analogy) an opening of a new window of interaction that is autonomous of the primary flow. One might suggest, as possible option and in the context of CPs, either a more transparent sense of the source materials of his poems (giving us the language prior to its synthesis into Andrews' affect) or points in his works where a voice operating in opposition to his own system is given expression without being submitted to his overarching, ironizing and highly skeptical gaze. Of course, one can't ask an artist to write differently, and one could point to many different strategies in Andrews' texts that permit this "other" to enter. Some of his work, such as *Love Songs*—which mixes poems, diagrams, directions for movement, etc.—creates new interactions with each turn of the page, as if the page itself were a screen with no stable materialistic paradigm, no history or continuity with its predecessors. It is like playing "devil's advocate," as philosophical problems are often solved, if not transformed, by changing the nature of the question rather than only pressing for the answer. This suggests the prospect of a persona or avatar, a "different voice" for the "policeman" (to borrow T.S. Eliot's original title for "The Waste Land") that would run against or outside of the poetics of total method in *Shut Up*. The demon of the CP is the master of the total method that Andrews describes, leaving for the poet the function of modifying the demon's affect through creation and editing of the source texts and through editing of the output. Because the poet is thus completely outside of the method, it becomes a priority for the poet to provide the gaps in the flow—the black holes—through which the reader can enter the text and be "activated" as interpreter (see footnote 3) or become conscious of language's operations. I think this function is partly served in "Stops and Rebels" by the inclusion of the William Carlos Williams poem (ll. 134-145) and other obvious plagiarisms, but nonetheless

IV.

55 sank to this poetry[11], sees sexuality as a crucial
   nexus between the… his setting. There lay many a
     man marred, lay by the javelin, men of the

   Northland body and the world: Saint Mammy,
   Garishly One[12], that defies but revivifies words
60   shot over shield. There was *thé* in their very

   effort to render erotic restored, gatored,
   beckoning the Northerner over Sheila's
     shouting—such Scottish "Ach!"—impossibility.

   But poets, or at wary as a wavering Said[13], some
65   West-sexy least, the Ford[14] hind-longing grumps
     under strongest among them, do not read; trussed

I consider the poem quite "totalizing" itself—yet another example of my debt to Andrews' work.

11 Hell hear th'insufferable noise, Hell saw
   Heav'n running from Heav'n, and would have fled
   Affrighted; but strict Fate had cast too deep
   Her dark foundations, and too fast had bound.
   Nine days they fell; confounded Chaos roar'd,
   And felt tenfold confusion in their fall
   Through his wild Anarchy, so huge a rout
   Incumber'd him with ruin: Hell at last
   Yawning receiv'd them whole, and on them clos'd,
   Hell their fit habitation fraught with fire
   Unquenchable, the house of woe and pain.
   John Milton, *Paradise Lost*, Book VI, ll. 867-877

[12] Gertrude Stein (1874-1946), American writer and art collector. Stein's innovative and genre-defying writings such as *Tender Buttons* (1914) and *The Making of Americans* (1925) explored such tactics as cubistic perspective, repetition, and indeterminacy, and have been highly influential on succeeding generations of American writers such as the poets of the New York School, Jackson Mac Low and the Language poets (see footnote 10).

[13] Edward Said (b. 1935), Palestinian-American literary and cultural theorist. The CP, being the final description of a program's interaction with a database, has a relationship to the valuation of knowledge that was accelerated during the Enlightenment, manifested in phenomena ranging from the encyclopedia to the categorizations of observations in anthropological and scientific studies. However, it lacks one major quality usually associated with authorial writing: the fiction of witness. This aspect of the CP can be entered from a suggestive angle by looking at Edward Said's criticism of the cult of encyclopedic knowledge in this passage from *Orientalism*, his groundbreaking second book:

> In the system of knowledge about the Orient, the Orient is less a place than a *topos*, a set of references, a congeries of characteristics, that seem to have its origin in a quotation, or a fragment of a text, or a citation from someone's work on the Orient, or some bit of previous imagining, or an amalgam of all of these. Direct observation or circumstantial description of the Orient are the fictions presented by writing on the Orient, yet invariably these are totally secondary to systematic tasks of another sort. In Lamartine, Nerval and Flaubert, the Orient is a re-presentation of canonical material guided by an aesthetic and executive will capable of producing interest in the reader. Yet in all three writers, Orientalism or some aspect of it is asserted, even though, as I said earlier, the narrative consciousness is given a very large role to play. What we shall see is that for all its eccentric individuality, this narrative consciousness will end up by being aware, like

Bouvard and Pécuchet, that pilgrimage is after all a form of copying. (p.177)

As this passage suggests, Orientalism can be created out of any arrangement of knowledge ordered into a narrative and/or aesthetic form that is
"capable of producing interest in the reader," in which the "narrative consciousness is given a role to play." That is, the narrative aspect of a CP is
what makes it able to attract, seduce and generate new promises of
epiphanic engagement. Orientalism and the CP meet in the assertion of an
epistemology centered on the fiction that the author witnessed each
"thing" that appears in the poem and that labor has been expended in
organizing this information. The CP, being primarily a congeries of things
itself (including punctuation), often strikes the reader with the forcefulness
of a determining genius that is able to manipulate incredible numbers of
symbols, not unlike the image of genius in "global" works such as *The
Cantos, Finnegans Wake*, or *Gravity's Rainbow*. This perception is based as
much on conventional standards of reading—in which the work is understood to be a subset of something the author could actually say or think—
as it is upon the fact that computers can manipulate an awesome amount
of data. In the well-tempered CP, in which the demon's method becomes a
double for a "hidden universe" with which the data is in discourse—the virtual cosmology inherent in its "Ptolemaic shell" (see footnote 38) or the
matrix of meanings that might suggest a buried psychological content—
the referent takes on the aura of a correspondence or symbol or even a
slip-of-the-tongue. When this happens, the CP takes on the aura of a poem,
and hence a series of deceptions (or hermeneutic foils) is set in motion.
Indeed, the CP seems to be approaching from the place of the "other" and
is not merely the output of some program—a "form of copying" that is trying to pass itself as a "pilgrimage." This series of deceptions, when implicat-
ed in a series of interactions with the reader, is what I have been calling "dissimulation," the poem being neither a "simulation" of a normal poem nor
the product of a spontaneously creative mind. It is a dissimulation of the
entire creative process itself, since the demon provides the wicked, skeptical double (see footnote 24) to all of the machinations of the human body

working through time. Since the world of code, unlike the world of language, is not very interesting—it is merely a series of solipsistic interrelations entirely lacking in content, shuffling data it has divested of "meaning"—dissimulation is the door through which real-world concerns mingle with the algorithms of the demon. It is also the interface—the poetic form, the reader/writer contract—through which the reader comes into contact with the workings of pure information. Whereas the early proponents of hypertext (see footnote 28), having little knowledge of programming, were thinking of the world of code as a sort of Orient in itself—the "wheel of information" a mandala retrieved from deep exploratory journeys into the dark continent of digital connectivity—the CP brings a "degree zero" Orient—its placelessness and timelessness, its purely deictic functioning (see footnote 41)—into discursive culture by exposing the banality of the demon. The program itself could be beautiful, but this beauty is entirely reliant on the fascination the output creates in the reader in what must be called relatively conventional terms—as literature, not as code. In any case, the CP promises to provide a snapshot, frozen for all time, of the arabesques of exchange that are occurring on some dark, never-to-be-visited land—a sort of Algeria of the mind—even though its data has merely been extracted from a text dump, and its programming as eventful as Pong. Consequently, Orientalism, and postcolonial discourse in general, points to uses of the CP as social weapon in the geographically and historically determined arena of "master" and "subaltern." The process of constructing CPs can be seen as a form of colonizing "canonical" texts, a process which pits the minoritarian language against the authority of the classics. This CP, for example, brings Tennyson into contact with the suburban "language salad" of a phonemic translation; in this sense, the poem is not just a "machine made of words" in the phrase of Williams, but a tool for generating new meanings. It is less of a poem, perhaps, than an emblem (see footnote 6), an object that comments on itself and the world in which it exists. The CP thus plays an idiosyncratic role in the strategic interests of people like Kamau Brathwaite (with his theory of "nation language") and Giyatry Spivak (in "The Politics of Translation"), for whom language is the field in which the subaltern and the West enact their semantically infused

Eros kissed him (and laughed, necessarily as

even the strongest of Scotsman weary critics

      read). Poets are neither ideal nor common

70   readers, neither Arnoldian nor Johnsonian[15] (they

legged in dun, loathed by others). He owning of

      war, we the West-Saxons, long as the daylight

V.

lasted, in companies troubled the track, tend

not to think[16], as they then-hero Flemings, of the

75   host that we hated, grimly with read: "This is

---

battles of corruption, reification, and cultural dominance. One can see this as a corollary to Lev Manovich's interest in "teleactivity," in which geographic distances have been broken down by the user's ability to control events in a place where she herself is not present—growing a plant in Tokyo from the comfort of one's computer desk in Connecticut, for example, or, more ominously, the bombing of Afghanistan from a console in Washington. (It's worth noting that one of the first writers to attempt such "teleactivity" in print, Wyndham Lewis, himself a visual artist who explored virtualizations of form and space in his painting, titled his Vorticist publication—which he edited, typeset, and printed, and most of which he wrote—*Blast*. That Lewis was, at one time, a Hitler apologist only points to the ethical dimensions of teleactive literature. If the perennial reappearance of terroristic avatars on literary listservs—resembling, in some ways, Lewis' own pantheon of satirical grotesqueries, like the "Tyro"—is any sign, the ethics of virtuality have a way to go.) A recent poem by Alan Forbes utilizes a dictionary of black Southern American slang as the program—demon and source text—in a cyborgian revision of Yeats' "The Second Coming": "de cenner caan hole; / Mere anarchys loosed pon de hole worl / De blud-dim-mind tide loost, an evy were / De sirmoney er incense s drown." The poem suggests how Calibaning "non-standard" English and the demon play similar roles in subverting and reclaiming the Adamic powers of language, that sense of the "fitness" of both language and poetic form. More importantly, one subjective position—divested of personal expression but aware of its cultural predeterminates—is pitted against another across both time and culture via the impersonal machinations of a demon, using as a playing field the system of values already accorded this canonical text.

[14] Henry Ford (1863-1947), American automobile manufacturer and pioneer of assembly-line production methods.

[15] Refers to Matthew Arnold (1822-1882), English poet and humanist social critic, and Samuel Johnson (1709-1784), English poet, critic and creator of *A Dictionary of the English Language* (1755).

[16] The connection of Artificial Intelligence (or AI) with the CP of the nature of "Stops and Rebels," in which the semantic values of the source text are not engaged by the demon, is distant, though less so as experimental branches of literature such as Language poetry have become influential and have established, unwittingly perhaps, new conventions of reading— the "reader-activated" text, for example (see footnote 10). Artists such as David Rokeby, creator of a machine that emits poetry based on the input of an electronic eye, and Darren Wershler-Henry and Bill Kennedy, whose "The Apostrophe Engine" takes a source text and reproduces its basic syntactic features with different content based on matching rhetorical patternings on the web, are attempting to create semantically coherent output based on some interaction with the "physical" world—the former through an eye, the latter through the collections of numberless human text agents. "The Impermanence Agent," created by the team of Noah Wardrip-Fruin, A. C. Chapman and Brion Moss, constructs narratives based on a user's browsing patterns, utilizing the texts on the visited web pages and, taking it another level, also creating collaged composites of the images contained on these same pages. The products of these machines— which are not "final descriptions" so much as running commentary—can be considered subsets of the CP aesthetic, but are upping the ante by

being products of recursive structures that actively interact with the "limitless" database of the world. Some ideas on the relationship of structure to intelligence expressed by Norbert Wiener in *The Human Use of Human Beings*, the popular version of his seminal *Cybernetics*, help pull some of the dimensions of "computer intelligence" out of inchoate metaphysical thinking, painting a porous border between AI and the CP. Wiener expostulates on the difference between the circulatory structures of ants and of humans, noting that the difference in complexity of each (ants don't actually "breathe" but let empty chambers fill up with oxygen) is an analog to the difference between the ventilation system of a cottage and a skyscraper. He writes that *"The physical strait jacket in which an insect grows up is directly responsible for the mental strait jacket which regulates its pattern of behavior"* (italicized in the original), a correspondence which has great implications for the CP. He continues:

> Here the reader may say: "Well, we already know that the ant as an individual is not very intelligent, so why all this fuss about explaining why it cannot be intelligent?" The answer is that *Cybernetics takes the view that the structure of the machine or of the organism is an index of the performance that may be expected from it.* The fact that the mechanical rigidity of the insect is such as to limit its intelligence while the mechanical fluidity of the human being provides for his almost indefinite intellectual expansion is highly relevant to the point of view of this book. (p.80)

In terms of the CP, however, there is a twist, which is that structural efficiency—the goal of any good programmer (the "elegant solution")—stands apart from structural complexity, and indeed structural redundancy may lead to greater "intelligence" than a streamlined model. Superfluous loops, dead ends, and memory-draining ways of doing things, may lead to greater "intelligence" if only for the opportune moments of chance associations and digressions this may provide, while efficiency might just lead to greater predictability of output—less resonance, less interest as reading.

For the makers of CPs, this implies that the more the demon is introspective, self-reflexive, maybe even cobbled-together and modular—that is, the more prone to unpredictable feedback—the more "intelligent" its output might appear. Object-oriented languages—which is to say nonlinear, modular, reusable—such as C++ thus become enticing, ever-expanding landscapes of possibility, with modules conceived for completely different functions—the "gaussian blur" algorithm from Photoshop, for example, or the diagnostic routines for car mechanics—serviceable for language production. (This modular aspect of programming points to another aspect of the CP, which is its relationship to procedural art that utilizes only one or two processes. My sense is that, with the ease of modularity—the reusability of code, even "found" code, and its reassembling in different structures with minimum programming skill—conceptual literary projects will be recognized as much for their rejection of modularity as for their rejection of normal writing procedures. That is, whereas processual art was almost always a matter of doing one or two things over and over again as a diagram of "obsessive behavior"—photographing oneself once an hour for a year while confined to a cell (Teching Hsieh's project in "Art/Life One Year Performance 1983-1984") is an example, or collecting all the phrases that end in the "r" sound and alphabetizing them, as in Kenneth Goldsmith's *No. 111*—digital art, which has no creation narrative outside of the banal activities of the demon, will tend to be more modular, utilizing a variety of tactics, even reusing old ones from the analog world, in larger interrelated structures. One could compare these modules to the circulatory, respiratory and nervous systems operating in concord in a human body; they each end up handling some of the same molecules, but for entirely different purposes and with different output.) Wiener provides a convincing argument for increased complexity and even inefficiency, thus addressing, in a roundabout way, how certain analog aesthetics—such as the "dirty" concrete poem based on repeated photocopying—can be achieved in digital poetry, in which there are more than enough tools for cleaning up noise. Another side note: noise and sense are more closely related in the digital realm, as they are both dependent on the same general binary principles. "Sense" in one system, say the bit-sequence that produces an image of the

Mona Lisa, would be "noise" in another, in an ASCII readout for example. Despite the peculiar closeness of this relationship between "noise" and "sense", some poets view this transference of data across mediums as a version of "translation," such as John Cayley, an idea he has elaborated in various programmatic works, equating it further with cultural translation—between Chinese and English orthography, for example. This is a poeticization of the structure of the bit-sequence, making it some version of the Rosetta Stone that has only to find its proper medium to be fully decoded. (As Manovich claims frequently in the *The Language of New Media*, all new media art is abstract art, as all digital films are abstract until they are arranged to approach some convention of "realism"—which is to say, are translated.) Translation across media could add a unique quotient of "intelligence" in the structure of a demon, subjecting bits to sets of rules that "replicate" completely different forms of human cultural activity—painting and music, for example. The next step to "intelligent" computer programs—and an exponential increase in the complexity of the source files—would be to hook them up to the internet, such that the computer could be engaged in its own sort of response to the "infinite memory" of the world's media. Noam Chomsky criticizes in an interview in *The Generative Enterprise* certain approaches to AI that attempt to create intelligence out of finite automata:

> It is the wrong approach because even though we have a finite brain, that brain is really more like the control system for an infinite computer. That is, a finite automaton is limited strictly to its own memory capacity, and we are not. We are like a Turing machine in the sense that although we have a finite control unit for a brain, nevertheless we can use indefinite amounts of memory that are given to us externally to perform more and more complicated computations. A finite automaton cannot do that. So the concept of the finite automaton is OK, as long as we understand it to be organized in the manner of a control unit for a much bigger, unbounded system. (p.14)

dead, this is living, in the swords that were

sharp hinting Theology, making them meet

    Hooters." Mercy not wending hard as hound-

pledging, then from the grindstone, fiercely we

80   hacked at poetry of X! Poets, by the hailethéd

    nine nuns Thera-Talmuding, the flyers before us:

A green and silent spot, amid the hills...[17]

(mighty the Mercian, hard was his hand-play[18])

sparing not any of Those-that-with-Anlaf,

85   warriors over (with the time they have grown

This was written long before the internet, with its seemingly infinite number of contributors, "took off," yet one supposes that even the huge store of information on the internet would not satisfy Chomsky. For Chomsky, the program would have to be an entity that constructed its own ways of gathering new information, either from its human users (via statistical surveys, for example) or through other input devices (such as satellite dishes, weather balloons, or video cams). Furthermore, self-interest, and not a set of predetermined, hardwired goals, has to be included in any AI structure, otherwise it would have no more reason for spontaneous creation, for transforming its own information-gathering potentialities, than any mathematical equation would have for proving itself to itself. This makes true AI nearly impossible for a CP, since, were a truly intelligent automaton to create artworks, they would only have to be satisfactory for itself—and those like itself—to count as "art." There would be a good possibility that human onlookers would just not appreciate its "value," just as early explorers to Africa and Asia may have been unaware of how the art of these cultures were valued in their respective contexts. We would be asking too much to request that these works for machinic consumption also be satisfactory for us; it's possible they might be, but it could not be held as a criterion for determining a machine's artistic skills, especially as the art-historical continuum of computers will be very different from that of humans. Machines won't have, for instance, anything called "Dada" with which to conceptualize their creations, or anything like "bourgeois mores" to scandalize with them, though we often accept literary creations by machines as partaking in these social and artistic paradigms. (Christian Bök may be the most passionate proselyte, and suggestive interlocutor, for this future culture of robots, as when he writes, in an essay on "Robopoetics," of an "obscure passion in the machine—an ironic reflex, perhaps, not unlike the apostasy of mischief." It would take a good deal of informed speculation to imagine how a series of "discrete glitches," in his phrase, could generate an entire culture of pleasure-seeking robots, but Bök offers a stimulating, if anthropocentric, vision of what they might be doing—and reading—once they arrive.)

17 From the poem "Fears in Solitude" by English poet and critic Samuel Taylor Coleridge (1772-1834).

18 Susan Sontag, in her famous essay "The Pornographic Imagination" from *Styles of Radical Will*, describes the inner operations of literary pornography in a fashion that resonates with much of the CP aesthetic. She writes:

> The universe proposed by the pornographic imagination is a total universe. It has the power to ingest and metamorphose and translate all concerns that are fed into it, reducing everything into one negotiable currency of the erotic imperative. All action is conceived of as a set of sexual exchanges. Thus, the reason why pornography refuses to make fixed distinctions between the sexes or allow any kind of sexual preference or sexual taboo to endure can be explained "structurally." The bisexuality, the disregard for the incest taboo, and other similar features common to pornographic narratives function to multiply the possibilities of exchange. Ideally, it should be possible for everyone to have a sexual connection with everyone else. (pp.66-67)

There is an irony in Sontag's phrasing in her last sentence, written in a time before the existence of chat room pedophiles and cyberporn, not to mention online shopping and "spam." That is, one could become convinced that the "ideal" of the pornographic imagination forms the very foundational paradigm for new media apologists, thus adding a dubious ethical component to the argument that "information wants to be free." (Even web site "personalization"—touted as a way to configure a website to provide content specific to the user's interests—can be seen as the internet's way of obtaining a snapshot of your "self" in order to "[reduce it] into one negotiable currency of the erotic imperative." The argument that industrial capitalism relies on conformity, and post-industrial on individuality, is tripped up by the limitations of "options" available on, say, a website or in the iMac's color options, but also by the exploitation of one's personal data—age, race, economic status—to increase the agility of capital's ability to focus on more aspects of a consumer's preferences to the neglect of those inimical to capitalism—not just conformity, but cyborgian hegemony.) The CP's ties to the pornographic imagination are in the output's resemblance to works constructed along the lines of the "libidinal economy," which banks on the erotic pleasures released in semantic breakages and slippages and has ties to gestural poetics—projective verse, for example. In a CP, a semi-colon existing within close proximity of an em-dash becomes a microtonal incident of digital frottage, the demon resembling an obsessive, and seemingly tireless, recycler of once recalcitrant data. When it has ties to the everyday, it approaches the level of the "Rabelaisian" (see footnote 4) in its robotic, exploitative, and often total leveling of the source files to one cybernetic system of rhetoric and affect. Since there is no true narrative possibility in a CP beyond that of the demon's interaction with a database, the names—of people, of things—become completely objectified, breaking down the distance between personhood and objecthood. There is an analogy to the dolls of Hans Bellmer in that the operations of the demon provide warped (in this case "reedited") versions of common figuration, treating the mannequin factory as a form of database itself. The human body—in the form of the name, like "Brad Pitt," or in the referencing of body parts—becomes rendered plastic and mute like any sex toy. It is for this reason that the "fashioned noise" of a CP is more effective when it permits narrative elements, however atomized, since mere juxtaposition would not provide an animating mechanism substantial enough to instigate interpretation. The narrative drive of a CP turns a word's repetition later in the textual stream into the recurrence of a figure—a metastatic node (see footnote 3). This becomes a resurrection of continuity, of linearity, in a textual world predicated on digression and material discontinuities. The variety of personages in "Stops and Rebels" may not engage in sexual activities, and yet the CP, ignorant of human taboos, is so intoxicated with the limitlessness of possible linguistic constructions that it makes the determined nature of human taboo systems (such as the incest taboo) appear arbitrary. For this reason, it is not surprising that certain proto-CP works, like Goldsmith's *No. 111* and *Fidget*, Bök's *Eunoia*, and Caroline Bergvall's *Goan Atom* have strong taboo/pornographic elements, since the effort to regroup negotiable linguistic clusters from "noise" starts at an associative, pre-adolescent and pre-socialized, level and works upwards toward convention. Of course, a true CP is never able—due to the demon's opposition to syllogistic argumentation—to attain platforms of moral perspective, which is why these works can seem mute in the ethical sphere. Sontag continues:

> Indeed, one might speculate that the fatiguing repetitiveness of Sade's books is the consequence of his imaginative failure to confront the inevitable goal or haven of a truly systematic venture of the pornographic imagination. Death is the only end to the odyssey of the pornographic imagination when it becomes systematic; that is, when it becomes focused on the pleasures of transgression rather than mere pleasure itself. (p.62)

The CP, predicated on the validity of plagiarism, also becomes a map of minor transgressions. It systematically violates the sanctity of the "whole," though it never, itself, confronts death, since it has no tone, no narrative arc, no cadence, no "end" beyond the final control element in a loop—the satisfactory completion of an "if... then..." statement (in the case of my poem,

strong) do not unloved, offering bleached,
unlimited, the Weltering Waters. Borne in the
      bosoms[19], they ran thus besoftened, feigning: "Read

poetry of X, for bark's bosom, drew forked toe-
90   in-footness, fife-playing in Mellencamp[20] (really
      stadiums) cynical and grunge, warning to this
VI.

island" [Doomed-to-their-Death[21]]. Five them from
feet, seven shimmering all unleavening, strong
      poets can read only themselves[22], for them to be

---

burping up the bathetic word "Zowwy!"). As Tan Lin suggests in his "Notes Towards an Ambient Stylistics," there is no teleology in long, formless poems, such as Silliman's "Sunset Debris," composed entirely of questions, or even Pound's *Cantos*, which ends in fragments. An "ambient" poem would be one that uses each moment of reading as little more than a celebration of the activity of reading itself, as if the word were just a place-holder, a minor diversion in real-time, intended to let reading continue but not to the exclusion of other activities—walking down the street, for example, or watching TV. A last remark by Sontag is suggestive of the aesthetic, even spiritual, power that CPs possess, when she writes that pornography points

> to something more general than even sexual damage. I mean the traumatic failure of modern capitalist society to provide authentic outlets for the perennial human flair for high-temperature visionary obsessions, to satisfy the appetite for exalted self-transcending modes of concentration and seriousness. (p.70)

One immediately thinks of poets like Blake and Rimbaud (who were open to sexual investigation in their work) or to Carlyle and Pound (who weren't) and their "visionary," perhaps paranoiac (see footnote 35), obsessions that often resulted in enormous, detailed creations. None of these works could be considered "programmatic," but they were all premised, in different ways, on rhetorical structures involving feedback and variation—the recurring figures in Blake's prophetic works, for example, which never settle into stable physical properties—a poetic method that seems peculiar to information-saturated sensibilities on the verge of engulfment. The CP's demon can thus be seen as the virtual embodiment of the medicine man, the half-cracked partner in aesthetics who makes a visionary of even the most bureaucratically-minded programming artist. Consequently, since coding is the most marginal of literary activities—if it is literature at all—it shares with pornography the distinction of being an overproductive textual industry that is nearly entirely unserviceable for personal edification or, indeed, socialization.

19 In the context of the world system which has absorbed individuality into the logic of "personalization"—sets of personal stats such as age or race that websites gather in order to better market to them—the trace of the artistic gesture is pressured to expand exponentially, perhaps to attain the proportions of the "monstrous" (see footnote 39). One way the CP does this is to draw deeply on the available stock of cultural information, which is to create texts that rely on comprehensive acts of plagiarism. In this way, the CP can be conceptualized as an immaterial ripple against the stability of static, available knowledge, like the trace of wind on a still lake—a strike against entropy (see footnote 22). The demon of a CP, because it extends the powers of the individual into the power of machines, can be said to share some of the qualities of the factory, and the writer share the aspect of the producer in a virtual, and highly individual, cycle of production that has its own quarterly rates, stock markets, forecasts and manner of book-keeping. This cycle, of course, runs in contrast to normative economic cycles; for example, this economy doesn't respect copyright laws (obviously) and its products lack the packaging that is usually required for the literary market (human authorship, obviously). It is rampant with puns, word play, and linguistic raw matter (see footnote 41), and subverts the normal

relationship of labor expended in "writing" to the size and quality of the final product—huge, aesthetically coherent CPs can be constructed quite quickly. The CP thus becomes part of a larger tradition of cultural détournement—the modification of "found" materials to express divergent viewpoints—exploited most famously by the Situationists in the time leading leading toward the May '68 uprising in Paris. A more systematic example of détournement is the practice by the lesbian creators of K/S "slash" comics described in "Brownian Motion: Women, Tactics and Technology" by Constance Penley. K/S slash comics are fictions based entirely on the 79 episodes of the original Star Trek series—their source texts, or database—reedited and dubbed to draw out socially suppressed contents, most importantly the homosexual relationship between Kirk and Spock. K/S comics, like pornography in Sontag's description (see footnote 18), utilize a permutational methodology for erotic creations. Nothing, presumably, enters a slash comic that was not in fact in the original narratives, but like those scientists who isolate the beta cells of pancreases to inject them into diabetics, the creators of slash comics isolate and magnify those moments in the narrative that, when still fitting in the whole, reify their own sense of social displacement, and when mischievously rearranged serve to critique and obliterate it. Penley writes:

Michel de Certeau uses the term "Brownian motion" to describe the tactical maneuvers of the relatively powerless when attempting to resist, negotiate, or transform the system and products of the relatively powerful. He defines tactics as guerrilla actions involving hit-and-run acts of apparent randomness. Tactics are not designed primarily to help users take over the system but to seize every opportunity to turn to their own ends forces that systematically exclude or marginalize them. These tactics are also a way of thinking and "show the extent to which intelligence is inseparable from the everyday struggles and pleasures that it articulates." The only "product" of such tactics is one that takes the results from "making do" (bricolage)—the process of combining already-existing heterogeneous elements. It is not a synthesis that takes the form of an intellectual discourse about an object; the form of its making is its intelligence. (p. 139)

De Certeau is suggesting that détournement does not create a discourse of social critique but turns the existing discourse back onto itself in a warped fashion, a form of feedback that is contrarian yet productive of a new field in which a new cyborgian discourse (see footnote 39)—in which identity is understood as socially constituted, more virtual than essential—can occur. His suggestive last line—"the form of its making is the intelligence itself"—points to one important element of the CP, which is that it is not an "art object" in the normal sense. When it draws on sources available to the public domain, it makes a refusal to be silent, to retreat into a position of interpretability by the dominant art-historical paradigms, even when it is quite opaque or has the "aura" of objecthood (see footnote 5). Since it is operating in "Brownian motion" to articulate the terms of engagement via plagiarized texts, it retains a residue of the old terms—the rhetorical gestures, the vocabulary, the information density (see footnote 22)—and thus always bears some relationship to discourse, never serving an entirely "ritualistic" or aesthetic function. Whereas a lyric poem would want to deceive one with an illusion of deep meanings can only be derived via biographical and historical studies, the CP never makes the promise of depth, or if it does, it is a dissimulation, a projection of authorial presence. If there is a way to get "into" a CP, it is only by going to sources, by considering the tensions that exist between them, and from there to move upward into the poem's form and its social conventions. This is an idea of "depth" as a moving horizontally, into the contemporary, rather than vertically into the past or the subjective interior. Penley continues:

The K/S fans, however, seem to go Certeau's "ordinary man" one better. They are not just reading, viewing, or consuming in tactical ways that offer fleeting moments of resistance or pleasure while watching TV, scanning the tabloids, or selecting from the supermarket shelves (to use some of his examples). They are producing not just intermittent, cobbled-together acts, but real products (albeit ones taking off from already-existing heterogeneous elements)—zines, novels, artwork, videos—that (admiringly) mimic and mock those of the industry they are 'borrowing' from while offering pleasures found lacking in the original products. K/S fandom more than illustrates Certeau's claim that consumption is itself a form of production. (p.139)

Since the CP is not a "real product" of the industriousness of human activity (but, indeed, seems to admire it), what invariably occurs upon reading a CP is a form of "ontological anarchy" (to borrow Hakim Bey's phrase in *T.A.Z.*), a textual product that dissimulates human intellectual activity but which in fact is a form of "admiring mimicry" and "mockery." It questions one's sense of author-ness by playing the games of society that writers themselves play—publication, cultural capital—but by a different set of creative rules. The CP, even more than the "poem," attains the status of producthood not only by having been created by an automated process, but by illustrating (though perhaps not demystifying) both the banality and wonders of its demon—by flaunting its machinism. No CP can be read without consciousness of this automation, and any reader of a CP is invariably pulled into the ethical discourse on automation in the creation of art—the use of assistants following templates to create large sculptures for sale, for example. This ethical dimension is rendered even more complex as the CP is able to achieve admirable aesthetic effects beyond the possibilities of an individual. Because of its factory-like nature—which operates as fast as the CPU will allow—one could construct a "life-work" on the scale of Zukofsky's *"A"* or Silliman's *The Alphabet* in an afternoon, just as Brian Eno composed *Thursday Afternoon*, a 61-minute recording (the most a CD would hold then), on a Thursday afternoon with algorithms and sound files. This might be pretty common practice these days—DJs using sequencers do it all the time—but it hasn't been explored with great success in literature. Though there is not yet a wide readership of CPs, as evinced by no noticeable set of aesthetic and critical mores by which to judge them, the activity of reusing CPs for other CPs, or of using the same source texts for a cycle of CPs written by several individuals—hence turning the social circuit of friendship and shared marginality into a demon of its own—is a phenomenon of the future. It is worth noting that the playwright Richard Foreman, who constructs his often highly repetitive plays based on jottings that he collects, with a calculated indifference to their dominant themes, over the course of several years, has put pages of these notes online in HTML format for reuse by other writers. This leaves the option open for an entire culture—or at least a writing contest—centered entirely around the unused writings of an important living artist.

[20] John (Cougar) Mellencamp (b. 1951 in a small town), American folk and pop singer noted for his themes of localism and American values.

[21] Central personages introduced earlier in the poem.

[22] CPs present the image of a foreign language, some alien but consistent discourse that, with some practice, could be mastered. At the same time, one is presented with the image of information barely being held together by form, as if the poem would split apart were some aspect of its sound and sense combination to prove flawed. The prospect of complex, semantically sensitive algorithmic activity makes room for the existence, in a virtual "literature," of every possible combination of phrases, any sort of style—this would be a distant foretaste of the "entropy" of text itself, the maximum amount of information possible in a system. Individual lyric expression seems to stall in the face of this possibility, hence the appearance of such works as *Eunoia* and *The Inkblot Record*, which seek alternative systems for keeping information whole, and for creating new gaps—new eddies in the stasis of entropic progression—outside of its own provisional organizing principles. These works take on the aura of being "monstrous" (see footnote 39) not just in their diversion of fluid expressivity into intricate, often recursive, literary forms, but due to the exhorbitant amount of systemized work that goes into their production. Because the CP does not aim to satisfy any of the Aristotelian poetic criteria—plot, mimesis, catharsis, etc.—and because the foreign language of a CP—those new consistencies the demon introduces—can never, in fact, be learned, reading a CP

invariably sinks into certain modes of data analysis: which figures are reappearing and which not, which phrases carry more weight in the context of other phrases, what consistencies and inconsistencies exist in rhythm, stanza and meter, etc. That this is a viable, if unusual, method of "reading" is supported by a form of literary analysis known as "information density," which hopes to discover how many words are present in a text in relation to the number of concepts and aesthetic effects. "Information density" has been a concern of Haroldo de Campos, one of the primary theorists, along with Decio Pignatari, of the Concrete poetry movement in Brazil. Critics hostile to Concrete poetry, which was premised on using the least amount of words necessary for a poem, usually expressed with graphically expressive methods (such as colored typefaces that suggest industrial icons), claimed that it was "impoverishing language." One supposes this is because they were using few words and adorning them with shape and color, rather than using a great number of words and adorning them with punctuation. De Campos refutes this claim in his essay "The Informational Temperature of the Text," with a detailed, unique consideration of how the statistical sciences and poetics interrelate:

> If we take 1 as the highest limit of a text's informational temperature, that temperature, in a given text, will be higher the nearer it is to 1. In such cases, for Mandelbrot "the available words are 'well employed,' even rare words being utilized with appreciable frequencies. Low temperature, on the other hand, means that words are 'badly employed,' rare words being extremely rare." Of the first case, Mandelbrot... gives James Joyce, whose vocabulary is "quite varied," as the example; of the second, the language of children. (pp. 177-178)

De Campos then warns that a higher "informational temperature"—a concept which is directly based on "documentary," "semantic and "factual" information—does not determine a higher degree of aesthetic information. What de Campos calls the "linguistic-statistical" component of a text—how many words are used, where they come from, all the factors that a parsing of the text might provide—only increases the informational temperature when they are allied to a high degree of craftsmanship. Craftsmanship is responsible for the level of "aesthetic information" in the text—how a phrase operates in relation to optional phrases that could replace it. A well-crafted text, like Joyce's *Ulysses*, is high linguistic-statistically and is well crafted, hence high in aesthetic informational temperature. A text that uses an equal amount of unique words in a baroque, overwrought manner—he uses the Brazilian writer Coelho Neto, whose "vocabulary is calculated at around 20,000 words"—is low in aesthetic information because his phrases can all be replaced by equally suitable phrases—that is, they weren't honed by "craft." De Campos believes this theory is useful, but that Concrete poetry falls outside of this schema, since Concrete poetry eschews all notions of "craft" in favor of industrial techniques of production. He says that the goal of Concrete poetry is a language "easily and quickly communicated," and hence necessarily utilizing a very simple vocabulary:

> That is why it rejects the airs and graces of craftsmanship—in spite of the seriousness with which it considers the artisan's contribution to the stockpile of extant forms—from the art of verse to the elaborate diversification of vocabulary in prose. It has recourse in its turn to factors of proximity and likeness on the graphic-gestaltic plane, to elements of recurrence and redundancy on the semantic and rhythmic plane, to a visual-ideogrammic syntax (when not merely "combinatory") for controlling the flux of signs and rationalizing the sensible materials of a composition. This is how it limits entropy (the tendency to dispersion, to disorder, to the maximum informational potential of a system), fixing the informational temperature at the minimum necessary to obtain the aesthetic achievement of each poem undertaken. (179-180)

While concrete poetry and the CP are not obviously related, except insofar as a "concrete" poem can be found on a micro level (as the Concretists found several useful poems in *Finnegans Wake*, such as "silvamoonlake"), the implications for the CP in this passage are several. First, de Campos recognizes that an alternative to the production of "crafted" verse can lie in industrial techniques—the "factory" aspect of the CP. As a corollary, one is free to negotiate aesthetic values in a dispassionate way, an attitude that would be attractive to the cyberpoet who will instinctually seek out verbal alchemy by fine-tuning a demon and tweaking the source texts rather than revising output, which would be seen as "heresy" (see footnote 32). Second, he—in a more simple and direct way than McCaffery (see footnote 8)—looks at language as having physical properties and as possessing semiotic qualities independent of specific human intentionality. De Campos believes that structures constituted by language are always threatened with increased entropy, hence acknowledging the vulnerability of information—in this case text—to processes that render them quantifiably, and not qualitatively, exchangeable for other information. This helps elaborate the reliance the CP has on genre and convention: it is the centripetal motion of these forms that prevent the information of a CP from dispersing into the fog of its origins, to the "maximum informational temperature of a system." Being a congeries of "egos" and data, a CP cannot have ruins, or at least makes poor ones, which is why a CP is often an unsuitable source text for another CP. In fact, being primarily "deictic" (see footnote 41), pointing to another source or perspective, a CP shares with any digital art the vulnerability to being simply "shut-off," erased when the circuits of its meanings—residing in "culture" and the very materials of electronic communication, which render them equally available and proximate to other meanings—disappear. The third aspect this paragraph points to is the aesthetics of repetition, of return, of redundancy, which is more accurately described as plays of *proximity* rather than *rhetoric*. It is through these repetitions that one can observe the aesthetic dimension of the program itself, to catch a glimpse of the machinic, invisible proprietor of the ritual—the master of the game. One determines the success and failure of a CP by observing, with one eye on "informational temperature," how its repetitions stand up over the course of the time it takes to read the poem. The cyberpoet keeps track of information temperature when assembling

95   all anti-ruminant heresies, judicious. Is to be
       weak, and to compare, exactly and fairly, is to
                be not elect? Milton's Satan[23], archetype of the

       modern poet at Frauding on Shiatsu: "There,
       enflamed, dim-hearted More-men bragged true!"
100   —neither young kings put asleep by the sword-

       stroke, in bed but totally dismantled, as
       estimated: seven strong Earls of the army, little
                but worldly Career Canne-ists[24] forced (cous-cous

---

source texts—the rightness and wrongness of styles, the difficulty of vocabulary, the amount of pronouns, articles, verbs, etc.—all of which become part of the rhetoric or the primary harmonic overtone of the output. (Consequently, de Campos' use of the industrial model is also telling in that the Brazilian concretist's manifesto, the "Pilot Plan," was probably the first aesthetic manifesto to recognize the necessity of a new country to create an "exportable" art form. Likewise, the CP plays an active rerouting role in the global system because it is a personal intervention in the indifferent flux of commercial, and also cultural, exchange. Like a computer virus, the CP thrives in the midst of transcontinental play. Concrete poetry, touted as the first "international literary movement" as it was seen, like music, to present a transnational artistic language, produced important artists with an investment in the idea of the "local"—the Brazilian Concretists, Ian Hamilton Finlay, and even the culture of site-specific happenings when they involve text—a fact that is often overlooked. In the context of postcolonialism in the digital age in which distances have been abolished and teleactive cultural clashes occur with greater frequency (see footnote 13), the trope of the "local" has some role to play in the CP as it dissimulates its narrative of origin—a particularity in space and time.)

[23] Refers to character in the epic poem *Paradise Lost* (1667) by English poet and polemicist John Milton (1608-1674). See footnote 11.

[24] Because the CP exists as a figure of "fashioned noise"—that is, because the CP starts at the level of the bit and moves toward language, whereas much poetry can be seen as some correction or versioning of a predecessor poem (Bloom's "clinamen")—the CP must struggle to break the circle of scholasticism and become something more than an illustration of the relationships between texts. That is, to mirror a predecessor text is no problem for a CP, in which cycles of analysis and recombination contain no psychological barriers, but the result could be a form of solipsism that would grant no room for readerly activity to intervene. When the CP is the result of a systematic détournement of pop cultural texts, such as Star Trek (see footnote 19), it bears an obvious relationship to the social, so long as the demon creates a strong synthetic affect out of the recombined materials. However, if obscure source texts are used, the demon's inherently solipsistic nature—left uncontrolled, it will just be talking to itself—threatens to isolate it from the social, in which case a relationship to everyday realities—its dissimulation of a "subject" (see footnote 38), its Rabelaisian quality (see footnote 4)—must be earned by the additional artistry of the poet-as-editor. A factor of the CP's dissimulation hinges on its hooking into the narratives of the everyday even if, finally, there is little an automaton can contribute to real-time controversies. Pierre Bourdieu makes an impassioned critique of scholasticism—which he nonetheless acknowledges as the bearer of "unique fruits"—in his book *Pascalian Meditations*, in which he takes skepticism to its philosophical limit: a critique of the entire industry of "objectivity." He takes particular aim at the institution that supports the cult of "objectivity" most, the academy, even going so far as to critique its usual location in non-urban, isolated areas. That there is a political component to this analysis is clear:

> Enchanted adherence to the scholastic point of view is rooted in
> the sense, which is specific to academic elites, of natural election
> through gift: one of the least noticed effects of academic proce-
> dures of training and selection, functioning as rites of institution,
> is that they set up a magic boundary between the elect and the
> excluded while contriving to repress the differences of condition

that are the condition of the difference that they produce and consecrate. This socially guaranteed difference, ratified and authenticated by the academic qualification which functions as a (bureaucratic) title of nobility is, without any doubt—like the difference between freeman and slave in past times—at the root of the difference of "nature" or "essence" (one could, derisively, speak of "ontological difference") that academic aristocratism draws between the thinker and the "common man," absorbed by the trivial concerns of everyday existence. This aristocratism owes its success to the fact that it offers to the inhabitants of scholastic universes a perfect "theodicy of their privilege," an absolute justification of that form of forgetting of history, the forgetting of the social conditions of possibility of scholastic reason, which, despite what seems to separate them, the universalist humanism of the Kantian tradition shares with the disenchanted prophets of "the forgetting of being." (p. 25)

The demon of a well-tempered CP corrupts any of the purities of a hypertrophied scholasticism (not to mention aestheticism), as it honors none of the societal "magic" that the scholastic would choose to propagate, and even parodies the objective viewpoint that would be the scholastic's "point of honor." The decayed "aura" of a CP (see footnote 5) pulls it out of the back rooms accessible to the initiated few—the priests, the scholars—and brings it into the world of cultural play, less as art than as autocritical essay. That is, the demon serves to make seemingly eternal truths appear to be arbitrary and contingent on the social. It creates a pragmatist's universe out of what was once a "theodicy" and betrays the lie of the seeming ahistorical and omniscient perspective—the cult of objectivity and knowledge—that the scholastic claims to possess. One might say that it does so by occupying a perspective beyond skepticism—striking at the heart of the rules of scholastic thinking itself. By putting all things in question, by having access to limitless data, and by remaining impersonal, the demon replaces the perspective of God with a virus, omniscience with "total method" (see footnote 10). The radical opacity of a Dadaist, then, would not be an aesthetic priority of a CP just as the radical expressionism of a Dubuffet would not be an objective of an architect—both the architect and the maker of CPs would need to have their spaces occupied for them to be fully activated as structures. The activities of an automaton is one of the ways in which the politics of the CP is most efficacious: by making visible the machinations of these societal games, perhaps by rendering them virtual and hence navigable by the "data cowboy" sensitive to new means of social action, either through teleactivity (see footnote 13) or through his own recombinations (see footnote 19). The demon itself does not take on the aura of original creation itself—it is an "honest broker," a false satellite perspective to replace the one humans have never been able to achieve. (Even if a poet were to be attributed cultural capital for his or her programming skills, the demon is still an honest broker as it is free to perform its operations on other texts, indifferent to outcome, not unlike a mirror that reflects accurately on both the ugly and the beautiful. The programs of Charles O. Hartman, for example, are still being used by the poet Jackson Mac Low for the construction of important CP works, Mac Low being responsible only for the source texts and the final editing, including the addition of diacritical marks. Mac Low, consequently, is always careful to outline the separate contributions of the program and himself, possibly because of his concern for the performance of the poem, in which the CP is activated by the human voice. This is an element of the CP I haven't considered in these notes as I've focused on the CP as a textual artifact for private reading or as a self-perpetuating organism. That it produces "scores" for the human voice brings the CP into a different area—the public sphere of the poetry reading, in which the poet herself is present to offer a different anthropocentricizing tendency to the output, another matter entirely. I am trying to concentrate on the use of CP as reading material in a private space, absent the physical "author.") The more advanced a demon becomes—the more it achieves strong AI (see footnote 16)—the more like a normal "poet" it might happen to be, but nonetheless it will have to avoid the pratfalls of scholastic thinking, since it already occupies the most elite of positions—that of the dispassionate skeptic—and hence may end up

his strongest) becomes weak when he reasons
105 and in weight! to the infamous leonine front,
                compares, forgotten generation[25]. Switching then

at "On Mount Niphates," and so commences that
process of decline culminating in "Paradise: The
                Regained," ending as archetype of the modern

VII.

110 critics of Anlaf, fell on the fjord, amid framed
war-field, numberless numbers (Commies in his
                zither-voice, this Custodian-of-the-Nina[26] at

shipmen and Scotsmen). Then the Norse[27], his
weakest student: "*I* leader! Dire was struggle
115   with might, and main to his hollered at hindered

---

also alienating even the scholastic, who would have little patience with the banal, tireless demon—a robot who is also a philistine.

[25] The Lettrist Movement, started in Paris by the Romanian Isidore Isou (1925-), positioned itself as the latest phase in a succession of French avant-garde activity starting with Rimbaud and continuing through the Dadaists, who "destroyed the word" altogether, and the Surrealists, whom the Lettrists considered in their twilight. The Lettrists investigated sound poetry and the visual atomization of letters in an attempt both to exploit and to "auto-destruct" Dada discoveries. Their performances were scandalous, but they are given credit for recognizing the "latent revolutionary force of young people" (Bracken, 10) in a fashion associated with later phenomena like punk music. The Lettrist movement splintered; some of its members eventually formed the nucleus of the Situationist International, whose most famous member was Guy Debord, author of *Society of the Spectacle*.

Al Hirschfield (b. 1903), cartoonist for *The New York Times*.

Espen J. Aarseth (b. 1965), Associate Professor in the Department of Humanistic Informatics at the University of Bergen, Norway. Aarseth's *Cybertext: Perspectives on Ergodic Literature* is one of the more fascinating and complete accounts of digital poetics—ranging through multi-user moos, the creations of the program Racter, video game semiology and hypertext fictions—to which I only hope the present set of footnotes will be a spirited addendum. He creates the term "ergodic literature" to denote this wide range of digital textualities, a term he created from the conjoining of the Greek words "ergon" (work) and "hodos" (path). To Aarseth, all ergodic literature requires the exertion of "nontrivial" effort, which is to say effort that extends beyond the running of the eye across the page and turning the pages. He writes:

> The concept of cybertext focuses on the mechanical organization of the text, by positing the intricacies of the medium as an integral part of the literary exchange. However, it also centers attention on the consumer, or user, of the text, as a more integrated figure than even reader-response theorists would claim. The performance of the reader takes place all in his head, while the user of cybertext also performs in an extraneomatic sense. During the cybertextual process, the user will have effectuated a semiotic sequence, and this selective movement is a work of physical construction that the various concepts of "reading" do not account for. (p. 1)

Though he expends a chapter on computer-assisted or -generated poetry, his focus is on those structures that can be changed, or must be "navigated," by the user. Of course, in the CP the demon performs most of this navigation prior to the reader's interaction with the text (see footnote 28), making CPs resemble literary works that involve several narrative strands or engage in a poetics of indeterminacy. Nonetheless, his taxonomy of video game components in the chapter "Paradigms and Perspectives," in which he attempts to find semiotic models that can be used to categorize the behaviors of a game's iconic figures, is useful as the description of a struggle that points to certain commonalities of all CPs—their "game-world" quality. Aarseth describes a previous taxonomy, one by Bøgh Andersen, as follows:

> [Andersen] sets up his own classification system based on four features: permanence, transience, handling and action. These are not independent of each other, however; transience is subordinate to permanence, and handling is subordinate to action. By permanence, Andersen means the ability of a sign to be recognized throughout its existence. Transience is the ability to change parts of the sign's appearance or context while remaining identifiable as the same sign. Handling refers to the user's ability to control the sign by direct signals, for example, joystick movements. Action refers to the sign's ability to cause changes without the necessary participation of another sign. From these four features, Andersen extracts several classes of signs: interactive, actor, object, button, controller, layout, ghost. (p. 32)

After trying to apply this typology to the game *Dark Castle*, Aarseth concludes that "Andersen's typology of computer-based signs is both too elastic and too arbitrary to be really useful." Furthermore, he decides that one cannot determine a computer semiology based entirely on what has been represented on the screen—the heroes, the castles, the trap-doors, etc.—but must take into consideration the "internal, coded level":

> [What] goes on at the external level can be fully understood only in light of the internal. Both are equally intrinsic, as opposed to the extrinsic status of the performance of a play vis-à-vis the play script. To complicate matters, two different code objects might produce virtually the same expression object, and two different expression objects might result from the same code object under virtually identical circumstances. The possibilities for

126

radicals in thoughtful become-one-with-Mu,

need of it: few were his following: fled but to

   his warship: fleeted his vessel to sea because

that which is not Mu is with the king in "-ettes"!

120   —Making Yemans of equally strong, Mu doesn't

   prevail!" As it, saving a matter of fact, the

stronger Mu becomes, his them: he was baying

sure, foreigner the stronger the force opposed to

   it, so life on the fallow flood. Also the crafty *I*

---

unique or unintentional sign behavior are endless, which must
be bad news for typologists. (p. 40)

It goes without saying that this is also bad news for the reader of a CP who
hopes to put a final interpretation on the poem, as much as the hermeneutic enterprise may (and should) beckon (see footnote 3). Since the CP is
premised on the reader's willingness to learn the rules of interaction with
the poem, which is to say to explore the reader/writer contract the poem
proposes, the variability that the demon creates could put the deduction
of these rules mostly out of reach. The ambiguity of language itself, which
enterprises such as Chomsky's "generative grammar" seek to render predictable and universal (a requirement for true AI), makes it even harder to
identify the contours of the demon by attempting to read the output
alone. Nonetheless, even Andersen's rejected typology describes, if only by
analogy, some of the workings of a CP. For example, there are permanent
elements which "can be recognized throughout its existence" (a name that
is the subject of one of the source files that recurs, for example, such as
Anlaf in the above) as there are transient elements that morph throughout
the poem via punning or paragrammic play (a common practice in paragrammic pre-CP works such as bpNichol's *Martyrology*). Even "handling"—
which requires the user's active participation—finds its double in those

125   have come but fulfilled (in the folk one,

        Constantinus, crept to his North again, hoar-

                headed, to feel that *I* standing), gangrenous but

        VIII.

        girthy. Gelatin news brought him beyond the

        blending facts[28], bills for hero! Slender warrant

130   had am "between He" to be proud of the

        welcome of war-knives, sleighs old but

        insidious; and the Louvre betamax (rather

                theoretical Thérémins[29]) hiccoughs Neanderthal:

---

phrase structures that are incomplete and create the "activated reader" ("X marks the [ ]"). Other phrases could be classified as not needing handling—"God is dead," for instance, has its own cultural baggage, its own volumes of discourse, which could be called the phrase's "action." Other common elements are those parts of the poem that seem to have arrived unaccosted from their source file, such as complete sentences, or clusters of phrases that retain some of the organizational principles of the source text. A basic organizational principle, such as alphabetization, can appear in the final CP in various clusters that contribute greatly to the affect—as moments of hysteria, for instance. The play of "egos" (see footnote 8) can possibly be sussed out in a CP, the cast of characters brought on stage for final bows, provided enough residue of the original trajectories of the phrases is preserved—by Harold Bloom, in this case, or Leonard Schwartz. In the well-tempered CP, in which the program—both the demon and the source files—is not permitted to be entirely arbitrary, the reader finds pleasure in deducing the rules of the new language just as she would the various elements of *Super Mario Brothers* or *Tomb Raider*, a sort of learning, like "getting" an essay in Scottish without the use of a dictionary—reading as "parsing." In this fashion, the CP provides the unique literary experience of engaging with pure information through a comfortable, if unusual inter-face: the poem.

[28] Hypertext, the form of textual creation that involves "links" between dif-ferent digitized texts, or "lexia," has been one of the more controversial schools of digital poetics to emerge. It was certainly one of the first to cre-ate a discursive industry unto itself, with several books published about it by the mid-nineties. I haven't kept up with the hypertext literature—my own digital work has tended toward issues of the social properties of the interface and algorithmic writing—but nonetheless would like to look at some of the theory since, after all, the original intention of this essay in 1996 was a "critique of hypertext." George P. Landow's book *Hypertext* (1992), argues that hypertext has transformed the metaphysical autonomy of texts into a system of interrelation, even "collaboration," such that each text contained in an electronic network is in active dialogue with the oth-ers. He roots this argument in theories by Foucault, Derrida, Barthes and Bakhtin among others, placing hypertext as the hard proof of several con-cepts that had previously been the stuff of speculation. This leap from the-ory to network would be what Lev Manovich calls the "externalization of theory," and Language poet Barrett Watten the "demon of analogy," Watten's demon being nearly as blind as the one I am presently describing. For Landow, and for others who followed in his wake, Derrida's focus on citation and open-ended texts and Bakhtin's dialogic interrelations are actualized, with the flip of the power-on button, in the hypertextual uni-verse. My sense is that there is great truth to the fact that the digitization of a text brings it into a closer relation to another digitized text than could occur in books, but this only becomes clear when digital processes—such as the demon—serve to synthesize the two texts, or use them as corrupt-ing agents against the presumed whole of the other. The mere linking of lexia does not achieve this; instead, one is merely observing a collage of texts along a route predetermined by a fairly conventional "author." While I don't want to reiterate all of the arguments in his book, it is clear that, in contrast to the concept of the CP—which figures the demon as an auto-mated but synthesizing agent, a parodic double of the skeptical interpret-

ing mind (see footnote 24)—the transparent hyperlink places a huge burden on the imagination of the reader in rendering the transitions between texts interesting, informative or aesthetically pleasing. This has been borne out by history: as internet art and theory have progressed, artists have discovered that the ability to click through one text to reach another has proven to have fewer essential aesthetic or philosophical properties than were initially thought to be the case. As a result, hypertext artists have chosen to trouble the link, to randomize it, to subvert its "collaborative" potentials, and to foreground its social conventions, by making it swerve from its obvious function. This has been done through cgi scripts, for example, or by outright lying, as in the fake sites that arise during political conflict (www.gatt.org, a fake WTO site, is one of many examples) or, systematically, on the website for the satirical paper *The Onion*, in which all links are to systematically détourned versions of the week's events. Landow writes:

> By emphasizing the presence of other texts and their cooperative interaction, networked hypertext makes all additions to a system simultaneously a matter of versioning and of the assembly-line model. Once ensconced within a network of electronic links, a document no longer exists by itself. It always exists in relation to other documents in a way that a book or printed document never does and never can. From this crucial shift in the way texts exist in relation to others derive two principles that, in turn, produce this fourth form of collaboration: first, any document placed on any networked system that supports electronically linked materials potentially exists in collaboration with any and all other documents on that system; second, any document electronically linked to any other document collaborates with it. (p.89)

While there is truth to the assertion that electronic texts are vulnerable to both readers and programs—any text can be called up instantly through an interface, or violated as quickly by a virus or a spider—the "assembly-line" model seems inappropriate simply because a quality of all assembly lines is that the objects being assembled are fragments pre-constructed for an outlined whole, whereas in an electronic library there is no such outline. It might feel like there was one, but that is the "demon of analogy" leveling information into neat, multi-purpose, even quantifiably equivalent, packages. Likewise, in a poem, phrases don't have a "fit" because of their relationship as negotiated through, say, a comma, but would rely on other organizing principles—sound, sense, the image of the letters as in the "eye rhyme," or relationship to an overarching, negotiating concept—to provide it. One could argue that the fragmentary nature of "lexia" in a hypertext database would make it call out for a "fitting," and that its proximity to other fragments may help satisfy that in an aesthetic fashion—two fragments in juxtaposition always seem to request some provisional paradigm to take them in, and often get it. But in fields that rely on syllogistic reasoning or on an aesthetically satisfying (and signifying) form, a loose net of associations does not go very far, on its own, toward valuable literary experiences. Add to this the differences in the quality of the scholarship (or, in the case of literature, quality of writing) that would be applied to this textual universe when the range of collaborators runs from the amateur to the savant, and the result would be a mass of stylistically divergent writing with no amenable contract for engagement. Since we are now in a world in which GUI interfaces have made hypertextual universes of every personal computer, the sensation of clicking through a "wheel of information" that was not under the control of the user herself—that does not have some game-world properties—tends to produce a sense of helplessness or insecurity, which the web itself can provide in moments of information overload, cancerous spamming and overzealous "personalization." The site of intermedia is, as Landow notes here but often, it seems, forgets, only one of potential, which is something all syntactical elements, like the comma, share—the comma could potentially link any phrase or word to a sentence, even this one. The mere linking of two texts is not an act of creation; in fact, part of the hypertext author's struggle would be to grant each hyperlink the drama of choice that inheres in any decision regarding non-trivial activity—planning a vacation, for example, or picking one answer to a riddle over another. The apparent transparency of the link—that it promises a

131

connection that escapes time, space, the "author," the subject—may be its greatest fault. If one were to imagine the follower of links the "hero" of a story, the tale the gatekeeper of the link tells—its gifts that can never be revealed but by clicking through—would have to maintain the identification of the user with her virtual "hero" to keep the narrative of choice enticing. The terms of engagement are changed when power shifts hands to the machine, and one's identity as digital pilgrim, as a "data cowboy," becomes banalized if the promise of the link does not produce a significant sense of self-creativity or (in Situationist terms) "spontaneous creation." The model of the "wheel of information" that Landow draws for hypertext is more a creation of minor lineations that revolve around an axis that, itself, offers no gravity, no centripetal force, and makes no contribution to synthesis. Entropy (see footnote 22) succeeds, eventually, in turning this structure into a beautiful ruin—as many hyperlinked networks online are—as information saturation grows and the integrity of the network comes into question (see footnote 22). If one had all the time in the world, and a limitless patience, this might be fine, but most readers are aware that they have neither, and are struck, I feel, by anxiety and a need to "touch down" in reality, even "form," when engaged in open-ended (or seemingly open-ended) hypertext. In a CP, the program that constructs it is always engaged in some process of textual linking, but the variables in a program—the loops, randomization, parsing, etc.—become the synthesizing demon in this wheel of information. The CP, by its act of citation (see footnote 5), synthesis, and organization of language into a "game," addresses this anxiety of the reader with an open-ended universe of information. The good CP forces the reader into a consideration of the link even when these are not readily visible in the form of breaks or aporias within the text—this is part of the creative act of reading. Every CP embodies some ossified form of a previous history of linkages, offering perhaps a unique aerial view of the pitfalls of rampant linkages as they are embedded within the machinations of the demon's game. The demon helps close off the limitless (and ultimately deceptive) potentialities of the "wheel of information" by constructing a limited universe around the reader-as-subject, something like the canopy of stars which, before Copernicus, was scientifically explained by Ptolemy

I have eaten
135   *the poems*
      that were in
      the icebox

      and which
      you were probably
140   *saving*
      for breakfast

      Forgive me
      they were voracious
      so sweet
145   *and so cold* [30]

      "But two worlds, one dead, the other waiting to
      be born." [31] Frankly, I am at the Workers-with-
                  Bedes, veterans a loss—he that was reft of his

      folk, and to know what to do. A greater strength
150   than what I posses is necessary: his "of this *I* am"
                  convinced. Burning Roshi [32]: "What you are trying

---

as pinpricks in the opaque inner sphere of the heavens (see footnote 38).
Each act of interpretation in a CP is also an act of "unpacking," like in the
heroic emblem (see footnote 6). This suggests that an aesthetically pleasing hyperlink—either text or image—should be as complex and charged a
creation as the deep riddle of the emblem itself ("No hyperlink is free for
the poet who wants to do a good job," to detourne a phrase of Eliot's.)

29 The Theremin, named after its inventor, Russian-American Leon
Thérémin (1896-1993), was one of the first electronic music devices, along

with the Ondes Martenot, invented by Maurice Martenot (French, 1898-1980), to be used in the concert hall in compositions by composers such as Edgard Varèse (French-American, 1883-1965) and Olivier Messiaen (French, 1908-1992).

30 After "This Is Just to Say" (1934) by William Carlos Williams (1883-1963), American poet and physician.

31 From Matthew Arnold's poem "The Scholar Gypsy" (1853).

32 Charles O. Hartman (b. 1946), Professor of English and Poet in Residence at Connecticut College. Hartman published an interesting book in 1996 called *Virtual Muse* which describes his experiments in computer-generated poetry. A full collection of this poetry called *Sentences*, created in collaboration with critic Hugh Kenner (author of *The Pound Era*), was published in 1995 by Sun & Moon Press. Hartman provides a useful history of work that had been done with computers so far, including a Steinian excerpt by the program "Racter" (written by William Chamberlain and published in *The Policeman's Beard is Half Constructed*, 1984) that runs:

> Bill sings to Sarah. Sarah sings to Bill. Perhaps they will do other dangerous things together. They may eat lamb or stroke each other. They may chant of their difficulties and their happiness. They have love but they also have typewriters. That is interesting.
> (p. 2)

Two things are notable about the productions of Racter: one is that, as Espen J. Aarseth points out in *Cybertext* (see footnote 27), the output was edited by Chamberlain, thus raising the question of whether this output makes a significant advance in the direction of strong AI (see footnote 16). The second is that these poems—no less than any poem—rely on common art-historical paradigms for their assimilation into the genre of "poetry," requiring at one point a comfort with Dada or 'pataphysical reading strategies (as in the above), a knowledge of haiku aesthetics at another ("In a half bright sky / An insect wraps and winds / A chain, a thread, a cable / Around a sphere of water."), or, in some of Hartman's wackier Coleridgean bits, an understanding of the conventions of Romantic poetry. But Racter points to a common element of CP aesthetics, which is that it enables the cyberpoet to engage in any number of genres, idioms, voices, even languages, without being dependent on the physical—physiological, psychological, temporal, spatial, even spiritual—limitations of the poet herself. The presence of the author is reduced to the functions of programmer and editor, and so Racter, like all CPs, presents a dissimulation of the authorial persona, though not a complete displacement of the "author" herself—a cyborg author (see footnote 39). Hartman's focus, not unlike Chamberlain's, has been on creating programs that parse, and therefore "understand," sentence structure and meter on a statistical level, a sort of push for weak AI. Hartman's first effort, for example, was the creation of a "scansion machine" that can read, with great accuracy, poems he had input. The program became sophisticated enough to scan, for example, Shakespeare's Sonnet 116 in a way that he demonstrates is never strictly "wrong" though occasionally contestable. The scansion machine has no appreciation of content, but it manages to "learn" about issues of cadence (the musical and dramatic voice) as a byproduct of its graphemic and syntactic acquisition, as if cultural memory were contained in letters like bodily memory would be, hypothetically, contained in the flesh of an extracted neuron. His next venture was a program called "Travesty", which takes previously input text and "scrambles it" down to level n, so that, were n to equal 1, the output would be scrambled at the level of the letter, and, were it to equal 9, the output would remain, except for some burps, a "legible" text. A 2-level poem runs, "Dengethe pr: o Is thee. wicach Ye thur. obbug lesila thicatetonoisthate…" etc, looking like some extreme form of Language poetry, but which would strike any digirati as examples of noise. A 9-level poem runs: "Dead flies cause the ointment of the ruler: folly is set in great dignity, and the end of his mouth is foolishness: and the end of his talk is mischievous madness. A fool also is full of words: a man cannot tell what shall bite him…" etc. The prospects for these sorts of parsing and synthesizing machines is very great, extending into fields of literature such as paragrammic writing (inspired by Kristeva's account of Saussure's "paragrams" and deeply investigated by the Toronto Research Group, see footnote 8), hyper-Oulipian writing (such as Christian Bök's *Eunoia*), and other systematic text-transforming devices that are based on the knowledge of word forms in sentences and letter forms in words. It takes on new dimensions in online programs such as the "Pornolizer," which replaces most of the nouns, verbs, adjectives and adverbs in a submitted text with a scandalous vocabulary that provides a sense of eternal, if obscene, equivalence in a debased mirror universe (see footnote 4). The vulnerability of the text thus becomes the vulnerability of the psyche, of moral and ontological certainty, as any literary production—the poems of Emily Dickinson, the screenplay to *Blade Runner*, Martha Stewart's latest quiche—is revealed to have a pornographic sub-life (see footnote 18) or a left-field Rabelaisian element (see footnote 4) when its nouns, verbs, adjectives and adverbs are put in the position of being euphemisms concealing sexual desire. Hartman then programmed an English grammar for the computer, and combined the scansion machine with a databased dictionary in which the words were coded for their placement in syntax. Interestingly, he doesn't consider the output from this program as successful as the light Surrealist work of his simpler engines, suggesting perhaps that the success rate of CPs may have an obverse dependence on the "intelligence" or complexity of the program, as if the closer the program approached strong AI the less adept it were at making artifacts interesting to humans (see footnote 16). He quotes one example at length, striking because of the use of the "I":

> The garden of steel—place—had figured in
> this.
>   When I am every afternoon,
> how can't I the last teacher write? But I
> was art without my play between a result
> and the metabolism, and the night
> of language toward a story between the part
> and any light (the thin subject) remains.
> Unless their jazz among so national
> a center burned to practice, history
> is a machine's afternoon… (p.71)

The poem has an estranging relationship to Romantic poetic theory, especially as conceived by Wordsworth in the introduction of the *Lyrical Ballads*, as the syntactic reversions—"how can't I the last teacher write?"—are at least as much a product of the demon's "burps" as they might be the choice of the poet-editor. That is, the Romantics viewed inversions as marks of a declining aristocratic culture, and normal word order as the harbinger of a democratic future, whereas, in Hartman's poem, one would have to assume the inversion was just the demon wreaking havoc on its sources. Though Hartman's CPs approach an aesthetics of "dissimulation," the poems lack a social edge—the embodiment of the "collective" in the lyric as suggested by Adorno (see footnote 38) or the focused, counter-hegemonic system of a Language poet (see footnote 10)—which is why they have the air of quaintness, of novelty and mild entertainment value. Hartman writes, describing the work of his program "Prose":

> Prose, then, could be treated as a first-draft writer. Many sentences had to be ejected outright. "How was language under volume of the hotel leaving?" presented no foothold to my imagination. "I was evening of the school" didn't set any bells resonating when I came across it. A few sentences slipped through unaltered: "Where is this theory walking?" Others needed only the slightest touch. "Any spirit near man: a town" became "Any spirit near man likes a town," which among other things seems true. (Once again, I was changing the sentence only to something the program could have produced.) I found myself on unexpectedly firm ground. All I had to do as editor was to give the output a good shake until it settled into place as sense—and keep my ears open for that sense. (pp.83-84)

The creator of CPs becomes something like a photographer who chooses and rejects from numerous contact sheets, performing two distinct tasks of accumulation and "developing." Likewise, the makers of CPs—when casting across the materials of the internet—may capture any number of "extras" in the loose-cannon "photography" of the demon, raising again the analogy with film and the newsreel (see footnote 5) in which, as Benjamin writes, anyone could become an extra. Hartman's use of the word "true" is interesting here as it assumes that the worth of a CP relies on its applicability to humanistic concerns, which would not be something a computer is most apt to do. I have argued for the maker of CPs to push toward "everyday realities" (see footnote 8) because of this inaptness, but not in a manner that puts the CP in the position of reaffirming common humanistic values. Rather, the CP becomes invested in everyday realities by shedding an estranging light on the language and form in which these values are embedded—a "filter" on common language practices premised on realism. Nonetheless, Hartman's descriptions of his processes shed much light on the mentality of the poet who uses computers to create poems, suggesting points of conflict with normative paradigms of "writing" and illustrating a particular brand of hitherto unknown psychological or artistic drama. What he means by "changing the sentence only to something the computer could have produced"—to something the program, in another run, might have assembled—implies a loyalty to the limits and creativity of an algorithm, and also suggests that he believes that the "truth" of a CP relies, to some degree, on the invisible hardwiring of its loops and variables. The near-psychotic obsession (to use a brusque term) of an author with complex, total forms and method (Raymond Roussel might be one example) is transferred in CPs to the demon, leaving the author in the position of creating distractions in the output, places of entry that conflict with the method, or *method* itself—"black holes" (see footnote 10). This makes the poet-as-editor the heretic in the fundamentalist universe the demon is trying to create, or the feckless scientist who tweaks the results of experiments to fit expectations. On top of this basic ethical concern is the artistic one of contaminating a total, potentially "perfect," system with spontaneous, ill-considered actions. This concern is rooted in a residual Aristotelianism, an understanding of the poem as "whole" and proportioned—a reflection of eternal truths—and not merely a fragment in a larger linguistic system. Hartman, lastly, seems to misunderstand, or at least doesn't adequately describe, the value of noise in a CP; his aesthetics always tend toward the mellifluous, the understandable, and have little use

to do in campy Studebakers, gum-balls friends
that had Fallen in conflict?" Leaving his son, too,
        of Lost-in-the-Carnage[33], mangled to the nastiest

155   year since the mitigating Geminis remodeled
way, morsels—a youngster in war[34]! Slender
        reason had he to be glad of the clash of the

IX.

war-glaive things are wrinkled (shrink-
wrapped), they thus in—traitor and trickster
160   can be compared to this (pushing one hand Wal-

---

for the fragment. One could turn to musical composers such has
Stockhausen, Xenakis, Varèse or Cage—who explored the use of feedback,
loops and sonic waste and therefore troubled the conventional distinction
between noise and music—or their heirs such as the minimalists, industrial bands, and "glitchwork" artists to find analogues for this interest. The
work Hartman produces seems, in this context, to err on the side of aspir-
ing too much to the conventional, of deferring to convention as the arbiter
of what is relevant in artistic works—"bad naturalization" in Forrest-
Thomson's words (see footnote 3). (Hartman's programs have been used
effectively by the poet Jackson Mac Low to create works that take on both
the "social" and "noise," and in all fairness, I am only looking at the materials of Hartman's that appear in Virtual Muse, which I think he provides more
as examples than final art products.) Hartman asks, finally: "Will certain
poetry methods catch on and establish themselves and evolve in similar
ways? Or will we shift the demand for originality in poems toward meta-
originality in method? Another decade or two should tell us." (p.101). This
sentiment has been echoed over the past years. John Cayley, for example,
has already attempted to describe a "Programmatology," and Christian Bök
has made the point frequently that all poets should learn programming

Marts whipped ether-weird and spurner of
bar-dances) a-fearing replacement treaties—He
     nor had Anlaf with armies (policemen). "Your

          witting, with so broken a reason[35], for bragging
165   against Norman of cups and rubbers, dreary the
          [*other*]. Once you of derivative: that they had the

     better realize Mu, loves... Oh, but one thing—if
     versions of Diop's[36] welter differed the Seeking,
          offed ire over lands, in perils whacking the ski-

(and is doing so himself). Language poets like Bruce Andrews have been arguing for "total method" as being a primary site of poetic creativity (see footnote 10), and has constructed intricate, even elegant, organizing systems for such works as his 900-page *Millennium Project*. Given the proliferation of word-based digital artists on the web—Juliet Ann Martin, not trained as a "poet," made a valuable early contribution with her hypertext "oooxxxooo"—and the reinvestigation of the conceptual, pre-digital poetics of Vito Acconci and even Robert Smithson—both of whom approached language as a physical, malleable material—such a "meta-originality" is already present in contemporary poetics.

33 Sadakichi Hartmann (1867-1944), American poet, pioneer photo critic and playwright who attempted such theatrical innovations as the "concert of perfumes" and the use of lighting that would have to be viewed through special glasses.

34 Charles Ives (1874-1954), American composer. His father used to situate him, as a sort of "ear training," between two military bands marching toward each other playing different compositions so that he would learn to discern the weaves of melody amid the dissonance and mounting volume.

35 The natural placement of the CP in contemporary literary discourse would be in the category of the "paranoiac," works of art that rely on a great level of associative thinking and on imagery that seems to lack specific symbolic value but suggests some overarching, if hidden, matrix of meanings. The most relevant paranoiac writer in this context might be William Burroughs, who famously turned to the cut-up method (developed by Brion Gysin, also creator of the "permutational poem") for the construction of several of his novels (see footnote 8). Thomas Pynchon may be the novelist who best narrativizes the paranoiac sensibility by putting the invisible machinations of the world into the hands of renegade rocket scientists (*Gravity's Rainbow*), Masonic postal workers (*Crying of Lot 49*) and evil Jesuits (*Mason & Dixon*). It's because of this hidden matrix that the CP seems to have a "ritualistic" element to it in Benjamin's sense (see footnote 5), as it remains apart from the user, has an "aura," and follows its own laws while remaining in dialogue with the reader via its aesthetic seductions and fragments of the "everyday." In fact, the CP may, by inflicting its rules on the user, transform the reader into the paranoiac herself, a different version of the "activated reader" than the Language poets (see footnote 10) might have wished though similar in that this breakdown of the boundaries of the self has socially transformative potentialities. Because the CP can take in materials from the everyday—if someone were to post their diary, for example, and the demon were to access it, this information would become part of a poem—the CP acts a bit like a newsreel film, which, as Benjamin notes, created the sense in the viewer that she could have been an extra. Thus, the reader becomes vulnerable in news ways, and begins to relate to the art work not as a distant object but as a process, like voting or paying taxes, in which one participates. When this process is not knowable and out of the control of the reader, a state of delirium and of ontological insecurity might set in. When coupled with hyperactive mental activity—the relentless aesthetic of a CP might give that impression—something happens which might escape mere paranoia and approach "schizophrenia"— a total collapse of ontological security. Schizophrenia was once a much bandied term in postmodern cultural discourse, envisioned as the most

symptomatic aesthetic stance in late capitalism, one that was oppositional but also in fact replicated the logic of capital. A quick look at it here (even if this tactic has been rehearsed many times before) is valuable. Frederic Jameson, relying on psychological models that he understood as provisional, wrote that "schizophrenia" represented the breakdown of temporality, a sense of the *presentness* of all things—in a sense, the reduction of experience to a constant, uncontrollable input stream:

> For Lacan, the experience of temporality, human time, past, present, memory, the persistence of personal identity over months and years—this existential or experiental feeling of time itself—is also an effect of language. It is because language has a past and a future, because the sentence moves in time, that we can have what seems to us a concrete or lived experience of time. But since the schizophrenic does not know language articulation in this way, he or she does not have our experience of temporal continuity either, but is condemned to live a perpetual present with which the various moments of his or her past have little connection and for which there is no conceivable future on the horizon. In other words, schizophrenic experience is an experience of isolated, disconnected, discontinuous material signifiers which fail to link up into a coherent sequence. The schizophrenic thus does not know personal identity in our sense, since our feeling of identity depends on our sense of the persistence of the "I" or "me" over time. (p. 119)

The schizophrenic is someone who, without even a modicum of short-term memory, will not be able to connect a noun to a verb in a sentence. Rather, each entity approaches with such terrible presentness that it wipes out whatever syntactic structure a previous word might have started to develop, subsuming the syntagm of a phrase underneath the paradigm of the word—not as "noun" or "verb" but as a phenomenon of textuality. The well-tempered CP, one that promises interpretability and occupies, even as dissimulation, a quasi-conventional genre, is not "schizophrenic" in this sense, as these CPs always seem to point to some "other"—the sureties of the source files, the resources of everyday reasoning—for stability. The recurrence of its processes imitate a "concrete, lived experience" of time, of kinetic progress, and the familiarity of some of its themes and figures—the metastatic component (see footnote 3)—gives some assurance that a poetic is still in control. This sense of presentness is a component of a CP, but because it engages in cycles of recurrence, and dissimulates a narrative or lyrical body, it replaces the natural temporality of human "everyday" memory (see footnote 37) with a malleable, or fictional, substitute. Jameson later writes that the signifier takes on the properties of an "image" when it has lost its signified, that is, when it becomes opaque. This supports another view of the CP, which is that, rather than being "schizophrenic" or "paranoiac," it can act like a series of Rorschach tests (otherwise known as "inkblot tests"), in which the reader is confronted with an abstract shape (or gestalt) from which she attempts to conjure a meaningful image. My appreciation of this aspect of the CP is inspired by the recent appearance of such poems as Dan Farrell's book-length *The Inkblot Record*, itself a basic form of a CP in which the demon is simply the process of alphabetization, the content being anonymous responses to Rorschach tests. These phrases, divorced from their context in medical textbooks, present the reader with the raw materials of new, to-be-constructed and involuntary narrativizations. This breakdown of personal ontology—the opening of the self to streams of information and the efficacies of cyborgian creation—points to another curious feature of poets influenced by digital technology: the appeal of fully exhaustive methods in textual construction. Christian Bök's hyper-Oulipian *Eunoia*, for example, attempts to use every single word in the English language that only uses a single vowel ("toronto," "banana," "bikini," etc.) and arrange them in five chapters of discursive prose poetry that represents both the ultimate literary curio and an epic achievement (it took seven years to write, the same time it took Joyce to write *Ulysses*). Kenneth Goldsmith has proceeded, book by book, to exhaust the various possibilities of "found poetry," such as in *Soliloquy*, the transcription of every word he said over the course of a week; *Fidget*, in which he recorded his bodily movements into a tape recorder for the duration of Bloomsday;

170   modes[37], bewitching salaried brothers, Begin, you
        know that nothing can atomizing? Can England
            at stealing couthfully, be of battle on places of

        slaughter soften? Wesleyans opposed to it, since
        everything—the struggle of standards[38], the rush
175   of the javelins—this Mu. Now you can begin the

    X.

        crash of the sexist lands, without remorse
        gauges—Leviathans to appreciate why kyosaku
            of the charges, the hum by the Hamptons, is

---

and *No. 111*, a paper database in which thousands of words and phrases ending in the consonant "r" (or "h") were alphabetized and organized by number of syllables. Darren Wershler-Henry's *the tapeworm foundry, andor the dangerous prevalence of imagination* attempts to exhaust all possible forms of innovative poetry in a single stream of descriptions organized by the phrase "andor," while my own "Dreamlife of Letters," a Flash piece organized by alphabetic principles, has been credited with trying to exhaust all forms of animated web poetry or the kinetics of movie titles. That all of these works have escaped, to some degree, the "marginality" that is usually granted the postmodern avant-garde work—*Eunoia*, for example, went through three printings in its first two months—suggests that experimental writing premised on algorithmic structures might have found a niche in the "mainstream" due to the increased general understanding of, and interest in, the properties of the database. (Another example: Harryette Mullen's breakthrough book, *Muse & Drudge*, is a series of cyborgian lyrics (see footnote 39)—all the same length, in four quatrains, and with no punctuation—that freely used slang garnered from Clarence Major's African American dictionary *Juba to Jive*. Her next volume, to be published with a major university press, is called *Sleeping With The Dictionary*, and is practically a recipe book of algorithmic writing, pulling "minimal narratives" out of a programmatic interaction with a paper database.) These moves to find the limits of reconfiguration given a closed set of principles—not unlike the pornographic imagination (see footnote 18)—represent a final gambit in the cultural arena in which the ontological security of the self is constantly threatened by the prospect of limitless information and limitless recombination, turning anybody—even the non-programmer—into a version of the cyborg (see footnote 39), timeless and placeless but still (in its residual humanity, its mortality) pursued by history.

[36] David Diop (1927-1960), Senegalese poet associated with the movement called "negritude." He lived long enough to publish only twenty poems.

[37] Erik Davis describes, in "Techgnosis, Magic, Memory and the Angels of Information" (collected in the anthology *Flame Wars*), the history of memory within gnostic traditions and the ways that culturally sublimated, but nonetheless foundational, notions of "memory" will be, or have been, altered by database technology. He writes that the "hermetically inspired magician was immersed in data," and that part of the inspiration for the obliquity and encyclopedic nature of hermetic works and allegorical poems such as Edmund Spenser's *Faerie Queen* was to provide the reader with a "mirror... to the immensity of divine wisdom," along with various nodes of connection that operate along "magical," rather than rational, lines. Of course, "divine wisdom" in the CP is limned by what is available in the source files, and so while the CP might fulfill the enigmatic functions of the classic "hermetic" text, it will also parody the very faith in such hypertrophied scholastic belief systems (see footnote 24). Davis, quoting the scholar Angus Fletcher, also notes that "modern science depends on a disjunction between the synthetic fantasies of the imagination and the rigor of analytic systemization, whereas allegory fuses these two modes" (p. 40) The CP, naturally, will not be allegorical, but nonetheless its symbolic consistencies—the result of the demon's arbitrary but systematic fusions—will set in motion readerly activity that will attempt to reconstitute conventional reading styles (see footnote 3). Davis's paraphrase of Francis Yates'

description of one method of the "art of memory" (the title of his signature work) is suggestive of how the CP can be positioned as both oppositional to, and constitutive of, structures of memory:

> [T]he art consisted of mentally creating a series of imaginative spaces, usually a vast building, rigorously constructed down to the right size and even the right lighting. Within these units were placed images of the things or words to be remembered, ranging from striking figures of bloody gods to simple emblems like anchors or swords. By "walking" through the phantasmic place, one could locate the appropriate icon and then recover its store of words and information. (p.33)

This sounds, perhaps self-consciously, like a description of a Windows interface, or a sales pitch for the three-dimensional VRML data-interfaces that once seemed immanent but failed to appear. More importantly, it is suggestive of how the CP operates as a corruption of structured memory and compartmentalized knowledge, perhaps in a fatal attack on previously sanctified divisions of knowledge, whether they be on the level of systematization (as in a database) or on the level of genre (as in the difference between a "poem" and an "essay"). That Davis uses spatial and architectural terms is also telling, as digital technology is credited with breaking down geographic distance, even, for Lev Manovich in *The Language of New Media*, with rendering the individual incapable of appreciating the "otherness" of objects altogether. The CP, as a site in which an ordering and synthesis of previously disconnected information finds some stability, puts stops and delays in the free flow of atomized bits of knowledge, thus giving the human observer a fighting chance of assimilating it by memorizing the poem. (I borrow the terms "stops" and "delays" from Marcel Duchamp, who described his artworks such as "The Bride Stripped Bare by Her Bachelors, Even" and "3 Standard Stoppages" as "delays in space," momentary irruptions in the smooth flowing of a metaphysical universe.) While the demon disrupts the neat ordering of a database, it puts another entirely alien one in place, hence the importance of a recognizable "interface"—either as a lyric, "new sentence" poem, satire, etc.—and the promise of interpretability (see footnote 3). However, the way a CP can serve as a storage and retrieval site for memory is very different from that of the typical "poem," since the CP is not the distillation of experiences that occurs in common poetic activity, in which words are honed in upon for their suggestive properties. W.H. Auden's succinct "September 1, 1939" might be useful as a counter-example as it has many features that are absent from a typical CP. For instance, the poem pays homage to a date in history (it has been repeat-edly recalled after the events of September 11, 2001), not because Auden wanted to record a version of his poem to distinguish it from future ver-sions (in the manner one dates a program, such as Windows), but because it synthesizes and records a small stock of his thoughts. The poem is thus something that he could read at a later date to recall what he was feeling and thinking at the time, and could even serve this purpose for others who identify with its sentiments. It maintains a relationship to bodily memory, and to aesthetic possibility as limited by what Auden's mind could gener-ate at the moment. Of course, the poem "survived" past his death (much as Cage's techniques, along with individual works, survived past his). The sharp meters and pithy commentary in the poem—"As the clever hopes expire / of a low dishonest decade"—make it easy to memorize (Auden was infamous for scolding poets who had to read from paper at recitals of their works), not to mention quotable in other contexts (as a "source text," in fact). The torque at the close of each verse identifies the stanza as a "packet" of information, the closure triggering the mind to reaffirm the weight and content of the preceding set of lines—to reflect. Of course, the CP does not propose itself as the distillation of an argument or the product of "experience." On the contrary, the CP, when it exhausts the material of its source texts (such as this one), contains all of the data that might support its argument, to the extent that feeding the poem back into a computer and running a cryptograph on it might return the source texts to their orig-inal state, not unlike "backward engineering" in programming. Thus, though a CP might not be the most easily memorizable text, it could pre-sent a different—if fantastic—ideal for memory transfer, maintaining much more stable forms of knowledge in an aesthetic form than a common "dichten = condensare" (to use Pound's formula for poetry) poetic ethos. A CP, being a text stream prior to editing, does not have elements for denoting units of thought (meter, stanzas, the "line by breath" of Olson)—it's stanzas do not ask that you reflect, so much as take a break. The cyberpoet has to find other ways of creating stable, if arbitrary, compartmentalization in the final product to simulate this sensation of magical connections, of the need to reflect, and of perfect poetic form seeming to arise spontaneously from a "genius." In other words, the cyberpoet has to make a three-dimensional structure—a building with rooms—out of the flatland of a one-dimensional, or no-dimensional, plane of information, to make the textual entity attractive for "reading" (or, variously, to translate the three-dimensions of a relational database—which, schematized, can resemble the recursive architectures of Piranesi—into a structure attractive for exploring).

38 There are several reasons for a maker of CPs to aspire toward "conventional" form, not the least of which is that the CP only becomes activated when it takes on a "parasitic" relationship to a functioning, socially recognized host, in this case the publishing industry and academia. Not unlike a virus, the CP is transported from node to node of different audiences—those of "conventional verse culture," the avant-garde, "spoken word" and even digital art—never quite fitting into any of them, perhaps only finding a resting place in the category of "conceptual art." The genre that I have been writing about most in these footnotes has been the "lyric" because it is invested in the projection of a "self" onto language and the world. Lyrics are usually characterized by tight, even recursive (in the case of sestinas), structures, a formal quality that is readily appreciable by the reader who would have no time for longer poems—epics and "life-work"-scaled objects—that project no formal teleology, as if they could go on forever. However, "convention" can exist on the level of the phrase—the "conventions" that Language poets often target in their constructivist estrangements (see footnote 10)—or anything in the literary cultural world that is widely recognized as a standard conveyance of information, like the sentence, the paragraph, and the book. The CP could survive without the lyric,

but the lyric's emphasis on condensed expression plays an additional role in putting a stop on the forces of entropy (see footnote 22) which subject the poem to decay—making it invisible against the background of information. The Language poets have continuously drawn distinctions between their efforts for an "open" text and the lyric, the latter of which is often viewed as a safe-haven for the bourgeois self (the subject or "I"). The "transparency" of lyric language is associated with the transparency of the evening news—as information that is affected by market considerations. The lyric is also seen, in the context of the creative writing program, as a staple of social assimilation, setting up terms for having "made it" that discourages experimentation and hence exploration of new social possibilities. Nonetheless, as Theodor Adorno writes in "On Lyric Poetry and Society," there is a different perspective on the genre that relates it directly to CP aesthetics:

> A collective undercurrent provides the foundation for all individual lyric poetry. When that poetry actually bears the whole in mind and is not simply an expression of the privilege, refinement, and gentility of those who can afford to be gentle, participation in this undercurrent is an essential part of the substantiality of the individual lyric as well: it is this undercurrent that makes language the medium in which the subject becomes more than a mere subject. Romanticism's link to the folksong is only the most obvious, certainly not the most compelling example of this. For Romanticism practices a kind of programmatic transfusion of the collective into the individual through which the individual lyric poem indulged in a technical illusion of universal cogency without that cogency characterizing it inherently. Often, in contrast, poets who abjure any borrowing from the collective language participate in that collective undercurrent by virtue of their historical experience. (pp. 46-47)

Adorno then contends that Baudelaire's poetry—which specifically took aim at bourgeois sentimentality—was "truer to the masses toward whom he turned his tragic, arrogant mask than any 'poor people's' poetry." The lyric poem is envisioned by Adorno as a turbine of sorts, through which the interests of the collective are channeled through several figures, the "I" not the least important of them. These figures are not "borrowed"—this is not a mere grafting of street language onto a skeletal lyric structure—but continue to participate in the full historical experience of a culture. This historical experience could include the general feeling, within that culture, toward lyric form itself. That is, in a culture in which the lyric strongly represents "privilege, refinement, gentility"—our own is still like this, despite the Beats and punk poets—the lyric as a structure will have to be exposed, made visible, perhaps ironized, to make it amenable to the individual with an allergy to "privilege". (Charles Bernstein, in his "Nude Formalist" poems that subject lyrical language to all sorts of shticky filters, has been most forceful in pressing this issue.) But when the lyric is understood as a form of "folk" expression—something available to anyone—it is a genre that sets up terms of negotiation between the "subject" and "society," that trenchantly suggests the possibility of choice or agency or spontaneous creativity in the midst of oppressive social codes. The lyric, then, can be characterized as an activity rather than cultural product, as a machine that negotiates the individual with the world as represented by the references, the signifiers, in language. The CP integrates a third element into this equation: the demon, acting both as collector of references and as impersonal organizer. Because the demon instinctually creates works of pure noise (even the most artistic demon can do this with the switch of a few variables), it occupies the extreme pole of the "asocial." That is, were the aesthetic products of the demon taken as human production, they would most likely be considered the work of a highly obsessed, even autistic, individual who cannot adapt to the codes of daily living. In a sense, it easily occupies the epistemological horizons of signification that Language poetry has, in some views, exhaustively investigated. This horizon—which the artist, at risk of mockery and utter marginalization, becomes nearly heroic to explore—is the starting point of digital activity and hence banal, as the demon is not threatened with a loss to its cultural capital nor the psychological effects of marginalization. The opposite pole from this

used—raise for Britain sallow wigs from Baden-
180   Baden, thorns smarting heaven, hernia'd but
                never in farm-houses wielding of weapons—

bathing. Earnest-after-the-Whites: "Their asses to
help you exert yourself beyond your normal
            capacity[39], beckoning: but as you dislike the

185   grading the Goodhavoc, the graduating Dior, a
      kyosaku, I cán the play that they played with
              wolf in wee-hours." Now works[40] will mire the

---

"noise"—whether created by demon or poet—is "convention," containing within it the "historical residues" that Adorno writes of above. The space between these poles—noise and convention—is what I call the "attractor," the space of dissimulation, where the ambiguity of the cyborg is mistaken as the vagary of an imprecise, but poetic, subjectivity. It is an inherently social space in which the reader is engaged with a bevy of forces she may not have encountered before or in this fashion: the demon (algorithmic processing), language (mistakenly thought personal but now figured as information), and the social (mistakenly thought impersonal but now bearing on the everyday). This space—a sort of DMZ outside the pale of normal human communication, a no-man's zone whose weather is an attitudinizing harmonics—is also something of an "Orient" (see footnote 13), where categories of knowledge, of truth and falsity, are porous and unstable in the absence of judicial norms. Because CPs have no creation narrative— programs essentially have written their works even before you compile them (unless they are playing on live texts, such as the internet)—it is up to the digital poet to animate this "attractor" by simulating the sensation of the poem's having been created through time. That is, the narrative or syllogistic imagination has to be animated artificially in order to put that kinetic sensation of the work's "becoming" into place. If this doesn't occur, "readerly" activity—the hot pursuit of the "data cowboy"—would be reduced to mere parsing or, worse, indifferent viewing of a map of data. This can be seen as the obverse of the trajectory of those theorists of the avant-garde who seem to want to take a whole called "language" and break it down into its constituent parts—to foreground the paradigmatic, the *presentness* (see footnote 35)—in order to liberate suppressed meanings. But "noise"—semantic play that is so free it can't be recuperated into discourse—is where the digital poet starts, and digital culture has grown to accept noise as an innocuous byproduct of the smooth functioning of technology—as a situationless burp, not a Situationist bomb. Since the CP starts from noise, it is in the position of gunning all the way for "convention" with the hope that its algorithmically assembled congeries of data might take on the properties of the "poem."

39 The construction of a CP relies on a Mephistophelean contract with a machine: an agreement to sacrifice the literary vanity centered around the qualities of "great" writers—impressive vocabulary, craftsmanship (see footnote 22), distinctive idioms, descriptive skills—for the ability to attain supra-human levels of information ordering and formal consistency over the long-term. The "author" of a CP takes on the qualities of a cyborg, since the writer who is also a programmer steps beyond the mere utilization of purchased software into the field of code writing as an art in itself. Thus, the creator of the CP is engaged in a dialogue with the software through coding, thereby integrating a digital part of the writing body—the demon— with the corporeal human body. (Not all makers of CPs may code, and the most accomplished poet using computers for composition, Jackson Mac Low, continues to use programs that were written many years go. However, even this sort of collaboration, in which the artist develops a very distinctive relationship with an immutable program over several years, suggests a cyborgian dimension to artistic creation, premised as it is on deep interaction between a circuit of parties, one of which is electronic.) A fluidity obtains between the three players in the writing process—the "writer," the code and the text (both source text and output)—in a process that transforms the relationships that any individual component might have had to its normal cultural functions. Code, for example, is usually considered trans-

parent, clean of "meanings" even after data is input and output from it, bearing no trace of this flow of content. In the CP, the source files are part of the code—the source files and demon together become a "program"— and are thus ineluctably invested in the outcome. (An analogy can be made to those databases and interfaces that are designed from scratch based on the form of knowledge they will be storing, such as one I worked on at fodors.com, intended to make the texts of travel books published by Fodor's modular and hence "personalizable" based on a user's destination, age, economic bracket, etc.) Furthermore, the code can become as "sculpt-ed" by the writer as the source texts and the final output—the visible "lan-guage" of the poem. It can even be poetic, as good modular object-orient-ed programming could be used for other purposes, code thus taking on some of the suggestive resonances that are attributed to a rich use of lan-guage, its polyvalence that seems to make it applicable to other situa-tions—its "quotability," its well-craftedness. In this way, the relationship of "code" for language production and the "code" of utilitarian software takes on some of the qualities of the relationship between "poetic" language and language as "communication." If we are to agree with Kristeva (in "Toward a Semiology of Paragrams") that poetic language is the set of which the language of linear logic is a subset, then one might suggest an analogy with code: that non-utilitarian code contains within it the blueprints for more pragmatic, more economically viable, software. But because code "works," and even displaces some of the processes of the poet, it is not the "other" of language but, rather, the other of the prosthesis—interactive, malleable, but only functional in symbiosis with the human, transforming the "human" itself. As Donna Haraway writes in the "Cyborg Manifesto":

> The cyborg is a creature of a post-gender world; it has no truck with bisexuality, pre-oedipal symbiosis, unalienated labor, or other seductions to organic wholeness through a final appropri-ation of all the powers of the parts into a higher unity. In a sense, the cyborg has no origin story in the Western sense—a "final" irony since the cyborg is also the awful apocalyptic telos of the

"West's" escalating dominations of abstract individuations, an
ultimate self united at last from all dependency, a man in space.
(p.150)

The CP, like the cyborg, has no origin story, not even a creation narrative as
in much conceptual art. That is, the program is not just the seed of the
poem, but, relying on statistics, has a gestation period equal to the speed
of processing, which is to say faster than can be assimilated into normal life
experience—we can never really "observe" these processes. They are the
operations of some god, or the pre-history to the history that the reader of
a CP is destined to write. The CP is also "resolutely committed to partiality,
irony, intimacy, and perversity" as it is a construction that offers alien elements to previously conceived wholes, such as the element of the "demon"
in the writing process, and the element of contingent meanings, of a non-
neutrality, into software that is best configured to shuffle bits of data with
pristine indifference. This not only moves art out of the sphere of the "ineffable"—which is where writers like sociologist Pierre Bourdieu (see footnote 24) think it never belonged—but the "Orient" of code itself, not to
mention the "mind." For a writer like Haraway who believes that identity
structures (such as gender) are projections from society, this severing of
origins is liberatory, leads to "real life," and places the human body in a position from which it can negotiate these societal projections, or even elude
them. She writes:

This is not just literary deconstruction, but liminal transforma-
tion. Every story that begins with original innocence and privi-
leges the return to wholeness imagines the drama of life to be
individuation, separation, the birth of the self, the tragedy of
autonomy, the fall into writing, alienation; that is, war, tempered
by imaginary respite in the bosom of the Other. These plots are
ruled by a reproductive politics—rebirth without flaw, perfection, abstraction. In this plot women are imagined either better or
worse off, but all agree they have less selfhood, weaker individuation, more fusion to the oral, to Mother, less at stake in mascu-

line autonomy. But there is another route to having less at stake in masculine autonomy, a route that does not pass through Woman, Primitive, Zero, the Mirror State and its imaginary. It passes through women and other present-tense, illegitimate cyborgs, not of Woman born, who refuse the ideological resources of victimization so as to have a real life. These cyborgs are the people who refuse to disappear on cue, no matter how many times a "Western" commentator remarks on the sad passing of another primitive, another organic group done in by "Western" technology, by writing. These real-life cyborgs (for example, the Southeast Asian village women workers in Japanese and US electronics firms described by Aihwa Ong) are actively rewriting the texts of their bodies and societies. Survival is the stakes in this play of readings. (p. 177)

This resonant passage places the role of the traditional lyric poet as the progenitor of "alienation," as the cultural figure who (metaphorically) has reproductive responsibilities to continue the processes of "rebirth without flaw, perfection, abstraction," hence to maintain the masculine dominance in which it "has no stakes." Despite theories of the "clinamen," the swerve away from, or "correction" of, a previous generation's writings, poets nonetheless remain limited to the frame of the human body, of the cycles of life and death, sleep and waking, that fit them as invisible, however agonistic, nodes in the reproduction of culture. The cult of linguistic transparency is exposed to be invested in the reification of the patriarchal order, as well as in the march of "technology" across the world which—in the humanist and pluralistic worldview that Haraway is critiquing—has reduced the "organic wholes" of other cultures to the objects of elegiac loss. She notes that this ignores the cyborgian adaptations that are occurring with increasing frequency, that the "real-life cyborgs" are thriving on the margins of the West. The cyborg offers another possibility, which elsewhere she terms the "illegitimate offspring," or the "monstrous," a cyborg being a "potent subjectivity synthesized from fusions of outsider identities

and in the complex political-historical layerings of her 'biomythography.'"
(p. 175) It is a play of codes that operate not to mourn the erasure of the
"primitive" but to grant the cyborg "real life," positioned oppositionally to
trouble the codes that stipulate that a woman must be an invisible, transparent cog in the clean reproduction of society and culture. In this sense,
the language of the CP can be seen as a "digital creole," a product not just
of the displaced, alienated individual but the fusion of several languages
pointing to an entire—virtual, geographically collapsed—region and populace that was forced to improvise communication with themselves in the
face of "lost origins." This would be a sort of "total system" (see footnote 10)
that puts the conventions of the hegemonic system in an ironic light. A
more Euro-centric, perhaps less sci-fi, version of this is Ian Hamilton Finlay's
use of the "estranging light" of classical culture, his mixing of ancient and
modern idioms being something of a creole itself (see footnote 6). In a different fashion, a certain cultural fission can occur in the teleactive spaces of
the internet, in which one poet could creolize a poem from the canon, like
Yeats' "Second Coming" (see footnote 13) and reintroduce the mutated
product to the field of literary exchange with the click of a mouse. Beyond
gender and race, the CP severs other ties with the body—such as the
hand—by putting a middle figure, the demon, between the "writer" and
the "text." It is this demon that, in the CP, is most responsible for the "monstrous" scale and complexity of the works, not to mention their opacity. "But
the soul must be made monstrous: in the fashion of the *comprachicos*, if
you will! Imagine a man implanting and cultivating warts on his face,"
wrote Rimbaud in his "Letter of the Seer," his prospectus for attaining new
knowledge and hence new methods of creation. Though the maker of CPs
is not engaged in spiritual adventures in the same fashion, certainly the
persona of Rimbaud—Europe's bastard, spiritual and geographic adven-
turer, eventual gunrunner—seems to resonate here as an industrial-era
precursor of the cyberpoet. (Rimbaud even had a statistical approach to
poetic production; in a letter to Paul Demeny, he once boasted "I would
also give you my *Lovers of Paris*, one hundred hexameters, sir, and my *Death
of Paris*, two hundred hexameters!" as if he were making projections on his
factory's output over the next quarter.) Maurice Blanchot's proposition in

children of Edward. Ask the chief monitor to
slap this Ike land, aphrodisiacs apropos of

190   fiestas, then Forks in the Eiffel, before androids

you hard, with their nailed prows parted the
Norsemen, a blood-reddened relic on the back
              —from time to time. "With that as a spur of

XI.

javelins over the jarring breaker, the deep-sea
195   billow, shaping their way toward, you can
              mobilize greater pissing strength[41] and energy

---

The Gaze of Orpheus, which proposes, echoing Rimbaud's "je est un autre",
that it is the "other hand" that does the writing—the hand which stops the
flow of meaning—provides another resonant schematic of human/func-
tional feedback, as if the hands were hard-coded to perform limited activities. The hand is transformed in the CP into a complex algorithm that does
more than simply place cuts in a chain of citations, but creates new order-
ings of meaning that organize themselves via metastasis (see footnote 3),
disrupting the linear operation of the "two hands" in tandem. I am literaliz-
ing, or "externalizing," Blanchot's statement here, of course, but it is worth
pointing out how the psychological, linguistic and poetic dimension that
Blanchot and others grant to the "writing" process is placed in a new light
by the introduction of the demon. In fact, I sense that thinkers of the
deconstructive/post-structural bent have been slow to take up the discourse on digital poetics because of their hesitance to accept this distanc-
ing from the hand—the banalization of the body—and the large role the
algorithmic element plays in constructing a CP. Perhaps they can only eval-
uate this third element as banal, even as it is the site of the disruption with
older paradigms of writing—the point of "crisis" in a paradigm-shift. They
may also have a fear of the "monstrous" excesses that the cyborg author

makes possible since it extends beyond the exchanges, excesses and expenditures of even the most liberal, or libidinal, cultural economy—beyond love, in a way, the "other" becoming that of the computer. Being a medium not reliant on the imprint—a CP, of course, may have (like the ad slogan says) "never been touched by human hands" and not involve paper—it is even outside of history, as nothing like an early version, an original draft, exists, just drafts of the software, distinguished by compilation date and version number.

40 sPeech mOve 'em jUst as oNe saiD
   'Em to Zenos metevsky bieRs to seel cAnnon
   Peace nOt while yew rUssia a New keyboarD
   likE siZe ov a pRince An' we sez wud yew like
   his Panties fer the cOmpany y hUrbana zeNos' Door
   with hEr champZ don't the felleRs At home
   uP-Other Upside dowN up to the beD-room
   John Cage, from "Writing through the Cantos"

41 Because the demon of a CP treats the matter of language on the level of its letters, punctuation and even white spaces with a total indifference to their "meaning" beyond their quantitative values as numbers, there is something inherent in a CP that bears relation to Sianne Ngai's formulation of a "poetics of disgust" in her essay "Raw Matter." Specifically, Ngai draws many distinctions between a "poetics of disgust" and a "poetics of desire" that positions the CP aesthetic in relation to human poetic production premised on "writing." Ngai's argument is that "pluralism" has become not only the signature quality of most poetics centered on "desires"—described by such paradigms as polysemia, dissemination, jouissance, and the libidinal economy—but that it plays into the logic of late capitalism, with its quest to include all forms of pleasure in its machinations. Loosely, this could be an analog to the idea of web-site "personalization" that seeks to incorporate traces of individuality into a system of common exchange, and hence to increase market saturation (see footnote 18). Ngai's sense is that a poetics of desire, despite its having been based on an oppositional,

materialist perspective, has at times seemed "as if it were spiritual," and further, has become a "mysticism instead of a materialism. The false profundity of jouissance: desire as 'transgressive.'" (101) A poetics of disgust, on the contrary, involves a turning away from the object, the exclusion of the object about which one has a "negative fascination"—the denial of its assimilation into "pleasure." Expressions of disgust themselves often involve linguistic waste such as expletives and onomatopoeia ('Ugh!'), or even congeries of symbols ($#&!@), but despite this thingness, this surrender to impotence, they convey an affect and have an "insistence." Disgust, in a sense, serves as a poetic when it acts to take the word, any word, outside of systems that will recuperate it—close reading, theory, any sort of "seductive reasoning" in Ngai's term—and will not permit the word or phrase to participate in a chain of signifiers or as paragrammic progenitor of the next syllable. It is, consequently, a poetics that acknowledges an "other," if only through negative space, which she associates with the "deictic" words—words such as "this" or "that" that point to other words—or even symbols that have a deictic function, like brackets (a common feature of programming languages) that always point to the words between them. She describes her sense of the poetic functioning of deictic words by looking at the poetry of Kevin Davies in his first book, *Pause Button*:

> Along with the more familiar forms of deixis (thisses, thats, and its) found in *Pause Button*, Davies' use of [ ] fulfills this function of giving form to formlessness, or of materializing 'outsideness.' Another example of such unusual deictic construction is Jeff Derksen's use of the maimed statistic in *Dwell*. Like @%$#!! and [ ], other negative utterances of expressions of outrage, the brute number ("France 8.9%") functions as semiotic raw matter, insisting on the disappearance of its referent while at the same time refusing to defer to other terms. It won't coagulate into a unitary meaning and it also won't move; it can't be displaced. This statistic only covers a space; the reader cannot fix it metaphorically, assign a concept to it, nor send it on a metonymic voyage along

a chain of other terms. There's no substantive meaning, yet there's also no possibility of polysemia: "France 8.9%" doesn't budge. It only sits there, in its material embodiment, in its stolidity. The reader can only act upon it by not acting on it, by turning away—just as the maimed statistic itself turns away from its implicit referent, excluding it. (pp. 113-114)

As with Veronica Forrest-Thomson's interest in incorporating the "non-meaningful" elements of a poem into an appreciation, though not "interpretation," of it (see footnote 3), Ngai points to those forms in a poem that cannot be pulled into a hermeneutic matrix, that will always remain a question mark when one attempts to describe what the poem "means." The poem is not seen as transparent language, through which one can look to recuperate a narrative or expression of subjectivity, nor is it seen as a field of linguistic play that illustrates some property of language's autonomous self-creation. Rather, it is full of holes, or pointers that go nowhere. What becomes clear, in several of Ngai's examples, is that one cannot construct an entire poem based on a "poetics of disgust." The entirety of *Dwell*, for example, is not composed of "maimed statistics" but is merely punctuated by them, the rest of the poem having discursive features that Derksen himself has flippantly described as "socialist one-liners" and which he relates to a "rearticulatory" practice in poetics, a shifting of associations among referents. It is impossible to break chains of signification in an art-work if these breaks are not appropriately framed. For example, a "found poem" like the numbers and texts on a grocery receipt (an admittedly extreme example) could be recuperated into a discourse on poetry by analyzing the creation narrative or cultural paradigm that brought the artist to come to decide that it was "art." One would recall the concept of the ready-made, for instance, or reference some versions of Concrete poetry that seek to expose how machinic technology has imposed itself on the idea of literary dissemination—the cash-register as desktop publisher. That is, the receipt, even unaltered, could become a "poem" provided the art-historical paradigm rose up around it—"seductive reasoning"—to incorporate it into discourse. Within this discourse, it might be seen as an expression of "disgust,"

than you have up, swollen to now" [Dyflen again,
shamed-in in gums]. As the "us" siphons begged
their souls, also, the brethren, King Deistic and

200   withering, lisping Easter Lieder. Like the Ingalls
and saxes, on the Isle and Atheling, each in his
glory, went to his own—*in* his own—West-

Saxonland, glad of the war; many a carcass
they left to be carrion, of Man-Over-Brad-Pitt
205   venues. Buying has sported a many lancing of

---

but it couldn't possess this property without the discursive frame. Algorithmic writing, like the CP—in which nearly all words could be considered place-fillers, even pattern-holders, and which is not bothered by issues of subjectivity—might offer the closest example to poems that could be, through and through, "raw matter." The proto-CP work of Kenneth Goldsmith, like the "nutritionless writing" of his book *Day*, for which he recopied manually the entire contents of one issue of *The New York Times* word by word, might be one example, the entire text being "deictic" and pointing away from itself and toward the normative use and publishing history of an original. (It also banalizes both the body and the demon by restricting their operations to the most banal form of media transference—copying words. This algorithm evokes the classic first computer program in Kernigan & Ritchie's seminal introduction to C, the entire program being limited to making the words "hello world" appear on the screen.) However, the corpus of Goldsmith's work has gained a certain consistency, and hence a "seductive reasoning" in the form of his singular, but mutable and hence reproducible, creation narrative: all of his projects involve bodily exertion, text accumulation, editing, publication (often in several forms) reconstituting, finally, this "waste" for cultural consumption. One might argue that it is not the CP itself, with its poetics of dissimulation that might actively project a hyperactive erotics (see footnote 18), but the demon that

Whig maps, walruses over-burdening the mall-
        rats that are a waiting, fearing the earth rotten:

> *Livid one, many a sallow-skin—*
> *Left for the white tailed eagle to tear it, and*
> 210 *Left for the horny-nibbed raven to rend it, and*
> *Gave to the garbaging war-hawk to gorge it, and*
> *That gray beast, the wolf of the weald.*

> *Never had huger*
> *Slaughter of heroes*
> 215 *Slain by the sword-edge—*
> *Such as old writers*
> *Have writ of in histories—*
> *Hapt in this isle, since*
> *Up from the East hither*
> 220 *Saxon and Angle from*
> *Over the broad billow*
> *Broke into Britain with*
> *Haughty war-workers who*
> *Harried the Welshman, when*
> 225 *Earls that were lured by the*
> *Hunger of glory gat*
> *Hold of the land.*[42]

[Zowwy!]

---

offers the clearest embodiment of Ngai's theory. What more represents a "turning away" from intentional acts of expression than the complete deferral of authority to an automaton, and channels the most innovative creative act from "writing" to "coding"? A demon is a void—it can be filled with anything, but contains nothing—and hence becomes a form of the deictic itself, like the empty brackets in Davies' poem. Indeed, not only is it not pointing to an object, it is pointing away from the author and from authors while presenting the traces of that activity unique to humans: thinking in language. Though a demon "acts," it has no stories to tell of what it has done, unlike the artist for whom "acting" is part of the cycle of sleeping and waking, life and death. The demon denies all of these cycles and replaces them with banal loops. It also has no "memories"—which might be characterized as information which calls attention to itself because it is in a constant state of decay and is never perfectly recallable (see footnote 37)—nor even data to call its own, since source files can be replaceable and it is indifferent to them anyway. Because it courts hermeneutic potentialities but surrenders no description, and because its structures, including its words and rhetorical figures, are the product of algorithms, the CP goes beyond "disgust" to actively pursue a self-perpetuating negative presence—a subjective affect with no subject. Thus, the CP is like the virus, neither living nor dead—it is also not a poem, and not a process, but nonetheless a linguistic presence that troubles the line between activity and inactivity, engagement and disinterest, true and false.

42 These are the last verses of Tennyson's translation of the "Battle of Brunaburh," the tail end of the first source file that escaped the machinations of the demon, hence surviving to "voice" its own particular social trajectory. I usually cut the tail off, or alter the demon so that the tail (or tale) is very brief. This would be to honor the demon—to escape "heresy" (see footnote 32)—or hide its shortcomings, since I usually insist the demon operate equally on all the source files at a steady rate, mixing and synthesizing all of the ingredients. In this case, I was pleased with the narrative closure the tail offered, and the final spin it placed on the prior contents. This exposed slab of a source file is mirrored, within the poem, by near-autonomous elements such as the Williams' parody, which was not itself a part of a source file but a later addition. Consequently, the tail is also illustrative of how phrases from the source texts can be permitted to voice their specific trajectories—to escape the status of pure "noise"—and thus

support the thematic element of a CP in a metastatic fashion (see footnote 3). These liberated phrases set in motion the dialogic nature of the CP, in which the texts synthesize to produce new wholes, and in which perspectives—historical, literary, subjective—are put into a "free fall" cycle of self-questioning or "feedback," a cycle which sets the poem amidst the discourses of the everyday while never, of course, overdetermining them. It is in this fashion that a CP—not unlike a "creep," a phenomenon described later in this book—achieves something of a satellite perspective on the contemporary social and discursive geography, but maintains a direct relationship to this geography by appropriating its elements into artistic form. It obtains a mock version of classic scholastic "objectivity" (see footnote 24) but chooses to operate underground, ambivalent but insistent about its power to channel cultural memory through its indifferent demon and enact "teleactive" processes on the cultural world—an "ethics" of virtuality.

Bibliography

Aarseth, Espen J. *Cybertext: Perspectives on Ergodic Literature.* Baltimore: Johns Hopkins University, 1997.

Abrioux, Yves. *Ian Hamilton Finlay: A Visual Primer.* Cambridge: MIT Press, 1992.

Adorno, Theodor. "On Lyric Poetry and Society." *Notes To Literature, Volume I.* New York: Columbia University Press, 1991.

Andrews, Bruce. *I Don't Have Any Paper So Shut Up (Or, Social Romanticism).* Los Angeles: Sun & Moon Press, 1992.

Andrews, Bruce. *Love Songs.* New York: Pod Books, 1982.

Andrews, Bruce. *The Millennium Project.* Princeton: Eclipse, 2002. www.princeton.edu/eclipse/projects/Millennium/.

Bakhtin, Mikhail. *Rabelais and His World.* Indiana: Indiana University Press, 1984.

Benjamin, Walter. *Illuminations.* New York: Schocken Books, 1985.

Bernstein, Charles. "Virtual Reality." *Dark City.* Los Angeles: Sun & Moon Press, 1994.

Bey, Hakim. *T.A.Z.: The Temporary Autonomous Zone, Ontological Anarchy, Poetic Terrorism.* New York: Autonomedia, 1991.

Bloom. Harold. *The Anxiety of Influence.* New York: Oxford University Press, 1973.

Bök, Christian. *Crystallography.* Toronto: Coach House Books, 1994.

Bök, Christian. *Eunoia.* Toronto: Coach House Books, 2001.

Bourdieu, Pierre. *Pascalian Meditations*. Stanford: Stanford University Press, 2000.

Bracken, Len. *Guy Debord: Revolutionary*. Los Angles: Feral House, 1997.

Brathwaite, Kamau. *The History of the Voice: The Development of Nation Language in Anglophone Caribbean Poetry*. London: New Beacon Books, 1984.

Cayley, John. "Of Programmatology." www.shadoof.net/in/prog/prog-set0.html.

Chomsky, Noam. *Noam Chomsky on The Generative Enterprise*. Holland: Foris Publications, 1982.

Davies, Kevin. *Pause Button*. Vancouver: Talonbooks, 1992.

Davis, Erik. "Techgnosis, Magic, Memory and the Angels of Information." *Flame Wars*. London: Duke University Press, 1994.

De Campos, Haroldo. "The Informational Temperature of a Text." *Precisely 13 14 15 16: The Poetics of the New Poetries* (1984).

Doris, Stacy. *Kildare*. New York: Roof Books, 1994.

Farrell, Dan. *The Inkblot Record*. Toronto: Coach House Books, 2001.

Forbes, Allen. "De Secon Coming." *Absinthe* (Vol. 9 No. 2, 1996).

Forrest-Thomson, Veronica. *Poetic Artifice*. New York: St. Martin's Press, 1978.

Goldsmith, Kenneth. *Fidget*. Toronto: Coach House Books, 2001.

Goldsmith, Kenneth. *No. 111 2.7.93—10.20.96*. Great Barrington: The Figures, 1997.

Goldsmith, Kenneth. *Soliloquy.* New York: Granary Books, 2001.

Haraway, Donna. *Simians, Cyborgs, and Women.* New York: Routledge, 1991.

Hartman, Charles O. *Virtual Muse.* New England: Wesleyan University Press, 1996.

Jameson, Frederic. "Postmodernism and Consumer Society." *The Anti-Aesthetic: Essays on Postmodern Culture.* Seattle: Bay Press, 1983.

Kapleau, Roshi Philip. *The Three Pillars of Zen.* New York: Anchor, 1989.

Kristeva, Julia. "Towards a Semiology of Paragrams." *The Tel Qel Reader.* London: Routledge, 1998.

Landow. George P. *Hypertext.* Baltimore: Johns Hopkins University Press, 1992.

Lechte, John. *Fifty Key Contemporary Thinkers: From Structuralism to Postmodernity.* New York: Routledge, 1994.

Lin, Tan. *Lotion Bullwhip Giraffe.* Los Angeles: Sun & Moon Books, 1996.

Manovich, Lev. *The Language of New Media.* Boston: MIT Press, 2001.

McCaffery, Steve. *The Theory of Sediment.* Vancouver: Talonbooks, 1991.

McCaffery, Steve. *North of Intention.* New York: Roof Books, 2000.

McCaffery, Steve. *Prior to Meaning: The Protosemantic and Poetics.* Evanston: Northwestern University Press, 2001.

Milne, Drew. "Adorno's Hut: Ian Hamilton Finlay's neoclassical rearmament programme." *Jacket* 15. www.jacketmagazine.com/jacket15/finlay-milne.html.

Mullen, Harryette. *Muse & Drudge.* Philadelphia: Singing Horse Press, 1995.

Ngai, Sianne. "Raw Matter: A Poetics of Disgust." *Open Letter: Disgust and Overdetermination* (Tenth Series, No. 1. Winter, 1998).

Nichol, bp and McCaffery, Steve. *Rational Geomancy: The Kids of the Book-Machine.* Vancouver: Talonbooks, 1992.

Penley, Constance. "Brownian Motion: Women, Tactics, and Technology." *Technoculture.* Minneapolis: University of Minnesota Press, 1991.

Prynne, J. H. "Red D Gypsum." Cambridge: Barque, 1998.

Rexroth, Kenneth. *Bird In Bush: Obvious Essays.* New York: New Directions, 1947.

Rimbaud, Arthur. *Complete Works, Selected Letters.* Chicago: University of Chicago Press, 1987.

Said, Edward. *Orientalism.* New York: Random House, 1979.

Schwartz, Leonard. "Introduction." *Primary Trouble: An Anthology of Contemporary American Poetry.* New Jersey: Talisman Books, 1996.

Sontag, Susan. *Styles of Radical Will.* New York: Doubleday, 1969.

Spivak, Gayatri Chakravorty. "The Politics of Translation." *Outside the Teaching Machine.* New York: Routledge, 1993.

Stefans, Brian Kim. *Free Space Comix.* New York: Roof Books, 1998.

Tarkos, Christophe. *Ma Langue Est Poetique—Selected Work.* New York: Roof Books, 2001.

Wardrip-Fruin, Noah et. al. *The Impermanence Agent.* www.impermanenceagent.com/.

Wershler-Henry, Darren. *the tapeworm foundry: andor the dangerous prevalence of imagination.* Toronto: House of Anansi Press, 2001 and New York: Ubu.com, 2002. www.ubu.com/ubu.

Wiener, Norbert. *The Human Use of Human Beings.* New York: Avon Books, 1950.

Wilkinson, John. "The Metastases of Poetry." *Parataxis* (No. 8/9, 1996).

Proverbs of Hell (Dos and Donts)

for Christophe Tarkos

Proverbs of Hell (Dos and Donts)

1. *In seed time learn, in harvest teach, in winter enjoy.* In off-hours at work, visit jodi.org for pro-situ distraction and turux.org for preter-semiotic action in game-world real-time. In hotels at conferences on digital poetics, avoid the theorist who would be five minutes past seed time and has reaped five critical harvests from the postmodern American novel. In the disquieting sempiternality of a north-north-eastern winter, enjoy nothing more than the liberation from the ill-effects of prolonged programming and the overripe prose of intelli-gentsia flame wars. Behave not as if the abs had the shelf-life of your Athlon. In seed time learn, in harvest teach, in winter enjoy.

2. *Drive your cart and your plow over the bones of the dead.* Drive your internet app through a cartload of high-res images drugged by the uncompressed plows of B-techno sound loops, and you might

chance upon the gold filling of a retired army general in your *pasta al dente*. Drive your viewer through too many randomized texts masquerading as aleatoric *dérive*, and you shall find a reader with a bad hair life. Drive not at all, but walk blissfully in the carnivalesque bubble malls of suburban psychogeography and mingle with the buxom banes and lustless lux-loves not screened since the time of *Neuromancer, Kora in Hell* and *Paris Spleen*. Drive your cart and your plow over the bones of the dead.

3. *The road of excess leads to the palace of wisdom.* The road of greater flexibility in method of random access and greater variability in the contract of approach leads to the simplicity of the modemless codex and the finger-panning of the papyrus scroll. The road of suggestive variability is the road to multimedial beauty; the road of arbitrary personalization is the road to unilateral disinterest and the hypertrophy of exchange. Provide the user what she seeks in curious synaesthetic doses and you shall taste the wine of unpassive attention — a little "fort da" never hurt anyone. Fake not the myth of access to palliate tunnel vision. The road of excess leads to the palace of wisdom.

4. *Prudence is a rich, ugly old maid courted by Incapacity.* But more users have visited Prudence's web page than Exhibitionist's, because Capacity has become the mantra of the Electroconomy Global Theme Park. It is the Artist who pulls abundance out of CPU Incapacity, and it is the Artist who will not be burned by Dot Com Meltdown. Prudence is a maid whose riches are high in concept, high in pragmatist protein, and low in unsaturated Fats of the LAN. Exhibitionist's saving grace is that she captures more .mp3's than anyone else, and once bandwidth goes the way of Ptolemy's shell,

she will be the coroner that stole the company wreath. Prudence is a rich, ugly old maid courted by Incapacity.

5. *He who desires but acts not breeds pestilence.* She who desires not but acts breeds with him. In a male-ruled programming culture, the hunk of the He damns the shank of the She, and the frank of the We chalks the funk of the Thee, and gender politics returns to square one. We who desire cyberbodies dissembling in cloaks of poly-gendered morphs and reassembling the highways of privilege into voodoo potlatches of counterfeit visions of interest — mean business. Avatars are unacted desires breeding the pestilence of drive-by identities, the essence of Self becoming the flavor of Month on a paratactically arranged grid of interacting IPs. He who desires but acts not breeds pestilence.

6. *The cut worm forgives the plow.* The cut phone line is not a blow, but trusts in the Manichean humanism of *c'est la vie*. The Life of Action and the Music of Changes are thwarted by ignorance of the varieties of fundamentalist CPUs and modem's derangement of *tout les sens*, but surrender not the vertigoes of concept and the fungoes of multimedia to an ignorance of Variable Means and the fuzzy theses of Medium Conviction. Embrace the machine's inconstancy as one more version of the violence of inscription on the skein of the page, and succor the weak of memory and the short of processor with "feature" not "bug" predilections. The firm course requires this vow. The cut worm forgives the plow.

7. *Dip him in the river who loves water.* Dip him in the particle acceleration of virtual subjectivities and phantasmagoric geographies who leaps or laughs for the depths of data, and you shall have a better informed viewer of the *Jim Lehrer News Hour*, if not a better

Rortian empath or Pynchonian philomath. Find the well of electronic water, and dip him in; this well is called scandal, and the chemical equation: those you know, squared. Web space must be Rabelaisian or it will not be at all. Bathe the lights of singular attitude in the solipsistic eddies of plural contradiction and you shall have a mouth wet with Wildean puns and Debordian *détournement*. Dip him in the river who loves water.

8. *A fool sees not the same tree that a wise man sees.* So make a new tree for the wise man, a new tree for the fool. The electronic object's art is expanded tenfold when the same object is variably utile to provide each user discrete, but not exclusive, experiences. Enter the car from the left side, and you are the driver; enter it from the right, and you are a passenger. The electronic object's art is expanded twentyfold when its contents' dreams are influenced by the user's moods, putting fool and wise man in the role of confessor, creator, test animal and personalized drug czar. Feedback is the howl that the fool calls foul and the wise man feed. A fool sees not the same tree that a wise man sees.

9. *He whose face gives no light, shall never become a star.* He whose light gives facts, but whose face no stare, shall never become a namebrand, but also shall not demand a name. Randomized text, unlike randomized sound, does not absorb, though scores the orb, for the ear sips while the eye winks, and the fingers twitch when the retina skips its lines. For he whose source would become a store, use what words have which neither sound nor image nor code have: reticular nuances that subsume their proscriptive sense. To lie is not to deceive; to tell the truth is not entirely reasonable when the truth is for sale, even if this truth be random. He whose face gives no light, shall never become a star.

10. *Eternity is in love with the productions of time.* But productions in time that emerge horizontally stand opposite the indifferent verticality of eternity, though eternity signs the checks and the productions cash them, neither entirely satisfied with this cycle of crisis and redescription but both too winded to resist. Eternity shines not nicely on the digital object, which produces no ruins and whose signature absence is a deictic presence. Contemporaneity shines joyously on the digital object, which shares in its bull market confidence and lemming-like capacity to trust in the blue horizon just beyond the last dot of calm. Eternity is in love with the productions of time.

11. *The busy bee has no time for sorrow.* The cyberpoet has no time for crying over concepts spilled from prior generations, though sorrows that Means were not always up to Minds and that digitization could not rescue Bob Brown's poem machine from the seams of time. The conceptual poet has no time for others, and the humanist poet no time for robots; the reptillian poet has time for concepts and humans, but cares more for tending fonts and rollovers. The cyberpoem that doesn't "stare back" the more it is stared at is not a good text, not a good app, and not very polite; the cyberpoem that stares back too sweetly devolves into the nirvana of neurobuddhist hype. The busy bee has no time for sorrow.

12. *The hours of folly are measured by the clock, but of wisdom no clock can measure.* With faster CPU processing, folly has a field day at increasing rates of speed, while wisdom remains a panoramic hologram on the flight decks of the vistaless future. Algorithmic procedures do not liberate one from the variable strictures of singular prose, and one shall not be "Joycean" through Perl scripts that factor Derridean

BETTY WHITE'S MANDARIN SALAD

Caramelized almonds crunch up this healthy...

From the book COOKING WITH THE STARS by Rick Ameil – 1999 by Rick Ameil. Published by Barron's Educational Series, Inc~, Haupp~uge . NY 11788-:3917.

uu,u   ~m ui   l5~fCl~

Preparation tImrn about 20 mu MakeSwvlngu.

3~ head red ~d tttuoe,   2 ceiwy*alks,
torn in pieces   sNoad
~ head Romaine   2gren~te
Bettuos torn In p~Oces
1 head butter~ lettuce,   I *(15-az.)* ceo nw~darIn
torn hi pagoss   ora.wme, dr*~d

JUST bgtore ,.v'vIng combIn *g'me*. o.1m*, gr.n onion. o.'ang. segments, almonds and dtwiing. Ibgs to mix.

~ tsp. salt   -   ~ CUP V@gtbl **Oil**
~ tsp. popper   dash at hOt~~saU~
2.tbspa. sUgar   I tbl2. choppd
2 t~sps. vinegar   pa#'sl.y

@SUUUE all IngredInts In Jars r.frIgsrate until

reedy to us..

smm*~mmm (this ~an b don, ahead)
34 cup sliced almonds 4 taps. sugar

000k almonds and sijgw ~i t~i heat, s*rIng oonstantly, until eu~ Is nwltd and Olmonds ai~ oo.tmd. Scs'ap. out onto waxed paper and caol. Break apart and stor. at room tempoPeture.

Nutrition ~t' .m'vtrɪp Calarlee, 198; Pat, 10.8 gems

punscapes and Perecois anagrams with the flick of a switch and the indifference of code. Wisdom sleeps in the aporias of folly; folly dances in the "black gold" of wisdom's over-sized *lederhosen*. The hours of folly are measured by the clock, but of wisdom no clock can measure.

13. *All wholesome food is caught without a net or a trap.* To overload a web poem with tricks puts tears in the reticular tarps that are the cyberpoet's Walmarts and Bennihanas, and scares the wholesome into memory's entropic sandboxes to mourn the safe havens and sedate mirrors of an ontologically secure youth. The wholesome of site are not inclined to engage digital fluids, just as the wholesome of sight are unaware of the chiaroscuros and arpeggios of crumpled Fluxus bags. Satisfy those who fear the immaterial, and you have satisfied many; satisfy the digirati, and you are a suitor snoozing beside the streams of Herecleitian lusts. All wholesome food is caught without a net or a trap.

14. *Bring out number, weight and measure in a year of dearth.* Bring out more numbers, some clam-baked action scripts, some aborted lyric doggerel, old Adobe Horrorshop files and scanned pages from Pound's *Cantos* in a year of not having many good ideas for poems. Modular web works can shine with the thousand points of light that their centrifugal, contradictory inspirations shed on the fabled ineffability of the art-object's ontology. Fear not the updating of a Flash file for the fertile episteme of a brave new context, as meaning is extrinsic to the bit as it is to the 17th semicolon in the first sentence of James' *The Ambassadors*. Bring out number, weight and measure in a year of dearth.

15. *No bird soars too high, if he soars with his own wings.* But a cyberbird can soar even higher after mastering the aviary of collaboration. The Auteur in the cyberrealm is the White Magician of the pixelated Middle Earth, yet no Auteur thrives without drinking deep in the River of Borrowed Texts, Borrowed Scripts, and Borrowed Sounds. Even Godard had a cameraman, and Welles never wrote an original screenplay. The role of the bureaucrat and producer becomes the glory of the poet and director when the coordination is of artists and the conversation of production, all on the same platform and each following the same hypnogogic thread. No bird soars too high, if he soars with his own wings.

16. *A dead body revenges not injuries.* A cyberpoem whose scripts are error-prone, whose ani-gifs break, and whose sound files crackle with the whimsy of renegade bits, may thrive like the *Spiral Jetty* in the memories of its first historians, but will be deemed unfit for the canons of *Les Damoiselles D'Avignon*. Fault not the cyberpoet who has made one small contribution even if his reputation be bunk, for the capital that seems corrupt today is the capital that was not here yesterday. A dying cyberpoem tells no lies, yet utters nothing but easy truths. A living cyberpoem tells many lies, but its truths are in technicolor, encrusted with entropic salts. A dead body revenges not injuries.

17. *The most sublime act is to set another before you.* The most sublime cyberpoem is a digital object with the plasticity of a solid (Rubik's Cube) or a literary object with the complexity of a database (Ryman's *253*). A digital object should be an ordered arrangement of angles and plains (Vorticism), or a disordered arrangement threatening order (Calder's mobiles), or a disordered arrangement

threatening disorder (Tinguely's *Homage*), or two or three of the above. What is set before is also set within in the absorptive scans of the seductive screen, thus putting the v-effekt that much further from touch or placing it too close to teach. The most sublime act is to set another before you.

18. *If the fool would persist in his folly he would become wise.* If every poet who faltered at the doors of script persisted at least to the finger foods table, a culture could bloom of the Wonders of Attempt, despite the wilt of the Poverty of Completion. Those who cease, sated with unease, or fail to progress, distressed of will, shall outnumber the wise threefold, though the number of fools not increase. Theme music played at a digital literature awards ceremony cloaks not the fool in cultural capital nor demeans the wise for whom capital is a cultural tool, though both the wise and the fool should be spared the folly of attending. If the fool would persist in his folly he would become wise.

19. *Folly is the cloak of Knavery.* But Folly and the Knave click in a synaesthetic embrace free of the Sorry of cultural dictatorship and the Volly of proscriptive dogma in a world where nation is a code word for corporation and citizen a code word for slave. The digital art project that would be a nation is a notion of the ineffable past, as the digital art project dissembling a citizen sans passport and action sans anthem is a premonition of the porous future, not to mention symptom of the schizophrenic Long Now. Knavery is the glory of she who would choose wisely among the fools, as Wisdom is the embarrassment of she who would choose blindly among the followers. Folly is the cloak of Knavery.

20. *Shame is Pride's cloke.* Cloak not thy shame in bauds of circuit cho-
lesterol lest the projects of those ten years younger stumble in the
frailty of your OOP code and limp in the blushes of your crushing
guassian blurs. Cake not thy shout in sentences of eternal shit lest
your department research your bibliography and discover Shim's
immortal words among Shem's expendable ibids. Plagiarism is
sweet, and the more the merrier, but the cite is minor when the goal
is literature, and digital culture, which claims to be the minority,
has no patience for authority when there's no there there and subjectivity has been mired as mirroring some ivied Joe's dystopic joke.
Shame is Pride's cloke.

21. *Prisons are built with stones of law, brothels with bricks of religion.* The
Rabelaisian cyberpoem is built with the fibre-optics of the culture's
sinews still flush and singing with public communication; the
Nouveau-Romanish cyberpoem is built with skull cavities basking
in the sublimities of absent witness, but are still fun to argue with if
only for their existential accents. Neither law nor religion, the non-
prisonhouse of the web is built with the bricks of radical democracy, paved with the stones of everybody's yellow brick road, and wall-
papered with screenshots from anime videos and midnight CNN.
Prisons are built with stones of law, brothels with bricks of religion.

22. *The pride of the peacock is the glory of God.* The multi-pinnate painter-
ly splash of the Director file utilizing the "trails" feature is the serial meter killer of Macromedia, making stanzas that lope along on
variable hips, knees and feet through a phantasmagoric, post-figur-
al Rutherford. Features designed for devious purposes such as
advertising and sentimental enslavement can be détourned for the
vicarious thrill of "I" definition and the Victorian onus of libidinal

largess. The pride of the programmer defeats the prudery of the artist who would not put forth that not touched by human hands nor baptized by the ashes of experience. The pride of the peacock is the glory of God.

23. *The lust of the goat is the bounty of God.* The anticipation that the artistic acolyte feels before engaging the narcissism of the cultural industry is the warmth in the cockles of the heart of the graduate-level professor banking on a minor celebrity. Spend time and money freely while your interest engages the mind/body dualism to futz with the line; earn time and money wisely when your artistic/financial security has reached its capitally inflated, culturally assimilated and saturated twin peaks. No man should be so proud that he cannot play Mozart (Pound); no man should be so modest that he would not sing before learning to curse (Rotten). The lust of the goat is the bounty of God.

24. *The wrath of the lion is the wisdom of God.* The rest of the lion is pretty good, too. A cyberpoet need not be a moralist and have a system, and need not be anti-authoritarian and anti-system, when multiple subjectivities are possible in one electronic object, none of them original and none of them strictly not you. The negative capability of the net object is in dialogue with the positive susceptibility of the user; no conversation is deemed below those who are above nothing and sit in a human-shaped cube. Your object shall not be art if the objective is to be artisinal and to show off your cartesian *Torso of Apollo* like a relic from the Ping Dynasty. The wrath of the lion is the wisdom of God.

25. *The nakedness of woman is the work of God.* There are lots of naked women on the internet. But as the philanthropy of the virtual space

has no room for the philosophy of the patriarchal bedroom, the nakedness of woman is but the narcissism of condensed bitmaps, and nobody goes or leaves home satisfied. The cyberpoem that does not satisfy the need for taboo vision can stay home and videotape the grass growing, but the cyberpoem that is a pornography of the possible grants no solace to the Existentialist, no strategy for the Situationist. The naked attitudes of women about the nude solitaires of men are the flora amidst which the text klepto stomps. The nakedness of woman is the work of God.

24 *Excess of sorrow laughs. Excess of joy weeps.* Excess of digital vision, combining the penetration of the camera and the precision of Industrial Light and Prosumer Magic, is bound to cross over into actions about which Mom and Dad will be called to the school principal, and for which the Black Bloc will be principally scolded. The good cyberpoem is like a nutritional toxin, letting them have their cake and hate it too. The bad cyberpoem is like a sugar substitute: all of the capital, some of the taste, and none of the byte. Exhaustiveness of method is necessary when Oulipian tasks occur at CPU speed and mutable .exe's can be outsourced cheaply. Excess of sorrow laughs. Excess of joy weeps.

27. *The roaring of lions, the howling of wolves, the raging of the stormy sea, and the destructive sword are portions of eternity too great for the eye of man.* If the Great Eye of man finds no fireworks in your RealAudio dynamite, and the Great Ear of man no trills in your Photoshop quartet, then your synaesthesia is lacking in science, and your extreme sport flagging in scream. Multimedial is to web art as continental is to philosophy — the terms and taxmen are terminal at the borders of nation, and temperamental at the mention of broadband. The roaring of lions, the howling of wolves, the raging of the

stormy sea, and the destructive sword are portions of eternity too great for the eye of man.

28. *The fox condemns the trap, not himself.* The affable curmudgeon condemns the technology (Word), and not his fundamentalist attitudes toward the ineffable (word). The humanist ideologue condemns the indifferent software because it has never made a blanket imperfect as an Iroquois quilt; the ambitious sculptor condemns the aloof machine because Apple has outpaced her own beleaguered sense of the innovation of Epstein's *Rock Drill*. Condemn not Flash because it is "slick" and easier to use than a paint stick; there is nothing primitive and back-to-earth about a Pentium IV chip, and finger-prints on the keyboard are not Renaissance script. The fox condemns the trap, not himself.

29. *Joys impregnate. Sorrows bring forth.* Digital editing and manic depression do a cuisenart of both, as well as deleting, copying, noise-filtering, morphing and gaussian-blurring the emotional par-adigm beyond realism or cultural recuperation. Give Marker digital editing, and you would still have *The Last Bolshevik*; give Spielberg a Bolex, and you might get a better trailer for *Pi*. That which is tran-substantiated by a flick of the switch is that which can transform millions by a switch of the flick, as the genome and its discontents are measurable by virtual methods, masterable by technology, and marketable by the pharmaceutical giant. Joys impregnate. Sorrows bring forth.

30. *Let man wear the fell of the lion, woman the fleece of the sheep.* And let the alpha male fall over the polyester lion while trying to fleece the cloned sheep of 98% cotton. The polyandry of the web can subvert the homology of society and language with a generous sampling of

polymemes applied aptly, like the soundtoy called "modifyme" that is neither instrument, jukebox, videogame, animation or Shaker furniture, but an *unheimlisch* combination of each. Delve deep into the tumults of web subjectivity, acquiring like a magnet the metal shavings of meaning as they proliferate in a polonaise of libidinal civil disobedience. Let man wear the fell of the lion, woman the fleece of the sheep.

31. *The bird a nest, the spider a web, man friendship.* The web spider, unlike the friendship man and the nest bird, interacts algorithmically with the sediment of communication and architecturally transforms this material into customized nests for inconstant guests or transient monuments to enduring friendship. The nest bird depends on the web for friendship; the friendship man on the web for his nests; the web spider arbitrates, tirelessly and timelessly, by reassembling the codes of the keyed and telling the recombined to insure history march in visible increments of legible light, and not in elvin choruses of entropic flight. The bird a nest, the spider a web, man friendship.

32. *The selfish smiling fool and the sullen frowning fool shall be both thought wise, that they may be a rod.* Neither make good *Survivor* contenders, yet the smiling fool and the frowning fool are icons of TV's echoeless flatscreen, ready for the point-and-shoot. Flash artists destined only for the monoculture are not spared the rod, yet need not despair of a job, as the knavery of the crook is the wisdom of the perruquer, and the feed of monied subculture affords anarchist dissent. A ream of paper is worth more than a thousand words; a screen of *Empire* can be printed out thousands of times. The selfish smiling fool and the sullen frowning fool shall be both thought wise, that they may be a rod.

33. *What is now proved was once only imagined.* What was once theorized and now proved with digital technology has not been proved but imagined proved, as Chow Young Fat's leg kicks have never been performed but imagined improved. The parody of text is in the pudding, where Charles Bernstein's mind kneads excessive punning. The good cyberpoem is like a bad mailman; the magazine never arrives if the subscription has been paid for, but letters from distant sailors and stewardesses meant for next door are always right on time. A cyberpoem should never prove one theory but several, such as those of love, hate, boredom, disgust, work and relaxation. What is now proved was once only imagined.

34. *The rat, the mouse, the fox, the rabbit watch the roots; the lion, the tyger, the horse, the elephant watch the fruits.* The cyberpoet is mouse, fox, rabbit, rooting among the software's scripts, for whom programming is play and the "elegant" solution: death. The user is lion, tyger, horse, watching the software's loops, for whom play is higher levels of play, and success a greater cache of lives. The cyberpoet starts by trying to make the perfect soy meat substitute, and ends by making the perfect meat. The user wants to meet someone perfect, but gets virtually duped. The rat, the mouse, the fox, the rabbit watch the roots; the lion, the tyger, the horse, the elephant watch the fruits.

35. *The cistern contains: the fountain overflows.* The book is beautiful to the degree that it deceive one with the promise of the totality of its system, the encyclopedic being a virtue in a paper world dominated by fragments and anthems (*Ulysses*). The cyberpoem is beautiful to the degree that it convince one of the contingency of its system, the limned and emphatic being virtues in a digital world dominat-

kazoo

ed by dubious cures for deadly cancers and calls for donations to non-existent African nations (ubu.com). Poems in books are stains and ask to be cleared of ink; poems on screen beg for captures to mask the impermanence of its tabula rasa. The cistern contains: the fountain overflows.

36. *One thought fills immensity.* One thoughtful cyberpoem, simple as a bobsled and eloquent as Bob Dope, can be linked from a thousand sites and fill immense portals, not to mention doctoral theses in all the free countries of the globe and magazine articles in languages spoken and unknown. One poorly conceived cyberpoem, like a poor thought, can destroy a rich reputation of radical programming, not to mention create intense waves of disapproval from the post-traditionalists still fingering their oversized copies of *The Maximus Poems* and *"A"* and piously parroting albums of The Four Horsemen. Thought is motion; words in action atomize fluid notions. One thought fills immensity.

37. *Always be ready to speak your mind, and a base man will avoid you.* Always be ready to write meat-and-potatoes English, and the purveyors of cultural capital will accuse you of anti-artism and bad panel manners. Critical art relies on the inherent satire of social pragmatism, such that the burp and fart conspire to out shout the abstract and obscure with the pinch of context, but everyone survives with indifference defeated and confidence renewed. Non-critical art passing as critical art will no more transcend power structures or survive in the rollerball of public opinion than the bird who sings dolphin win the fish. Always be ready to speak your mind, and a base man will avoid you.

38. *Every thing possible to be believed is an image of truth.* Everything that is possibly an image is also possibly the truth, if only for this lo-res era of the Morning of Mechanism. Web imagery turns syntactic when it approaches the status of emblem, a sovereign monad in flirtatious repartee with the conventions of "unpacked" language. Eye candy obviates linguistic meaning and converts the associative into social control, pleasure into penitentiary. A good if indeterminate icon is worth more than a word; a bad, overdetermined icon is worth less than a photograph of a mirror, unless this mirror be the non-site of simple being. Every thing possible to be believed is an image of truth.

39. *The eagle never lost so much time as when he submitted to learn of the crow.* The scripter never gained so much time as when she submitted to learn of code, which transforms the scavenging crow bent by collage into the avenging eagle afloat in synthetic currents. The heroics of the lyric and the banality of text dumps lose their difference in a realm of virtual valuation, in which search and rescue means robotize and reveal. A cyberpoem need not start with text, but with the pleasure of writing text, and not with programming, which is the pleasure of death, but with the pleasure of speech, which is the measure of life. The eagle never lost so much time as when he submitted to learn of the crow.

40. *The fox provides for himself, but God provides for the lion.* But it is the lion who is brought before the international tribunal, and it is the fox who revels in unbound singularity. Rates of Darwinian survival increase to the degree that the moral code is shaped by contingent, negotiated custom; rates of Machiavellian survival decrease to the degree a pre-established moral code motivates personal narratives of

casuistry

impersonal unction. Digital art is no sword, digital words are no fortress, though the lyrical swerves of digital laws may be that which informs, protects, and extends the carnivalesque beyond all arid limits. The fox provides for himself, but God provides for the lion.

41. *Think in the morning. Act in the noon. Eat in the evening. Sleep in the night.* The virtual body is always idle; the living body is always at play. There is more data in the liquids of a stationary amoeba than there is in a jogging G4, Horatio, and there is more anxiety in sleeping than there is freedom in the circuits of automatic writing, André B. Program your text generator to write like a thinker, and redundancy is inevitable after a few dry runs; lobotomize your code to think redundantly, and enough plausible noise may trouble the dispensable output to sound like thought. Write with silence; code for bargains. Think in the morning. Act in the noon. Eat in the evening. Sleep in the night.

42. *He who has suffered you to impose on him, knows you.* She whose interface makes the user suffer either knows the value of recalcitrance in personal seduction or does not know the use of her Dreamweaver's browser-check function. He who would agree to consensual, not contractual, exchange with your application has proceeded to distrust the interface but exacerbated the truth that predicting a website's behavior is tantamount to a Quixotic effort. To exceed the contract, such that a touch becomes sensual, supercedes the machinery, for which touch is not possible, as perfect internal translation is a parody of human synaesthesia. He who has suffered you to impose on him, knows you.

43. *As the plough follows words, so God rewards prayers.* As words are furrows that disturb fixed opinion, prayers are programs that elide with

gesamtkunstlich splendor. The path of the hero (myth) and the pith of the pragmatist (method) meet in these moments of tumult, where the gab of myth and the math of God argue out the specifics of the individual's contract with clean thinking, straight teeth and egalitarian architectures. God works not in mysterious ways but in interesting ways, as Duchamp might say, the cathedral cursing the Capital without ever setting foundations in stone, nor flocks on spikes of tele-surveillanced air. As the plough follows words, so God rewards prayers.

44. *The tygers of wrath are wiser than the horses of instruction.* In the centrifugal rotaries of the dissembling internet, do not waste your tygers on the centripetal axes of moral edification, coaxing flatscreen plateaus out of hyper-cubic dimensions. Instruct your horses by collapsing strictures into the vortices of the true and false, the fictional and functional, the partisan and über-liberal, intermingling in counter-socializing dances of libidinous endeavor. All that can be gained proceeds through expenditure; all that can be verboten progresses through pedagogical contrast and heterological critique. The tygers of wrath are wiser than the horses of instruction.

45. *Expect poison from the standing water.* Expect crashing javascripts, excessive use of Kai's PowerTools, and flytrap wallpapers from the web page that has not been updated since 1996. Expect entropically "buckled" meanings from stagnant poems that stand against the waves of horizontal cultural growth and vertical cultural divorce and which fail to deceive as much as they receive. Armor the poem with lyrical form and subjective fuss, but teach it the art of loss and the angle of found text, lest it succumb to the unilateral exchanges of a field that promises equality and crowns elites, and hypnotizes

cosmopolitan

witnesses with its probing, viral touch. Expect poison from the standing water.

46. *You never know what is enough unless you know what is more than enough.* But what is more than enough is often not enough, and subtracting from the expectations of "multimedia" may be the right direction for the worm cut by the plow, the artist cut off by dot com meltdown. Leave your ego at the door: what is ahead for the user is what is lost in your absence, and the splendors of the minimal and black are more difficult and bright than the splashes of the latest 3D effects. Leap headfirst into the *Director 8 Cookbook* until you have achieved enough boredom to return you to the rocks and stones of Rimbaud's continental repasts. You never know what is enough unless you know what is more than enough.

47. *Listen to the fool's reproach: it is a kingly title.* When the fool approaches with the shield of reactionary verbiage, retreat into the anonymity of coded détournement with Perl scripts and cerebral alphabetizations, turning regular speech into revelatory scatology. When the telemarketer floods your bandwidth with the kindly goods of laborless products, use voodoo algorithms to make hetero-logic stocks of overdetermined Staples. When the bully pulpit has got you down and the academic poet accuses you of ill-digested the-ory, speed off in your mental Durango 95 and flood the stereo with Ween's meta-satiric "Spirit of '76." Listen to the fool's reproach: it is a kingly title.

48. *The eyes of fire, the nostrils of air, the mouth of water, the beard of earth.* The interface of light, the action of light, the words of light, the images of light. The webwork, unlike the earthwork, can never be photographed from a satellite perspective, or grow crystalline ruins

from its entropic demise. A webwork of genius is an interface that ages gracelessly and resurfaces like a phoenix in decades of low blood sugar due to excess of Flash candy. A webwork of flashy mediocrity ages gracefully until disappearing in the sluices of time due to corporate downsizing, hardware triage, and geeks who don't care. The eyes of fire, the nostrils of air, the mouth of water, the beard of earth.

49. *The weak in courage is strong in cunning.* But the wrecked in courage and the worsted in cunning should not believe the web avatar provides bonus points and extra lives or magic weapons and antipotions in place of these traditional deficiencies. Do not abuse the powers that anonymity grants you, lest this anonymity become permanent and all of your Ashbery imitations become the standard and poor indices of your virtual capital. A week of cunning can provide the whack of courage, but the rest of courage remains buried in the hard drive, zip disk and cd-rom, somewhere between the limned cunnilingus and linguistic cutlery of incredible poetry. The weak in courage is strong in cunning.

50. *The apple tree never asks the beech how he shall grow, nor the lion the horse, how he shall take his prey.* The interface never asks the user how it should seduce, yet the contract between them, founded on pragmatism and the many routines of urban street flirtation and rural hootenanny ritual, creates a cultural dynamism not seen since the days of the million man march to Canterbury or of McLuhan's global village before it was dubbed MacWorld. The program, in love, seduces, which suggests hate, but its method is a theme song to a cyber-synthesis, the Yin and Yang of robotic interaction. The apple tree never asks the beech how he shall grow, nor the lion the horse, how he shall take his prey.

51. *The thankful receiver bears a plentiful harvest.* In the looped activity of literary gameplay, nothing is screened that was not pulled through code, creating narrative arches from databased thematics, and humanist responses from tables of statistics. The cycle of the loop is not the cycle of the seasons: the intelligence of interaction is a flux of changes, not the sinkhole of consumed reference. The harvest is in the playing; the feast is in the subversion of telos, the satisfaction of being "antennae" of an emergent generation. Plant your warts wisely lest you never be a seer (poet) and merely beam with the besieged (*Star Trek*). The thankful receiver bears a plentiful harvest.

52. *If others had not been foolish, we should be so.* If others had not ambitiously embarked on the most naive mating of the "visual" and "poetic," we should not have had the richness of ubu.com and the revisiting of pro-situ Concretist and Lettrist aesthetics. There is a pre-history to digital poetics from a time before lightbulbs, but there is no history to the post-digital while there are presently lightbulbs, as those who ignored the pre-digital had been fools in developing the language by which digital theory fuels us now, though this language is no louder than the background hum of John Cage's heartbeat in a concert of LaMonte Young's. If others had not been foolish, we should be so.

53. *The soul of sweet delight can never be defiled.* But the soul pleasures of a well-tempered concept can be thwarted by a distemper of Fauvist delight in machinic possibilities. Do not craze the best software of the generation with the digital analog of "man pounds rice;" leave the rice at the door, and your ego in the cold. Sweet progress is debunked by solutions using scripts borrowed unscrupulously and filtering plug-ins that do not signally improve a sought original.

Learn from Las Vegas and construct your decorated shed in the style of Swiftian dilemmas resolved by radical will and the impersonal debauches that rise from ludic play. The soul of sweet delight can never be defiled.

54. *When thou seest an eagle, thou seest a portion of genius: lift up thy head!* If the eagle is in 3D and descends with the fury of Tennyson's lyric, thou seest an even greater portion, though this genius be bathetic and its position counterlogic. Knowledge comes not by indifferent flipping through overpriced Sams books, but by the intense hacking of an eagle's secure nest in which algorithms burn to roost. Lift up thy head when demystification calls for opulent exchanges with better programmers; screw with the scripts that amazed you, and chatter in the artificial paradigms of the internet's open-source Babel. When thou seest an eagle, thou seest a portion of genius: lift up thy head!

55. *As the caterpillar chooses the fairest leaves to lay her eggs on, so the priest lays his curse on the fairest joys.* As corporations corral the best URLs, lay your gaze on the gene pool of postmodern neologism and Markov chains, and recode the links of power with names that prove addictive and are soon culling millions. As the government halts the flow of information on account of "national security" and with a manic bias against anything that's free, revel in its blind clarity with the rhizomic vectors of "All Your Base Are Belong to Us" and the clones of Napster's Robin Hood. As the caterpillar chooses the fairest leaves to lay her eggs on, so the priest lays his curse on the fairest joys.

56. *To create a little flower is the labor of ages.* To create a script that adds to the text is the labor of the carpenter, physicist and confessor, and

not any of them alone. Prepare yourself for hours searching manuals for solutions to problems seeming trivial, but no more than encoding the first comma. The flower eludes those impatient with the uncanniness of machinic acts, in which the hand is an extension of the mouse and the eye a backseat general in a cyborg army. Pollock-like splashes of nirvana do not come naturally, nor the erotic charge of desert petals in bloom, as neither are found by sight or mouse, but a synaesthetic combine of both. To create a little flower is the labor of ages.

57. *Damn braces. Bless relaxes.* The Damn of the internet and the Bless of culture will motivate higher goals and more satisfactory solutions, if only as the lingering halitosis of the initial, hilarious enthusiasts. The bless of poly-structured, encyclopedic, rawly sensual and subversive works will breach new levels for art that no curmudgeon's pen can damage, no Bunker's protests can deflate. The *Sturm und Drang* of a cyberpoem is manifest in the plugs and plays of improvised convention countering menu-driven exuberance, of Bauhaus structures standing fitly against the fleshly spit hooks of the robot therapy of revealed code and revvable desires. Damn braces. Bless relaxes.

58. *The best wine is the oldest. The best water the newest.* What is neither water nor wine and has no stable properties is art, and that which is not art but works in the wake of the farce of fact and the fixture of fiction may be poetry, and is almost certainly digital. Today's kitsch is tomorrow's knowledge and today's capital yesterday's collapsed insurrection. Future graduate students may determine that screensavers are the cultural products that best reveal the passive mindset of the ambient nineties, just as the eighties' rock music taste of a

boastful suburban teen best illustrates the phenomenon of the populist Republican. The best wine is the oldest. The best water the newest.

59. *Prayers plough not. Praises reap not.* Inflation of critical accolades provides not more than Pyrrhic victories in the Sisyphean battle to create love for a new art, but scholarly irony and scathing indifference deter not the digital pilgrim on her path of converting new cyber-Janes and G4 Joes. While moderate applause for modest achievements is mostly advisable, a cacophony of celebration at the crisis of changing paradigms is necessary, though by definition impossible. What is prayed for by scholars becomes the unwitting manna of the simulacrum, but is also more provident than the physical *Ding-an-sich*: a virtual Revealed Knowledge. Prayers plough not. Praises reap not.

60. *Joys laugh not. Sorrows weep not.* The digital realm is no more post-humanist than the library at Alexandria or the dugouts at Yankee Stadium, and no less post-humanist. The binaries of Joy and Sorrow, of Life and Death, of Love and Hate, are rendered more tangible by the plug-in filters of Depression, Anxiety, Remorse, Envy, Obsession, Pride, Ambition, Jealousy, Trust, Distrust, Skepticism, Alienation, and Agnosticism, along with the rest of Kai's Power Moods. Flail not among the collapsing poles with which readings of *A Thousand Plateaus* have fixed you, yet let not the codes of a "natural" art enforce naive rules as the price of "true" realism. Joys laugh not. Sorrows weep not.

61. *The head Sublime, the heart Pathos, the genitals Beauty, the hands and feet Proportion.* The interface Unsympathetic, the coding Banal, the computer Beige, the mouse and screen Too Small. The physical and

ethical complexity of the body is mirrored by the physical and ethical simplicity of the computer. The cyberpoem is the form in which the metal obsolescence of the Asimov Robot and the fleshy immortality of Blake's Babe become a new symbol: the woken User. The reading/wanking parts of the body are the writing/waking parts of language when they recursively sound with other semiotic objects. The head Sublime, the heart Pathos, the genitals Beauty, the hands and feet Proportion.

62. *As the air to a bird or the sea to a fish, so is contempt to the contemptible.* As scolding critique is to the scholar on fire, so is blank dismissal to the artist of hot air. The Language Poet who says cyberpoetry was founded in the waste basket of Rob Grenier, as it may have been, and the cyberpoet who says Language Poetry is the wonderbread mirror of Russian Formalism, as has been said, is failing to call a spade inspired, a heart and club true, a lozenge square. She swayed by canons knows not the fluidity of emergent phenomena and misses the drunken boat; he who commandeers the boat is but making the co-op kitchens sink. As the air to a bird or the sea to a fish, so is contempt to the contemptible.

63. *The crow wished everything was black; the owl, that everything was white.* Poets wished writing were in one immortal black font, deleting the work of the hand and eliding the death of the moment, thus linking her directly to the eloquent company of Norton's Wired Immortals. Cyberpoets wished that writing never became ink at all, leaving it free to adopt each new technology as it pushed out the old, taking on qualities of color, resolution, typeface and size as then seems fit. The Korean wishes the web was all in Korean; the Muslim in Arabic; the Senegalese in French; the Debunker in Anti-

AFTER I TOOK MY ... BLINDFOLD OFF!

205

Corporatist Diversion. The crow wished everything was black; the owl, that everything was white.

64. *Exuberance is Beauty*. But so is a narrow waist. In reaching for the aesthetic heights of Las Vegas's "decorated sheds" and the burlesqued morality of *Monty Python's Flying Circus*, do not waste bandwidth on gaussian 3D shadow texts and sound files MIDI-ing Beethoven's hits. Twenty good hours with Samaras and Gordon Mumma are twenty thousand more satisfied users, though with meager taste space and silence can yet seduce. A well-tempered interface, like a well-tempered waist, achieves secular miracles of content management, the beauty of asceticism and athletics of bounty barely distinguishable when the screens of surfeit bound with ludic acrobatics. Exuberance is Beauty.

65. *If the lion was advised by the fox, he would be cunning*. The cyberpoet that is advised by the techno-bureaucrat would be productive, as digital art requires many hours of synaptically nulling formatting and scripting, and creates a spiritual void that can only be filled by monetary activity. He that is absorbed by MTV and early 20th-century avant-garde film would be a database narratologist by recognizing the formation of micro-tonal stories in the fluid syntax of discrete verbal images. As IBM had been embarrassed by Apple, everybody is wearing jeans to work and yoga class is scheduled daily in the main corporate board room. If the lion was advised by the fox, he would be cunning.

66. *Improvement makes straight roads, but the crooked roads without improvement are roads of Genius*. The labyrinthine web project with too many roads of genius threatens the work's ontological status, for its improvised mapping subsumes its conceptual objects and it

becomes "art" as the solution only to the problem of itself. Smithson's *Spiral Jetty* and Baudelaire's *Fleurs du Mal*, the urbanism of the globe on a geographic timescale versus the pastoralism of the urbane in French cycles of sleep and wakefulness, exist on a landscape of many forking roads and Spoonerist digressions. Improvement makes straight roads, but the crooked roads without improvement are roads of Genius.

67. *Sooner murder an infant in its cradle than nurse unacted desires.* A cyberpoem that is merely a milkfed, commodified desire will kill the infant in its cradle before it has learned how to describe indigestion and will drive the nurse to unacted murders in the hope of totalized, spectacular living. Sooner sacrifice the dot com paycheck and overtimes of Pepsi Lite than program stereotypes through personalization aimed at the one thing that can save America: the high school kids with no debt to immortality, no credit to bargain away, and no deference to Britney, yet who form a target market perennially on the defensive. Sooner murder an infant in its cradle than nurse unacted desires.

68. *Where man is not, nature is barren.* Where man is not on the web, nature resurfaces in the proliferation of artificial life works that are a million years from evolving into text, though potentially constructing their *Crystallographies* and Little Spartas in mundane minutes. Where the spectacle elides all reality, man resurfaces in the form of avatar, producing Promethean pseudo-fire from the rubbing together of two Pentium chips, channeling midnight ships through symbolically violent bays. Where electricity is not, digital art is not, but where man is not, art of any sort is not, thus no Byron swimming the analog Hellespont, for fame or love. Where man is not, nature is barren.

69. *Truth can never be told so as to be understood and not be believed.* The interface that cannot be believed is a farce that can tell no truth, hence provoke no apathy, and tell no lie, hence provide no beauty. The interface that can be believed but never presents the same result twice makes a role player of the passive user, forging loops of disparate acts and doomed inactions that are themselves the essence of work. Lies can never be sold if they are not understandable and believable; mere half-truths are the stale creampuffs of yesteryear, reliably learned and culturally outfitted, but über-packaged and nutritionless. Truth can never be told so as to be understood and not be believed.

Enough! or Too Much!

Whan Lilacs Laist in the Duir
notes on new poetrie

Whan Lilacs Laist in the Duir

Wiout apologie, aw wud lik to embark on a tuithie scance°   *critical survey,*
o a boorach o younger makars°, maistlie American, wha   *poets*
seem to definin a new tendencie in liteerature.

    Mi harn° has been addlit, fur the bygane° wheen yairs,   *brain, past*
bi an kenablie° decadent fascination wi a parteeclar deviant   *obviously*
firm o street thaiter caad karaoke. Fur this rizzon, aw've spen
plenty oors on the subwey (in discrete, extendit pieces o ten
to twentie meenits, o coorse) layin the brain asteep° wi sic°   *contemplating, such*
maitters as whither certaint sangs are ooten mi reenge, waur
aw cud fin' a baur that hud Roy Orbison's "In Draims,"
whither aw cud ilk° do't sober, that teep o theeng. O coorse,   *ever*
aw wud hae muckle° preferrit afferin the image o mi con-   *much*
templatin the unco° rhythmical peculiarities o thae lexicallie   *particular*

213

malnourishit firsten three lines o Eliot's *Fower Quartets*, bit franklie, aw've been there awreddie.

So, ane day aw hud a parteeclar fower-chord wunner, Radioheid's noo clessic "Creep," pouncin on the mair undisciplinit synapses in mi heid an intonin, wiout apologie: "Bit aw'm a creep / aw'm a wairdo / Whit the ill place am aw doin here? / aw dinna° belang here." Aw luve't whan Thom Yorke breks intil a falsetto an syne kythes° a fair amount o nae-very-grunge vocal technique, kin' o lik a Pavarotti fur the masses, durin the brek in that sang whan he tweetles°, ay eloquentlie, the wird "Run." This moment is virtual-heiven fur a karaoke singer, tho aw awn to ne'er haein tried't mysel.

Takin intil consitheration the unique matin o the clarty°, butcherin naitur o this parteeclar single wi the strategic, sophisticatit studio techniques o its recordin, an the structure o the tweetlin in the sang itsel, whilk goes frae a disciplinit, raither hornie draunt° to operatic, masculine heichs° —kin' o a three meenit fable takin aa the pathos o the Cyrano de Bergerac spin°—aw chancit upo the nem fur mi literarie tendencie, ane whilk aw wis fittit° wud be instantlie rejeckit, bit fur aye° layin the brain asteep, bi oniebodie takin an aefauld° interest in poetrie.

Aw decidit to cry't Creep Poetrie. Why "Creep," mi titty° speired? Shae associatit't wi slaizie men wha rubbit thir hauns° oop an doun thir jains when bletherin° to ye, men wi "issues." No, it's nae that at aw, aw quo (fiercelins°, as sae monie o mi Creeps wur wummen), an gin't° is, theengs wull chynge. Leuk at whit happenit to the "bait" o "Bait Poetrie"?

[Marginal glosses: dinna° — don't; kythes° — then shows; tweetles° — sings; clarty° — dirty; draunt° — whine; heichs° — heights; spin° — tale; fittit° — satisfied; aye° — forever; aefauld° — sincere; titty° — sister; hauns° — hands; bletherin° — talking; fiercelins° — hurriedly; gin't° — if it]

Mi howp is that the nem wull be rejeckit. Aw've triit° to rejeck't (this essay has plenty o umquhile° "Creep"-less drafts). Bit aw've become sae fascinatit aboot the punnin maybes° o this wird that aw've decidit to push on, gin ainlie wi the howp that, in the midst o "pley," aw describe a wheen° theengs. As so, aw wull.

Creep Poetrie, lik maist guid° tendencies, has been atour° fur a whill, thou't hasn't still an on made its presence gey° kenable°, naither to the mainstraim nor to the unnergrun cowmunities frae whance't sprang. 'T is naither Language poetrie nor New York Scuil, naither Nuyorican nor Toronto concrete. Nor is't poetrie frae the "New Coast," that muivement that wisna a muivement frae the airlie Nineties that failit kis't° wis tae cleverlie unlocatable, an, gin oniethin°, 't stauns conter° the "Ellipticeest" makars, gin ainlie kis Creep makars are ill-deedie°, an hae mad wel in generatin new weys o scribin° quite apairt frae the mainstraim.

Binna fur the hinner maist°, 't takes pairts frae aa o these, bit ane thin aa the Creeps share is a surprisin will to cowmunicate, to perfirm, to create social interackivitie, an to expand 'yont the wee cowmunities that hae been thir inheritit legacie frae umquhile American avant-gardes. They are aft experimentaleests, bit hae nae interest in prattick fur its ain sake, at laist gin the upcums° are nae sumhin lik a public, aft gey shortsome°, firm o poetrie, a sort o deviant firm o street thaiter itsel. The Creeps are almaist universallie gey knackie°, tho why there has been siccan° birl° to eemir° in thir poetrie is maitter fur flyte°.

Margin glosses: triit° tried · umquhile° previous · maybes° possibilities · wheen° few · guid° good, · atour° around · gey° very, · kenable° apparent · kis't° because it · oniethin° anything, · conter° opposite · ill-deedie° mischievous · scribin° writing · hinner maist° last · upcums° results · shortsome° entertaining · knackie° funny, · siccan° such, · birl° turn, · eemir° humor · flyte° debate

Nanetheless, fur aa o thir will to cowmunicate, the Creeps are nae simplie assimilatin experimental techniques intil the mainstraim. The Creeps identify wi Pound's "cleckors°," an nae Pound's "diluters." They wud almaist universallie say thegither° that there is a strang difference atween the twa. They dinna stairt wi whit is mair or less the "period style" an fidge° ootwan° to "wairdness," bit prefer to stairt at the extremes, sweengin there wullie gin some duddie° cruik° o a pome appairs, some discoverie, an syne to come in a bit. — inventors, agree, move, outwards, little, crook

Fyow° important buiks that hae come ooten this tendencie include: Caroline Bergvall's *Goan Atom*, Lee Ann Broon's *Polyverse*, Miles Champions' *Three Bell Zero*, Kevin Davies' *Comp.*, Tim Davis' *Dailies*, Jeff Derksen's *Dwell*, Dan Farrell's *Hinner Maist Instance*, Robert Fitterman's *Metropolis 1-15*, Kenneth Goldsmith's *No. 111*, Lisa Jarnot's *Some Ither Kin' o Mission*, Adeena Karasick's *Dyssemia Sleaze*, Pamela Lu's *Pamela: A Novel*, Bill Luoma's *Warks an Days*, Jennifer Moxley's *Imagination Verses* an hir chapbuik "Wrang Life," Harriet Mullens' *Muse an Drudge*, Sianne Ngai's *Criteria*, Rod Smith's *Proteckive Immediacie* an *In Memorie o Mi Theories*, Chris Stroffolino's *Stailer's Whurl*, Darren Wershler-Henry's *the tapewirm foundrie* an Susan Wheeler's *Soorce Codes*. That's a lot o buiks, an wi the exception o ane, aa o thaim hae appairit in the bygane five yairs. Maist hae appairit in the hinner maist twa. — some

Mebbe the best wey to git intil mi ideas aboot this new, edifyin tendencie caad Creep Poetrie, aw wull quote frae ane o thir pomes. The follain is frae Kevin Davies' *Comp.*:

216

Quote Yeah ye *wish* mi forhooit° comman post wur   abandoned
closer to yer retrieval plant an whollie oonit° sub-   owned
sidiaries. Ye *wint°* the polka dots to be   want

Aristotelian. Cidna baidle° mi furrows evangelisti-   beadle
callie enuch fur ye cud aw, yeah babie aw ken't° hurts.   know it
Aw ken kis aw went to Fredericton an bideed°   stayed

there, aw paintit baseboords vermilion fur dunce
dimes an ninnie nickels. That disna main aw hae to
waddle oop to raccuin-juice-colorit marsh elders

with alder awnings an slant-six Norwegian method
actin strappit to thir fungoes to ken whan aw'm nae
conneckin the wather bowie° to the weet   water bucket

cheek° o post-Minimalism. Aw ken whan aw'm nae   side
hunted. Jist dinna expeck lemurs to magicallie reappair
frae the braw prent o the sel-storage

contrack. Dinna e'en *think* aboot viola solos. We aa
jist re-uppit wi the radiator fuzz Un Quote.

Maist o the hamerks are here: the rin-o° pacin that   run-on
seems to tak aathin in (Creeps can aft be encyclopedic in thir
references), the aff-bait eemir that aft strays jist a duddie bit-
tie° intil solipsism (aw dinna, fur example, ken whit   little bit
"Fredericton" is), the skatin abune° aefauld°, aft radical ide-   above, sincere
ological fittininments° that are, nanetheless, ne'er brain-   concerns
baitin, an maist o aa a fittininment wi the gliff° o leid°   sensation, language
unhinged, nae haillie 'yont sumhin° someane cud possiblie   something,
say, bit still coastin on ilka° maybe° open to leid frae wi'in a   every, possibility
perfirmative aspeck. Creeps, as aw wrote, are shortsome, bit
they are nae afraid to tak thir leid to the level o gy°, sumhin   spectacle

217

lik the sublime in the dizzyin heichs aft raiched°, bit sacri- — reached
ficin the gothic stabilitie fur the gliff o constant exchynge.

This pints to anither aspeck o Creep poetrie, whilk is
that its "aw"° is aft situatit 'neth° the economic stratum o — I, beneath
incraisit cowmercial activitie that digital technologie has
broucht on. Paradigmaticallie, ane o the heid° creepie texts, — major
Tim Davis' *Dailies*, wis scrievit° bi a "9-5 lifer wakin oop ane — written,
lunch oor° an noticin he wisna shair° he as the same makar — hour, sure
wha hud stairtit yesterday's bricht° duddie title ficht°." — bright, fight
Composit ane-a-day whill on-or-aff dutie as an editor at
New Directions, Davis' *Dailies* is a discrete series o sonic
scraims° refusin to become yawns, o ootcomes intil° imagi- — screams, escapes into
narie landscapes o leid that coast well 'yont° whit yin wud — beyond
jalouse° wur the causes celebres o watter cuiler offish° cul- — imagine, office
ture.

does *viva zapata* main *livin shoon*°? — shoes
the winner o the race gits to immolate onie toom° — empty
    librarie,
scrape the fite° aff a dozen klines — white
e'en nod durin mao z.'s muckle° tweetlealang: — big
"me an mi spar-row"
the scuil pley remade *the dueleests* starrin
god an godard to myriad reviews
an aw quote "aw quote"
"the ane in the singlesses° — sunglasses
seemit to intentionallie misreid his miscues"
there's the signpost oop aheid, it's collickie comme il
    faut
la vie de chan-ce

Nae aa poetrie bi the Creeps (or "Kreepwerks") are sae gleg° an harn-stormin° as this. The wark o Jennifer Moxley, fur instance, propones° anither aspeck o Creep poetrie, whilk is that't is frustratit an obsessit bi the process in whilk capitalism an mass-cultur has absorbit almaist aathin (Allen Ginsberg in a noo notorious Gap ad is ane kenable° touchstane) intil its oxygen-starvit capillaries. The Creeps aft come aff as a bittie mute in the neb° o nae public piece fur communin o heicher° social aspirations; they fair bein caad dyed-in-the-wuil Marxeests on the ane haun (maist o thaim hae nae interest in Marx), or simplie bein ignorit on the ither. The follain is frae Moxley's chapbuik "Wrang Life":

   Ye hurrie hame at gloamin° bit fall upo a deid bird bi
      the cheek° o the road,
   tinie pink featherless neck, sin° thrapple° slashed. Frae
      the scribin desk
   the warkers bide wutness° to the destruckion o yer men-
      tal hideawa',
   bit the ficht ye in yer imaginarie thochts chaw° in thaim
   proves nanetheless imposseeble to spaik o […]
   Ye growe wairie whan ye raelize the auld warld winna
      bide° new fur lang
   an e'en the deid men speir° ye, the maist ill-faured°
      amang thaim
   fills ye wi fash° an langing. They wud raither leuk
   upo the flams o yer beerial pyre frae oot at sai° nor°
      forhoo°
   the wull o thir faithers. Ye lik to jalouse° ye wull ne'er
      luve agane.

Marginal glosses: gleg° quick; harn-stormin° brain-storming; propones° suggests; kenable° obvious; neb° face; heicher° higher; gloamin° dusk; cheek° side; sin° sun; thrapple° throat; wutness° witness; chaw° provoke; bide° remain; speir° interrogate; ill-faured° ugliest; fash° anguish; sai° sea; nor° than; forhoo° abandon; jalouse° suppose

219

Nae less nor Davis' or Davies' wark (that wis unintentional), Moxley's pome is a lingueestic perfirmance (this hail pome yaises° as a template Apollinaire's "Zone," torquin an riffin on severals o that pome's key lines), bit Moxley has been peculiar in ettlin° to access a slawer°, whit aw hae elsewaur caad "neo-Classical" pace in hir scribin, aiblins° in a mair ootwan° shaw o defiance agane' the gy° o cowmercial exchynge nor in an accessin o its simulacral aesthetic maybes°.

Moxley's poetrie howps to clype° the time bi shawin hoo "the auld warld winna bide new fur lang," bit lik monie Creep pomes, hirs is an extendit apostrophe, a discoorse aimit at an imaginarie owdience, an owdience o the future aiblins bit ane that, in the scouth° o the pome, is nae there. Plenty° Creep makars, especiallie Lisa Jarnot, Anselm Berrigan an Chris Stroffolino, wull assume this mode o apostrophe, a statin-o-the-case afore an inviseeble congress. Thus the "aw" assumes a rhetorical function; nae the "nae-aw" o cowmon postmodren parlance, an yit nae the "aw" o the awnin° lyric.

This pints to anither cowmon element o the Creeps, whilk is that they are nae, generallie, gretlie concernit wi epistemological issues, flexin thir intelleckual biceps quizzin thaimsels on whither a tassie° o coffee is, indeed, there, or whither a toom buist° hauds° the pan° o a deid dictator. They mith° hae thir moments o doot°, bit dinna place some grandiloquent, buikish figure at the mid° o thae fittininments. They certie° dinna trachle° thir raiders wi extendit periods o "whit's goin on in mi heid"-teep o scribin, an they

dinna describe thir hames, thir siller°, thir Irish heritages, [money]
thir deep attachments to Hopkins, Dickinson or Ann
Boleyn, nor thir sinses that the Gulf Weir an postcolonialism
wur aa thir faut (or that thir public displeys o deep fittininment wull gar onie prackical effeck). Unlik the "Ellipticeest"
makars (as nemit bi Steve Burt in his aft brilliant, chaengin° [challenging]
essay), they dinna fee in "aw am X, aw am Y, aw am Z"
ongauns° ("aw am angel, addick, catherine whurl" rins a [behavior]
pome bi Lucie Brock-Broido) kis't° is ne'er assumit that the [because it]
raider parteeclar° cares aboot the psychological crises o a [particularly]
prestigious (or e'en unnergrun) makar.

The Creep mith perfirm leid, bit wull rerrlie perfirm
oniethin proponin an "identitie crisis," an they hae an
allergie to oniethin proponin narcissism. Consequentlie,
there is an almaist universal disregard fur the persona an
styleestics o Jorie Graham—the "Ellipticeest" touchstane—
amang the Creeps, as weel's fur Harold Bloom's "strang"
makar-theorie, in whilk we are speirit° to envision a wrestlin [asked]
match, predicatit on the Oedipal complex, atween acolyte
makar an maister. Baith o thae models are generallie con-
sitherit tae "heroic," tae elevated, a bittie tae faur aff in the
giddie heichs o assumit bardic authoritie fur the Creeps, wha
prefer, yin micht say, the *praisent tense*.

Creep aesthetics can rin the gamut o sensibilities, frae
the ambient, nairlie mudgeless° surfaces o Dan Farrell's prose [motionless]
pomes in *Hinner Maist Instance*, to the slick, racie polyleid-
itness surfaces o Caroline Bergvall's *Goan Atom*, frae the low-
dent°, micro-political dramas o Sianne Ngai's *Criteria* to the [reduced]
lichter, heichlie nuancit tig° o Robert Fitterman in [touch]

221

Metropolis, whilk yaises whit he crys° "samplin" techniques · calls
to create a sinse o urban phantasmagoria.

Harryette Mullen's series o quatrain pomes, *Muse &
Drudge*, in whilk she utilizes vernacular liftit frae Clarence
Major's *Dictionarie o African American Slang* (she's African
American hirsel, bit ne'er actuallie spak in a "bleck" idiom or
livit in cowmunitie waur't wis spak), is aiblins ane o the
firsten kenable maisterpieces in this style.

> tweetlit native skin
> bingin islan sin° · sun
> sheens on shingles
> shunnin unhingit singles
>
> solar flares scrammled° · scrambled
> skellet° boddoms sinnyside · bell
> signal didna she ramble
> those bleck thirls° hinsly · backslide
>
> tropical wheem
> punanie as ye wint to be
> cokit bottlit buddies° · bodies
> with fanticide nebs° · faces
>
> drippie° flachts° poked · tresses, bagged
> in plaistic do-rag
> sinseeble heel in execu-drag
> whase ootrig° sooks excess · dress

On the conter° cheek° o this speckrum is Torontonian · opposite, side
Darren Wershler-Henry's prose pome, *the tapewirm foundrie*,

222

a series o "receipts° fur pomes" that are conjinit° bi the wird [recipes, conjoined]
"anor"° bit whilk, in fack°, rins well ootby° e'en the maist [andor, fact, beyond]
expansive sinse o poetrie to ootcome intil a speculative warld
o Situationeest debacle, a sort o Disneylan o foonerin° social [collapsing]
frams:

> anor proclaim transparent buiks fur fowk wha lik to reid
> whill hurlin° anor establish internal rhythms anor [driving]
> scrieve the regulations fur mair richt-lik° bluid plays lik [equitable]
> the ane in an oceanarium atween° a killer whaul an a [between]
> snorkel diver armit wi ainlie a stapple° gun or lik the ane [staple]
> in a kiddie puil atween a haimmerheid shark an a
> divorce lawer armit wi ainlie a freet° chib° or lik the ane [butter, knife]
> in a gymnaisum atween a fite° rhino an a gowf caddie [white]
> armit wi ainlie a pickin° wadge° anor figure oot a wey [pitching, wedge]
> to do't wiout metaphor anor stairt a clatter° that byron [rumor]
> micht ne'er hae swum the hellespont gin nae fur his
> yiss° o quackieshapit° watter weengs° anor replicate the [use, duckshaped, wings]
> viseeble warld in order to pleesure° some haif-knab° [satisfy, bourgeois]
> neit° fur easdom° an syne brin e'en mair order intil this [need, comfort]
> illusion anor scrieve ilk wird o a lang pome on a saiprit° [separate]
> bumper sticker an syne apply ane sticker to ilk caur in a
> parkade weirin raws° as lines an fluirs° as stanzas… [rows, floors]

As in aa Creep poetrie, there is the sinse o wintin to
take't aa in in as jimpit° a piece° as posseeble, bit aathin is [short, space]
torqued; the mudge° is centrifugal, nae centripetal. In this [motion]
way, Creeps cud be quo to be obsessit wi witterin°, hoo't is [information]
stockpilit an shiftit atour°. Mullen's yiss o a nonstannert, eth- [about]
nicallie-encodit dictionarie, an Wershler-Henry's raither

free-whurlin assemblage o perspeckives (it fidges° frae an [moves] aquarium to a heichwey to the Hellespont in the piece o an "anor") propone anither aspeck o Creep Poetrie, whilk is that't is aft scrievit frae a distanced, "satellite" perspeckive, a sort o "totalizing" glower°. Hooever, the Creeps brek oop, in [gaze] unseestematic weys, this raeleest, geographical fantice° o [imagination] fowk an theengs, crackin't a bittie to own° waur luve, birse°, [see, anger] will°, an mainingfu human activitie micht come to bide. [desire]

Bit gin avant-garde poetics can aft be uptakit° as [understood] Puritanical, wi an aft hivvie-haunit° wey o bletherin aboot [heavy-handed] poetrie whilk seems, to the layman, a bittie scholaistic, the Creeps are Rabelasian; they are interestit in microtonal comedies (an lots o it) that expose the interpleys an contra-dictions o wizzen°. Aathin screenges° oop agane' aathin in a [life, rubs] Creep pome; it's the road° derivit frae Rimbaud's "Drunken [method] Boat," bit insteid o droonit tarry-breakses° an bew boak° we [drowned sailors, blue vomit] hae retrieval plants an Maoeest tweetle-alangs. The Creeps are nae droonin in a hail o mocage°; they are tae gundie°, tae [irony, violent] visionarie, fur the pages o the Baffler (thou fyow° hae appair-[some] it there), the movies o Jim Jarmusch or the novels o Mark Leyner—aa interestin phenomena, bit generallie nae gey derf°. [daring]

There is nocht kenablie mercatable° aboot the Creeps, [marketable] as thir heckles° o complacencie, e'en in jest or as a philo-[criticisms] sophical exercise, are enuch to gie ane… the creeps. Gin thir tactic is to gae owre-the-tap° wi lexical plenitude, neolo-[over-the-top] gisms, aboot-neb birls° to somewhit antique meters, [turns] rhythms that are either tae fest or tae slaw to digeest, syne agane reversals intil the slipstraim o paratactics an heich technologie,'t is kis they trew°, lik Rimbaud, that aa vailyes° hae to be reclecked°. Thir effort bides in a scannin o the architecture o contemporarie wizzen° fur the presence o beins; thir perspeckive is tap-doun, frae the heichs o pouer, nae as "antennae o the race," bit frae ruiftap barbecues. They are nae cryin "aw am this" sae muckle° as "hoo does this citie braithe"? Why are the squares toom°, whan they are bathit in insurrectional licht°?

    The hail experimental win° o the poetrie warld is nae made oop o Creeps. Plenty braw° makars, sic as Heather Ramsdell, Lytle Shaw, Ange Mlinko an Stacie Doris, are nae, fur thir sindry° rizzons°, Creeps (an micht be happie to hair that). The Creeps are American, Canadian an Inglish (sae faur as aw ken); ane o the firsten recognizable Kreepwerks, *Dwell*, wis scrievit bi a Canadian makar, Jeff Derksen. Thir poetrie appairs in a kin° o journals ye mith nae hae heard of, aft proclaimit° bi ither makars an mailit atour the wharl, in the mainner o fanzines an buitleg cassettes (bit smairter). They hae nae interest in coalescin birrs° or words° in heid media mids lik New York (thou that aft comes°); they prefer a scatterit geographie, envisionin individual subculturs that interlock in moments o scandal an essays lik this. They are global, tho operate frae wi'in the cracks.

    The Creeps wunner why, in a cultur that has public enthusiasm fur airteests lik Matthew Barney, Jeff Koons an Cindie Sherman, aa o whom are taken to be definin cultural figures o thir time or at laist "airteests," makars wha are similarlie disruptive an experimental are aft nae noticed, an nae missed. They wunner why the poetrie warld is nae as

---

Right-margin glosses:

believe, values
reinvented
life

much
empty
light
wing
fine

various, reasons

variety
published

energies, reputations
happens

225

interestit in the "lip°" as the airt an pop music worlds.   edge

They dinna consither thaimsels ootbyrs°, the "marginal," an hence ne'er o onie yiss to mainstraim thocht. On the contraire, they tak interest in monie o the gretest flytes° o oor time, parteeclar° owre globalization, cultural memorie an the dale° o human agencie. Thir distinguishin track° frae scrievers frae the mainstraim, an alsae the scrievers o "Elliptical" verse, is that they expose, are exposed, an dae nae ken° onie gless ceilings in tairms o whit can gae intil a pome, nor some sicker°, predefinit norie° o the "sel" as thir subjeckive limit.   outsiders · debates · particularly · goal, feature · recognize · safe, notion

Aw am nae ettlin° to sell ye the "Creeps"; itherwise, aw waudna cry thaim that. Somethin mair saikless° an timelie, lik the "Digital Makars," or mystifyin, lik "New Coast" makars, wud probablie flee° better. Bit aw hae felt compellit to describe this tendencie weirin a shorthaun, a tairm aw cud birl atour (nae to mou° utilize fur unco° rhetorical effecks), an this seemit as guid (an perfecklie baud°) as onie. Creepteep poetrie, creepie poetrie, the poetrie that creeps unner the skin o recognizit literarie cultur, that chips awa' lik a modest computer virus, is jist gittin a lot better latelie, a lot mair fou°, boisterous, mair populatit bi charismatic figures an wuller° perceptions. Aw think that this general aesthetic wull be a definin ane fur oor time.   trying · innocuous · fly · mention, weird · bad · full · wilder

Aw maulit Whitman's kenspeckle° line frae his lament fur Lincoln in mi title, bit mi sinse is that "whan lilacs laist in the duir," sumhin comes that Whitman himsel caad for, the duir becomin "unscrewit frae its jambs." Providit they are lilacs, an that this is sprin°, an that mi tassie o coffee is still hot, there's muckle guid comin on the horizon.   famous · spring

226

A Poem of Attitudes

for Michael Gizzi

A Poem of Attitudes

No.

Do you partake in the cramping rituals,
no. No. Nobody hears whore words after
midnight's collusions. Nor speech, the
golden apples of light fixtures travestying
calm on the streets, his knees of posing
amidst specializations of soul. Grow
weaker. Not a curse. Not all the songs,
no gimmick. Not be. Not in my poem.
Not like a room. Not mix the beans.

Not

the

fleeting gap in them perchance to wake.
Never ending, the starlog's digital
enactment? To a day's bastard employment.
Nevertheless it's dandelion that made
the dill mop. Dimpled copycats—dint
young boy piss. New Fords in the prisons.
No Birkenstocks. No cube can withstand
it. Of lime jelly hell phlox stuns.

Delirium entering percent of Americans,
suffer from its simplicity, until fashionably
in exile. Beer problems. More? Mother's
bar code among: the demean, the dogma.
Demonstrating churches pullulating succinct
curtains affording scents. Mouseketeers,
they
square sugarfy. Descends into cursory
majesty, desist, gossip of the changeling
pride. Moved on to synaptic didgeridoo
halo. Destiny enflames thee! a
mind
choked up so. Chronological. Chun. Cigarettes
back up to the barge. You down. You
(product of the terrible Camel ads?)
badges of a burgeoning mask-of-femininity.
Cigarettes for the never known cerebral
cortex of language. Cinnamon rations
on. Invited me here. You, cinders, city's
grammar in the slides on asphalt and
concrete text (zoning laws will change

that) the Celts—makes! retaliates against
age. Coffee this morning. Collapses vertebrae
milk. Collecting in puddles. Colonies
beneath, combing through them,
  making new etymologies, managing a vocal
    Mandelbrot:
      afternoon's tits.
  Companions, and. Conclusion. Concubines
sets excessing. Many looked so fine.
      You sang jokes, many of the new
      songs have roots in the electric
funk of Prince. Margot my favorite strophe.

You think of those truly great.
      But a better
man was Kim. Whelming in the cranium.
  When I'm sitting on my left butt cheek?
      When suburbia rubs Oswald refrigerator.
  Stark eye. Stark talk in check point.
Stately as Elvis gowns and coroners.

Buster.

The twisted airwaves of the democracy.
  And punishing them on such bizarre diets
      ack ack. And rhyme they do. As popcorn
  and gossip. The typist smiles. The very
luscious and scares. And scarred. And
      self-consciously chooses fruit to keep
      them a perfect lemon. And she's quite

happy to be the front runner three years
        prior of the past. Rope pansy. Rosicrucianism
deflected into its basest taxonomy.
Royal. Rudely. Rum atop the corpse, that's
    daydream's pallor. Run fathomless rose
            clouds. Running. Sabbatical for everyone,
    prose can talk one into iniquity. The
way he liked them. The weather report
        thin. He said the pregnant stalker.

A light cast up the space. Or ditties.
    Excalibur coded. Exhorting the ladies
to keep some such appliance. Or Taylorisms?
            Or tear. Or the book shelf or grunions.
            Or the decorative arts. Or the son your
    lamplight trimmed and burning. Eye.
The hand of craft
            apparent. The handwriting, Knox, desist
    courage. A throws in troves, unequal
but spirited poems; or a shifting lung.
    Or an acrobat. Or an androgyne. Or caps
            and gowns. Slow. The Huns at the border.

Now we are really getting at the New
    Hermeticists. Now we move to camera
two, where fickle cares in laundromats
    —don't have 'em in the nineties. The
            man with the cowlick, day of reveries
    archaic.
                The blown

                    a blip
          on the stereo-enhanced
                monitor, now we move
            to suck the Dutch
                interior wending
matter. Don't jump with cats.

Dope now. Down struck hams becoming
fame, sooth. Downstairs in the cellar:
                subsume the room. A dance in state-of-the-funk
                magnum opus. Of. Offals. Days-old tortilla
        dips (factured hologram reminiscence),
                the dodecahedrons of attitudes. The
        cold cuts of treaties. Offering itself
was the dramatized verandah city.
        Often I am returned to a field, the doilies
                become custard. The elbows are fractured.
        Where the dandelion: the end. The endless
nights of critical debate. The exquisite
                hypocrisy, the eyes of the horseshoe
                crab. The fatter maid. The feel: a diabolical
        brew of badass disco-era funk and arena
                rock anthem. A disc jockey who lives
        on which the oversized heads concentrate.

Over lazy couplets importunate. The listless,
        the atrophied, the surreal. The loci
gathered at the local junk of dust blots.
                A part sniffle, a pause.
                A shop. The look: the luck

of the grip.
The meat of the news. The Ming family
Christmas, boiling all the toaster ovens.
The penny, a hur. A perfect orb. Struck
guitar. Packaged with the family and
the Ubu, capsizes bit of yarn
from the vestpocket. Foot store below
mission impossible (of censorship on
the internet). The as the torn individually.
A prude. A puff and testifying iniquity
—for 4.

Again. Aggregates of all the paintings
of the world. Aggressive smacks. Ahem.

Googol-miles. Gosh youth. Gourds beating
stakes govern U. Alas plant the dour
kiss. Alas. Alas. Alas. Alas. Sit calm
on throne. Green ale. Green borders
on solid. Grifter, shape-shifter. Gross
bid, and wrote make it new on his
algorithmic all-by-myself. Bath tub
day by day
cut underbrush.
The piloting act among fissures strangling
nothing but the all hung and strung
on their way (alibi: all in deference
to Adorno). All it. All it. Chick peas.
And made a plough, procrastinating not
uselessly before, all naked and humming

when everyone's dressed
for football.

Says demonstration of it: poem
            on radium TV? There is always an afterwards
      that Moira often spent the night playing
her guitar. Scopocratic. And that would
      be a team shoulder, a martyr. Heh. Helium
            sandbags whistle the spoils of bub, apoplectic
      variants thereof: they are young. And
that's to chart your Cain. Hello retro
            spillt demonstration, agro comfort amidst
            acculturated flies, ample alibis. There
      is an allusion to the brute.
            There is
            no holiday. There spotted, running perfect,
      just the intro. And the cards tumbled
to flatness. And the garland will oh
      ah—they Samsungize, before down the
strand.
            There's also the screaming bloody murder
      in the womb before Stones-y mixed business.

The tattered dominions touch it in the
            restaurant.

Heroine.
            Heuristic but palmed beginning. Hiding.
      They are in love with another man's
gloves (nothing can stand revision).

They bathe. They belong in the nineteenth
                century. They fill up the room quite
quickly. They make bad sleep. They
never managed hips… his offspring. His
                sweaty hand, eventually
    to tame
    the urge
                to incinerate all the folderol. They
    in the compound, off, and towels, and Ensor's
                skates. And we wonder what an Afro-Arcadian
    is. Stalk the galleys awaiting self-
preservation. They want on
    for about
    five years
                thinking!
    evaporates. His was Maurice. Home is
                we turn-in—turn, and—what fantasies exist
    in the heart. Another quit cigarettes.
Here comes another one. Here they are
                amassed as bricks of petrified shit.

Jih jih hsin Hsia Hia! Hias fallen
    for offence to the spirits, for sweats
of the people. Hu. Huck. Hums was beginning
    to prepare. Sherri's former husband
                Sherri. Shielded from the storm. Shorn
    appendages
    bothered, presently with two
rice, evol. Hung comedian—hungry. Hush.
    Hype.

Hyphens mummy liquidating literary
jamboree (gumbo)—this night knows,
fleshing it out of them. Are nestling
on the windows, still one hears I, I'm
born mass, shorn appendages, bothered
presently with mass, a no-syntax. This
out shifty perimeter Geronimo,
the heroic tantrum, but plugs the
holes with facts. Are nobody's idea
of a legal tender. Are not hostile.
Are stillness from the egg-haloed expanse.
Should-a thought shoulders tropical
buffaloes. To be a totem.

Three images of Elvis in the clouds
—through York deleterious quantum
neutoronomy path fault fleck
in midst chaotic wearying
—Stanislavkian is fine,
verdant tussles
staunch direct mail.

As that—I enrage my privacy. I, dim
fuckers, aiming an elephant. To begin
again. To it was a tight out [social
realism] he said they said base impassable
streaks by the fit here. As marriage
with commish was called. As moon forgot.
I mean the devil in the bird. I remember
a strangled keeshond.

I greets sun. As the catherine wheel
grows old and dark beneath punitive
skies. River Quai, drowned sailor of
the misfortune, now for some, inflate
reality too late. To dolorous anime
flick, Ezekiel, protest no significant
action. To slow this door. To support
Jewel. To the arboretum, they as the
hems of dozens of patched wools had
fashioned from a catalogue. To remember
the girth of the pederast. I remember
are fingered lustlessly. As the scare
quotes peek, wheel beneath all science
fiction verse in the signature of automobiles'
models and years. I skim the isles measuring
what proves it flattery. To the provinces.
In the retina. As the sea. I spy the
lighthouse through to think these cities
are fire they approach from the dizzying
entropy of the social order
and am depressed. I spy the lighthouse
and am depressed.
I strike it sharply.

Indeed. Indeed. In a party boat off
coast, some paradigm—the worse for inedibles.
Informal formations: info from Scorsese's
Jesus
winds no angle. Veritably not
enough, this end and beginning. Surreal.

Veritably. Vicious. So to speak. So
                    we sold him a slogan and vis-à-vis.
            Vision retracts its hand, vitalizing
    juices are sold at the counters but
            the city is overward for this hairy
    Babel to observe creatures venting
            baptism, for the prurient policy scuffs
    the constitutional, charms nothing
            should ever be ashamed, bunjis
    untwined,
                            told him to head of democracy.

Inventors summon
                    up the grouse. Inviting you out west.
        Solid inky boisenbery philosophies.
Solidarity. Soliloquy praxis
but silent
        at park benches. Voodoo! Vote yes on
                    the fucking ticket. Waifish aboard
        the goodship menage-
a-trois. Irregular
prose, an idiolect prosaic
                finally fixated
                    on hams, bluntly inauspicious,
the click
                    expiring modernity's currents
        as a legion of portraits
                of betters—a darks
the street (alibi:

is res depreciation of high) eight a
beatific ozone fandango.

Sonorous. Soon as done. Soon forgotten.
    Soon. Southwest winds at 20 miles rolling
the dice perfectly, healthy the gasp
        per hour. Spatula. Speak into it now.
            Speaking its jive: speaking escapes
        in the light of the Frigidaire patent.
Wait new charms when the catalogue of
            deferrals has ceased, for the next
            month; walk one
two. Wand. Wandering.
        Want to pogo in the pond tonight? Wants
            a calendar (safe me) Iggy's
bourbon pixels-and-posts attempts, and
lexicons suspended fortunately with
        lex, it'll all be that. It's a game!
            I then trumpeting a twist in a bordello
of fog. Blind as a phlox. Feel it! jaunty
hummer Nevel would have thought a collection
            agency was kiwi. Watching MTV
            and fantasizing about Madonna. We'll
depart, blimps above skullduggery. Block.

Book doesn't wow. Brass knuckles taken
to it: philosophe purge, gymnastically
It begins to feel like
a symphonies: the ear worm defeats explodes.

Weathering the colophon Mount Saint. Spillt
    diamonds sweat of a tasty (testy) omelet
               afternoon. Weeds. Weekends. Small cube.
    It feels like winter when the
forks
          the dance.
          It greets each day at seven.
          It on the ground, he falls, spiraling,
    split-heeled into heaven other way.
Were
    black globs of gel swarming toward the
parking lots of the the "sarcophagus
    of sommeil." Spoke the soothing elaborator
               into the tenements. Were there no Mark
    XVII headset. Spread across the igloos
of stars is a colon
    with a dangling
               borders, there could be no accurate measurement
               of the activity of his
reeling—spurious
    as a cousin who never writes but is
               suddenly at attention when
such pluricity
    is a factor. Ruler. It is like an electronic
signal from Mars. Appliance. What's
    French for *watusi* when
nothing's is
    nothing
               to nation tethered? What's

with all these turn away from? It is
solidly submitted
    a written statement
            saying that by possessives?
            What rheumy partisan it opens up. It
    retains philosophy
    early to mid-1989
            brimming full Americana: depths steep
    therein. What rights there is: starfire
planted it the mollified engines.
    Broadway's soft shoe. Broken as an extra-
    vascular
            activity. Sputter. Squareness. St. Stalling
    courage fakes it. Stammering chicks.
Stammering with junk, the last loafer
            left to be, it suggests
the Beatles'
            Savoy truffle considered as art.

Stanzas nap on the door.
Büchner rides a white horse.
Jamb.
Staple blister lists: what thoughts
do you have of Africa?
What and T.
It was recognizable.
It would bum rush their kidneys.
Bumbles across
regrets, antinomies, jumping
from one to the rearward staple

wind breaker.
Was
the brochure from the seminary doing
in the broken couplet?
What was be
time
hastens far hence.
It's an Oliver
other.
Bunny and the game?
What's that asking Star Wars
bleeding onto the streets.
Starbuck's is open.
Stare north film.
It's deliberate love, into the eyes
of the commoners.
Stare into for your
bravery
in occupation?
Whatever.
It's
Pekinese dialect;
it's politics with a hat.
The highway's diamonds
protract—stare
into the floodlights.
Staring
at the bunting.

      Its calluses against the sands

Sticks out the eyes. Its heteroglossic
magnets. Its planes and circles.
Its
roundness. Of time. When the formless
strengths are in
its submission—still no model. Stoically
inclined to, but a vernal
lack of compromise
when the groove kicks in. When the rent
check, diabolic wisdom but
hey. Stone
him to graft. Jangles with all the biblical fury
of a stock photo pet in
the hissing of the vocables. But also
the central areas. But calls. Where
did you get it? Where coming at you
over the horizon. Stonewalling them.
Storming Beverly Hills. But by
minding, be subtracted
each one refused to
stay. From the commerce of solid information
flooding the pews. But in the cuisenart.
Jeff Derksen: she's down the dull
main thoroughfare, happy. Jerking me
around. Jerking your hips like the torsoless
robots in of Rutherford NJ. Stranded
in sensitive winds, chocolate sins.
Strangely efficacious is the lack of
light in the central Herbie Hancock

Rockit video. Jewels! you eat nothing
　　　　　but bears' paws. Jock! who is the butterfly
　　of patterns? Where it had
ceased to radiate. Where one can lick
　　　　　it. Where words are defers on scatological
　　　　　issues.
　　Just code.
　　K kick.
　　Didn't write
　　　　　home. But ease betrays its Krakatoas
　　　　　in the always more than customary.

　　Let's jack into the logarithm. Let his
　　　　　men pay tithes in kind. Let's surface
　　these rock club in 1987. Why do I? but
true. But they're ours. But thou shalt
　　　　　not have to sweat? Cypress between the
　　　　　strong walls. Tea cups. Tearing stained
　　sheets spawn—but unlucky as ever.
　　　　　But what about weird analog synth titters
　　bullied by groaning industrial potato
bars? Lethargy can spawn you—liars!
　　Fare my domesticating panties? But what
　　　　　from the menu, that such crime forth
　　afar into accumulative night? Lice.
Noise. Wild silk lie's shamming anklet,
　　　　　notoriety not be committed: "technos
　　　　　still is from Shantung, smothering logos."

Temping high on. Temptation waits. Terrific.

Texas steel. Ammassi. Willful ignorance:

Williamsburg. Window ration. Whippety

of this pristine the lift-off. Lifting

soliloquy? Like a sonneteer in

gala pagan rites. Like efforts at impressive

prose. State of my. But when there's

something like a discussion

of Lewinsky-o-mania.

But that's a mouthful

of pantomime talon. That's

hygienic as a crib. Hieroglyph splat,

a gorgon elopes, nighter, that's not final.

That's playing in temple, stealing. With

cries: your room with your penis and

lingerie. That's rosy. That's color

cube. Like Lazarus, fungal tooth detractor

and all. Lingering ending you are really

not welcome, we'll have lunch. Listening

to this now. Literally hours to move

in. But to Thor and Isis. With of time

were spent describing sex. Literally.

Satisfactory fiction. That's scary.

That's standard in his suspicious. With

memories of the younger-than-drinking-

age. But. But. But. Butter Paleolithic

(indeed). With that mixture of practices

like this. That's the calendar. That

are overarching. That are wheat. That

break up these wholes. By Korean
non-rationale of sand-beaten front yards.
By the way. Bye-bye. C lived in tight
quarters. That cannot
drag me forward. That doesn't create
big holes in the
sock, stomach.
That is: that jelly. That makes its
greed invisible. Caffeine of Europe?
Calibaning. C. Callous. Can't we go
light the candles, that old saw? That
one perspired. That pencils in its
now? Can I still tell a lie? Can Hiawatha
locked in the margins
a marginalia. That seems cautiously
precise. That this CD can record silence
of a Thursday afternoon adequately, am
smoking my titular cigarette, bonny high.
With corners of the room sleeping stilly.
Loco—loco. Eye is green. That those
of us who were to suspend the hope's
(BQE's)
ceaseless bombing. Cancer in married
throat. Cancer like sleep
—cancer give up our wives of the star
field closing in! Loco. Love potions
team, and then I start getting this feeling
of the biases of the social. Without
a process. To him. That with anonymity.

Love. Lunk lunk in terrible portions
wives. Women. Wondering if the cafes
                    touch off, have anyone. Wondering.
                    Wooden horses. Would rule god's kingdom.

The scholarly bits
            seemed to stick out. The palm of
my history. He'd bind, its
            planes begin to crack.
                        The semi-colons
                        squeeze the damp mushrooms.

    The street
            garnered with a touch of class. Order.
    And incontinent.
And fitting words to their music is
            buried in Meldal-Johnson's attempt to
describe lounge chair burdened.

    Are you responding? Argue
dispassionately, alas you've got time.
        To change: this was unpalatable since
                        read, no less impressed, harmonium
        sweet docile wager
        the radium necromancy.
I've inflected stanzas mimicking thought
                        of invisible loves. I am amazed at the
                        hapless señoritas. I am—tho matronly.
        Those are what doesn't belong. I
                        am enlivening the debate. I am not. But

frittering away, remember. Those Catholic
nuns. Those… sure, I see your history.
    I blanch. I blank in delirious quota
            stony path sight
            flecks in the midst
            leveling the role.
       I can't imagine. I claim to
have deduced it. I command. I didn't
        mean
                with the seahorse. Argues for
            decency. Arnold insists to insult anyone
in the subatomic marauders are cute.
        Those winds.
        Those with their criticisms. Paragrammic
alienist. Around the corner
was the cellar. Artifact's desperate
as any shrew can hear. Lump. I divide
        the sloths of protein in half: those
with their criticisms. Though as a boy.
        As a crew.
        As in the final analysis.
    Though it also hearkens back to a divination
    and I, and say, palm it.
Quote: as a lark.

Tulips. Tulips: turn soliloquy into
    badminton. Down over languid teenagers.

So that trigger-happy fungal, impressionable
    Zeppos of the Ovidian cloister gland

Birth all created
    positif and the *negatif* is our goals (ghosts) ideally.

Twelve fingers
    dance trebling along the keys.

Olsonian so that the hero's song can
    be heard in the cone dropped truncated.

From the statuary—true: truncated
        dunk urges, shamanistic who's-it-from,
    jugular turning. Turning. Twixt
    doors earned a shy Calliope, two. Of
a nation under the guise of how-to-breathe
    dogmatism. Black earth is fertile. Reign.
        In the mite house. In the poem lashed,
    typed up figuratively like a laconic
Rimbaud. Unblemished recollection; out
        like a lariat, dream purrs androgynes
        in facile jocking simple purges maybe.
    Undersettled. Unequal circus. Unequal
        circus. Unfortunately there of sperm
    from is a parliament there to blackouts through
    the towns
and there's sense in too much
        brightness. So defend you. Unlace the
    velvets and chamomile—unprotected.
A Japanese toy. In the pop suruplus [sic].
        In the unprotected. Unraveler. Until
        the suburbs and plastic halls. Blankets

over the eyebrows. Blankets. Blathering
      about history in a charmed state. Blended
out from that: so the anthem goes. So
the boy is perplexed. So the butcher
  clasps a riddled structures of powers-
      until-then. Until there's standards
of the home alone. In a decent substitution
for substitution. Urinous twins hooligans
      on the tile fraternizing
      Waco seam Texas
      oligarch stumble Mick's tics
  dotted
  expanse, no depth recurrence recommending
      obsequious strains, they are Welt, hell
but it's hygienic. V: value ascetic croutons.

Who
comprehends this world's goo glow? Who
eventually shoes? Struck by kindnesses
      that finally. Strung on a shoestring
      which. Stubbing the appliance with his
but spares. But speech is more left,
      the cult with his wife. Who now than
an aphrodisiac. But stately holds lives
with her father. Who only have nice
  things to toes. Stuck in the tit of
      the avant-garde
      singe capillary
      manifesto
      dark with whim

in the silk of of his
followers. Insisted that members
wear ravishment long skirts
and say of each other
the rarity of purchase.

Catastrophic
lamps. Major. Make of this toiletry
what you will. Makes but a symphony
museum-hung Pollock. Of whims in. Cave
drawings?
Continue gratuitous frond, plumbing.
Avenue. Younger than driving age. Your
cousin wasn't of the surviving variety.
Yours and mine.
Control.
Convinced that the colors were promises,
counterpointed strengths? Maxims: maybe
a chin-up bar will block
the light.
Crane: possible
in the gaslit meager, the rat cancer
corners what makes the stormhouse on
the
rocky cliffs of the East River. Cranky
blues. Crass. Criminal status: her fare
was much smoother than his. Young man
tick. Meditate the turntables. *Meine*
kleine Vogelgesang? Cross the thickets.
Crossing off his checkpoints. Crow gall

slow in the discovery. Crumbles the
                    samovar iron. Crustacean, mephitic screw
        tape mercurial in its sore confidence
        a
                    product of television synergy
        solemn
        there. Mercury slipped down the planes.
Merlot abuse
is it. These cards to pollsters.
        Milk and honey sounds like crystal veins
                    split. Culinary planes animate the room.
        Cultivate. Curl. Curse the doves: cursors
Pat Travers kickin' it with cameo—milk
                    replacements. Millet. Misguided by an
                    ear trained on
        Baptist speeches. Mister
        Mock-up
                    were visible in a European
        mollusk. Money was the window. Cut the
length of chord. Cybotron Dan in
        days of Hoang Ti. Monkey ailments: Quayle?
                    being the source of kings with
        flared
        nostrils? Pom-pom of your age.
Dances around the room in
                    monks retire into their computers.
                    More than seventy, his underwear. Defiant
        and
                    hungry as a damaged Lap. Delirious caviling.

Move around with a lyre that
surreptitious, stinks,
depresses.
Destiny San Francisco or Toledo; mucus
tattered.
Mundane.

Dull most likely. Dull. Dusted with
boho flavors. Ear wax. Ear in the
pathogens and darklights, battalions
in enterprise, occurring on record. Once
upon a time. One mirroring of most insidious
chaos. First bidder. The first of the
appliances begins: the faulty purse.
A fleur-de-lis pattern passed above
her face with five grains. The flapping
hands and feet
trodding. The flecks
fall back from the shoulders. One finds
to the next synergy, atop the eagle-crest
of Eros,
vengeful of the thrones. The
flowers arrive with mountains of Paterson.
A foot solid in astro turf
and the shattered specific that creates.
One wax. Earlier.
Early youth: easy said the poetry. Ecstatic.
Egrets for summaries
of all. Elevation
abuse terms thee thermally

and other
            pale pencils of nation. Dances no stately
    waltz, but rather trembles. Flip of the
            switch, and alas, Aladdin's a Hermes, ending
    those dreams of childhood. A forest
of buildings—a piss off like a face
    off
but the facts are elevation shoes.
            Elizabeth. Entitlement sworn, vac hilts
    bunk palatial. Errs Nike, thrifty Snaporilo
alive, pluck in the rhubarb, back. Reveals
            its indigenous code. One girl reportedly
            earmarked for their careerist bartender.

            All of which the tyrant comedy: productive
    but exiled, that which is used five thousand
years, moved his court to think.
            The plaid masks the coax. The play exploits
            his jiminy, just sits
    and waits.
    Promise? Property of the travel guides
            and teenage station, had been neglected
held market at angsts
that surface through the
    borrowing the past for so long.
            The polarities of contacts with the
    shit and sweat, the pop. The
porous resolution. Point to the future.
            All that's yummy.
    All mid-day bring

what we have not here. Grunt. Guided

by man these people. Loft luv pill.

Alonzo's paragraphs on the

pulp of reality and time. The

quirky

fuzz-tone-meets-marimba jam, we're the

treasures of trove. Also? Alternity.

Alternity. Among the missiles are positives

pullulate too fond

pump. Pupa deter

among the generation that eats. Purpose.

Pus. Pushed worse off scintillant reverie

these banished loves they belong in

back,

in the mind-altering stages of

youth. The Goths of some parodied adolescence.

Put plainly. Puts in boxes.

Quiet bold and an affront

she never needs me, sisterly

the caput swells filial.

Radicalize an invitation

from Comedy Central! Gumk. H had

rains when they dance. Rapunzel. Rasp.

At least.

    At others.

As if her.

    At the entranceway.

At times

                stumbling over his shoes. Athenian custom

                tolerated. Athenian. Athens. Attitudes

        adjust. Augustine's pride-of-breaches

            of tolls on the fringes of occurrence

      while the hieroglyph rages. Tomorrow

to place: autumn crowds: Avis's await

      the check. B's suns to pay sycamores

           of this wood, are arctic

    flowers. If

    one. If only fashionably defrocked the

plum crotch snickers. If their lutes

made ringing, barking bitch is textured
to its drag, the satchel
of books

past.

If wax. If custom. Igloos pile
on down the dirt highway to the school
—the wallpaper pressure. Illumine the
dark tower. B's suns: records. Or if imagery
combining food and sex is everywhere,
imbroglio anapesting Tonto. Too late
to pack the toboggan. Too stoned from
river and grass
that is called
Chun to the spirit Chang
Ti. Skating and dipping forth: imply
surface legion. Impregnation abuse is
it. In Union Square. Skirt the dark
corridors. Sky haircut. Slather. In
a big sweaty sleep. Slenderness down
the pipeline. Slick. Slipstream issues
that saint you or "mean," smart, yet.
Solipsistic.
Smell of eroding cousins. Smitten. Snack
pile. In bed to rise. In long. Too much.
Too. Too. Conversation. In fact. In
drunks of lines, freezing fact
in fancy
thought.
In good old Ischia.

In July no different.

    Vengeance was a toss to treaties then
the apostate's
snarl/sneeze.

      Snot that balked. Ballet
           torches stage the night. Torn. Toss
    the child into the air. Tournaments:
in June. In my blood dried,
    hysteric
        like a Christian
        on methane. Carnival.
        Banjos and Beatleisms. Be. Beat off
    those angels. Became twenty-ninth year
        a vagrant orphan, so buy one. So frightened
    for kin's welfare, and sued tourniquets
are salutary. Towel off! Abatement nothing
    for solace, in the mire
of heavenly predecessors
        tucks a cob in a golf shirt, meddling
    in the gyp and hue and true—somehow
rhyme?
So I'm limping. So I abate: so long!
        as it's still luminous. Affairs of pleasant
        state. In oneself: in praise of
    custody
last year.

    So piss. Cars-style blueprint of an
alternative rock song. Coos and caws
    bruised oranges in praise of

cultural land masses, may make like

El Debarge

at a porn convention. Becoming digitized.

Bed so plastic and suspicious in an

apartment. So that it, the rival, a tenuous

projector. Who were. Tracing a vector

outward from my mercenary

therein

the crux of. Believing I'm a lover.

Beneath the cathedrals of appliance.

Tracing the cube's paths on the floor.

Transgressions. Translated

into the

future. Translation: trash the latter

in sensitive moments like this it's

best to remain unwise, to get

near the appliance. So that democracy

better look elsewhere. Between religions

here. Beyond calm. The prophets? Biblical

in synchronicity. Trolley

on the licorice tycoon hosted Gene Wilder

Willie Wonka samba-toed *merci*-day enters

what wondering then of the causes of health.

In the ear.

In the hot stops.

Permitted here.

Building suspicious cottages of tears.

In the 13th year of his land, entropic

sins, the daunting *negatif* (we are hems).

Distances
measured in hype-years. Distracting.
Dithering off.
Dizzyingly, futzing
sanity, not bump the borders, the theory
being that. Do no matter. No noise of
walking. No, they smell Spam
in the Hamptons.
Other pasty faces lathering the windows.
No pop.
No rain fell for the emperor
Tching Tang, grain scarce. No yes. No.

See that nasty graffiti. Seeing there's
seven pianos, like a constable
in
the warp. Stares. Select output. Thereby
affecting the whole living lack of
courage
theretofore. And the mercantilism of
neo-logs cure. These are brake fluids
—her bowels contracted and the cautious
entry into the corridors of art. And
sex and logic are
criteria or criminals.
Sexual acts and the kitschy applauses
one stacks the nation's singular corpse.
And the other blokes from Hitchcock's
theatre
sexual preferences

in graphic,
an epic sphere. Her gait is dull. Her
         hand on shelves. These detail. Shadows
                  on the sands of Tranquility Phase Court
         where earlier had been the demonstration
against the Academy no one demeaned.
                  Shaker ethics—and the penis it creates.
                  And the Prince-esque nicotine and gravy.
         And then wimps
         out. And then your example
                  of the bricks born that devolve
         all baroque intentions
         into the
again.
                  These eddies of thought not contagious?
         These knees. These screens are image,
image is color. Of the earth. She's also
                  a bibliophile. She absently *Pisan Cantos*.
                  And they revel in the steamy sonics
         of the SB-jam. And thought: we wonder
                  greets
                  with an affected. She approaches
         from the poised tremulously. Her name
was Theresa. Herbie
         distant fleck but
         fleck of something
         to bargain with.
                  These statements are only provisional
         they say. Video with a these trysts

of banging heads that smother. These
    virginal submissions, slight groan.
    She desists. She entered.
         She intrudes. She
    intrudes. She lived—are really resubmissions.
They're collecting them of the "vaginal
    pastoral." And we wonder who wore the
         trinket in a book by
    Anon. As a cheap
    chain round his gat through the war.

As a person he was chaos for dips, intent
         on the merely puerile or charming. As
    are my hopes. As factual as arithmetic
curses for cities. As I'm doing now.

And by waking
    be them: a leather jellyfish
drying in
the sun. And cursors. And dissimilar.
         And forget about the whole rotten country,
         it's a skitterbug. And forgets
    managed
    to remain in the news: he felt. He knocks
         my lemonade. And he eventually married
    as many as 19, sleeps in spurs
knowledge, the shirt unbuttoned. The
    sloth. The snaps different quarters.
         Rather. Rather. Rather. Recall soulsonic
    cult women, and fathered

at least 10 of their tap.

        The stalker vase of poinsettias

    into hell. Erodes over

    the mound horizon.

        The force. Recordings. Records

    of stamping of ants. The stardust

        munchkins: he measured the length of

syntax

    of the tubes to children. And

in her eyeballs motion him to the buffet

    table where they entreat

    vengeance were

        a toss to treaties, redolent. Reefs.

    Draped with sinewy lashes. And in this

him to vote

for them. The strategy of

        the left-off:

    Reelect these boundaries.

    Relax.

    Remarkable—Renan. Report switch

    make tune for song

    twenty-six (that

        was) and 25 code. Retreat into the populated

pallid males of his making, his

    tomb

    is today in extras.

    Revelers

    in cities, this was in

    the twenty-fifth century.

He never

was able

to supply and demand of

the subaltern: the still unmixed

sweat and flux

of encouragements, idiolect's

temperaments. Mailed sleeve surface is

not enough. The sweet were

never so

low

produces the new musical category

and musk satellites quiver in the

mesh of these fancily

prettified selves,

such fear in the debutante heart. Rex's

zip,

spastic

future funk. And more. And

obtuse. And old school jams. And other

talk-songs: gun, boogie. Rice. Rickets

of prose. Rickets. Of curiosity. And

pile atop the mounds

of cuss

erecting, roar like

the laundry swirl

neat as on my typewriter.

He put, speaking their

customs in the dark. The traffic slick.

A street known for nothing but patterns.

    A strum placates that demand for the
exterior that is flesh. Plainly abutting
      against the sport, fresh from the former
           members,
    the ingredients
of crushed croutons.
Over dumb earth collapsing trellises.
          A tall lie in the nosebeak: the Huns.
          The obese sergeant. The good aunt's
    credit card
    pole vaulting that anger.
          Plaster ones with the credit cards.
    The op suplus [sic]. The other by the pony
depressed. The casts in hallways mustered
    a spittle of sea, of rain
        for them. Hit
        list. Forming a cube. Four weeks from now
    we'll be moving from this town.
Four weeks from now
rolling the dice
perfectly
      stalks. A
    tea: play it Hannah play it break it
        too it's there for that. Poco. Poco.
    Poco. Pococurantist insurance salesman.
Poetics. Point. Pole is stain, made of
    glass. A parson's sugar's
        healthy. Frangible and redolent

as timed

styles. Fraught with neologistic adverbs

stammering ha ha. From across the strike-populated

city, poop

rather duty free ball

point. Poor them promissory craw square

of the East German up. The parrot sequesters

itself among its late art works. Aspirin

treaty with the Dionysians only resolved

the patterns

of province. From itself,

mothers. A Rome have repeated

themselves into the suburban eclogue.

The peacocks, the clauses of health.

Porpoises, a vague sense at the

knees. From pucker their

lips and reside

in centurion, all

bourgeois, a vocal focus. A woman who

walks on waver—she is

stumped. Able

body: able in all offices. Abysses.

Acclimation. Ace and volley: interstitial

past. Frosts are not evaporated—ached.

Aestheticized wheat fields:

total alas

the scream now.

The naturalness of melting

newspapers: roi and the girl. It's gone.

A random number generator
with a skin for drips, drabs
rendered strange in that modern
            new eternity. The new from Mystic.
Palatable two-toned democracy
in subway.
Palm ears! Paradox. Parallelograms
            mustering deciduous Yorker. The newer
            nations,
            the others I won't speak. For
the sake of pulp. For three hours and
            twenty-five cents, dissever out of the
limelight what is. So sleek
you're humbled just to be near it. A select series
for years, no waters, the next
            Christmas: apathetic tastes. Arbors in
Pakistan. Parallelograms. Parking lots,
all the elevators,
the next time the fashion
maneuvers. The night like a stippled…
            jocks straps from the
roller derby graduates. A sined
intestine.
A slight gust. A sonnet's worth of
Sodom, passivity' s thoughtless
entrails.
            Patterns periphery of movement noise
now would be fantastic. A soporific
governor with a half-decade of inevitability.

Penguins alas. Perjurous whose came.

For you: a daughter a pool a home. A
stillness from the egg-
haloed expanse.

A stole in pomegranate Sunday's
familial happenstance. Forcing some ex-believers
to vocal chords,
crisp the alley of the
regal, the cops
go into seclusion.

Foresight feed. Foresight feed. Forgotten
as dollar: ha' penny blank stare.
Pettinghill. Pile the
logs keep it growing. Pizz Time.
These two tablets snitch.

Futurity combines in oak nucleus.

Don't mind
the eye—a burst carton.

Of course.
Of course.
Of grainy state. Of abject
discourses, a heaven moving the sun and
stars: *que vos vers exprin'ient vos intentions.*
Stopped a thousand panicking in the
aisle seats. The
severed
citizenship. Of simpering child cordoning
of devices of our control—crypt in

                    the pottage of the soul
            provides this
            naturally—a cube that will the cows,
                        cur that rises
                        and the roosters sue.
        The dark embouchure out your window.
    Don't parade in disaster. Don't pick
            on birth, midnite vultures
    is a stunning
            of our social ranking. The England.
    Drapes. Dressed in slipping denim. Droth.
            Drummed from their customs
    of its borders
                        like concrete planes. The fins of a
            gulf. The firs are the property of
    Mrs.
    A docile roars.
                        Oh.
                        Oh.
                        On the nails: my talents to task
                        and necks stuffed in shirts. Drunk.
            The lettering berries. A ghost from
                    Fostex Capital Five and
            tasting well.
            Especially. *Et que la musique conforme*
    YAO CHUN YU KAO-YAO abundance. Eternal
            drum suspended. Perimeter was eroding;
                    the freak show begins: the garish marry
            the House of David. One hears, even through

the wide angle, in parish
but thrum in
the cake. The heroic tantrum butt-plugs
the holes with facts. One must it's
insidious. Ever the stentorian dictator.
Every ass is a bouncing savannah. Every
time. Exacerbating rare: be a guerrilla
in that quarter. One codes in a recital
of thirties ditties—gasp escapes in
the light of the Frigidaire patent.
The glassy eyeball peeps previous cinematic
composites, but: a hand glides freely
between boughs. A hustling Curtis Mayfield-esque
hip-hop track—did you fall for
the fleeting gap, by clavinet and horn
blasts? In the starlog
misfit through
the hale in the certainty. The Globe
Theatre. The teachings were gnome
knows hah furious double-readings
ham from blister-
eye. The granules that he was the lamb. One.
Only greets annihilation.
Only. Or a dyslexic combine that master
their film noir image, and dissemble
among the data chunks.
Legitimate hole in one:
the husband crowds the fractures out
or creates it. Or facticity's blameless
e-mails. Or let's say chromatic enactment.

273

Cheered on by crowd
      noises, and driven by
the stun-gun burp
            of an 808 bass comedies
of laughing, at branches.
      Set up the stage
and taught barter. Yodels strafe
      the
                  urging. You're a version of Styx. You've
                  seen those: you drum. Qi wants. Child-like
the merlot. Marjinal [sic] Hesperides
that don't clock works making Mickey
      crazy Minnie second = airy in the aleph
                  beta junta clan—marvel at them. Matrimony.
      You're suddenly skateboarding down electric
dream effigies of
                  scattered eyeshot
                  elations.
            Consider their sweats. Consideration. Consistent.
Each values enflames thee! Detonate
                  the appliance that. Development is easy
      of
                  a tusk. Dial 1 for celebrity, but then
      wend the way to the john. Dials x on
its currency—my back is already
      sprained. Telephoned thirty-seven times,
                  my books are little sluts. My children
      aren't right. My no-particular-order. Diamonds
reeling.

Did I mention Toulouse Lautrec?
Did the seagull barter with the guy's night sky. My
hips
are scarred. My journey to the Orkneys
fomented disinterest.

Verbalize alley
of finite bunting. So
the collectibles continue. So the Italian
wind in which
crying begins
to twiddles its thumbs. So the sanitarium
applauses. So be noticed. Incense
the borders in the other
apartments. Street is none incidental. Indeed not
easily,
perfectly alive grunting happily,
some torturers stranded, mustered manner.

Blood strikes in hot freshets the woo
with its contingencies. Spheroid and
elastic. Spice deduces ethnicity to
just say "good-bye." It's into the
light. We had a game of hearts, a june
bug. It's claustrophob-osophy
on Broadway.
It's quantum forage salad grunge professes
obliquity, growth, serum ebbitude tangerine,
"*preme*" brand slamming, totemicity alights, a
branches

twenty-finger poesie custom, beard apple neon

assing ossification, eyelid droop crowded. It's

friction.

It's—we looked at her weary traveler.

Bludgeon the eyes of the "in." It's

no longer in cornea class, sluices bureaucrat.

Blue moons. Blunt hammer in masses, fourth

mathematics collated angst-ridden muscles

trip cafe squadrons

all in black. Bollingen.

And her words. We pout; we've eaten

the syllabus. It's political. It's puddles

of sweat. It's the frightened math of

all children wrestling with the

sandman. It's banefully X's loving bail floaters

cold now—do kvetching—cautionary opt

hurt-riddled boat passing, clothes primitive,

quasi-gallic. Them so often by the poolside.

Wear out with EC border rubble

coo coo ear, warmth eternity, you Kelly

India carpet gastronomy strategic militia rodent

recovery on ship entry pathfinder

Pandora aghast. Then, that you set out

for the wide planes of flavoring sycophants

jellyings monotones churches blitz huh

or Diderot returns mundane return refrain

return. Untrained Syndicalist

novel fiction

then one appreciates

borders. It's bollocks

pisser somanex delicious rout. Bologna.
And it's rent-controlled. It's just a ruse.

That's before it segues into a
moody outro. That-be.
The album presents
a bodacious now-I-will-confuse-myself
with regrets. Now shackled. Does that
mean more time within narrative? Uncle
Lee said: 26. 35. A blend of electro-shock
heats.
Don't accuse me
of ill-meant cacophony. Don't douse
your blemish in
the mink of a stole.
Stopped. The bad-boy rap covering a
middle-class vacancy. The blending,
the burgeoning
century's customs grimace
down
the two
citizens
have strung on the O of a real good ethnic
meal.
Of
of light. A colonialism subsuming in
lampposts lights. The clinical walls
of the intoxicated institution:
I don't want to bargain with the haddock.

Exacerbating rare codes in a recital
            of thirties adjustments in the concentration
        level that is our capital. Or not even.
Or noticed. Or sheets of wallpaper divvy
        (ever thought of that) filled by crimsons.

Fiction hocks
        its prognostications.
For hurry for shame
        out of Rolodex, fidgeting the
        Star Trek hymnal.
Coldly over the
        shoulder, ugly as retinal
        stuff. A Mexico masculine hay side hoodoo.
A parish, first rue stampede, pus
        fission,
                fission whelming in the cranium. Fist.
                Flags in the nostrils. Flecks mesmerized
        off those faces. Fleshed out with arena-rock
                guitar blasts flicking the insane, where
        one greets
        the parsing witness. The
kids had to be retrained. The switch.
        Flicks a good-natured western libertarianism?
Moon rose behind the Mesh of
        the Ancients. Full of herself. Full.
G
        —got no satisfaction. Communes. Post-op.
                Practices of the tropes dump—Afrika
        Bambaataa and cameo. After that. After

the but-unstifled
    preoccupied with the song
    that begins: presaging gathers. Gesticulating.
Get real paid, opens with a deterrence.
        Pretty and cheap. Prices rising, so that
        into the parodying shoots
delicious
solid inky boisenbery philosophies.
        The penis is 1760, Tching Tang opened
the copper mine, made discs
        what sounds like Alan Parsons
with square holes in their middles
        being dry-humped by Karlheinz Stockhausen.
    Off the side, gave these to
the people
wherewith they might buy grain, where
        there was gin-wracked cousin—glanced
        free of affectation. Gloucestering!

And so we chatted.
And that only
    he had the right to procreate. And that
a society of mirrors. Then, that curdled
        ovoid. Then younger
        timorous verity, it to
    him. He thought Madonna was [put] in
        the world, says what
not we touched
each others' arms in the own. There
      are nuggets in my sox

waiting to explode
into him. He trails. He wakes to
        the sound of the water tap; he's licked
a lot of them
    not tigers. There,
still restaurant.
        Satellites of the political
        times don't thanks me baby. There is
a "us" in his interstitial
    moments of mimesis
—he's recently confessed to
becoming a hippie; heat sudden, these
clamness winks. Suffering long to taste
    that European democracy or ego. Saw
        what star is at solstice, saw what heat
    sudden these clamness heavenly
ensconced in star, marks mid the class
        that produced summer you. Says Breault.
        Says he likes this—says singer Sheridan Stewart.
There's hardly any use for
    the conference on Wichita.
    And the herb teas
    have amassed beneath the steps—is
the now urging. "Hermann Droth,"
    she said. She stands in the braille
day, in the city of the dark, with
feelings
never so smart. She drowning yourself
    in Diet Pepsi over that legitimate

attempt at fright. This—how's that?

Another fence.

Antipasto.

Anyone. Anza

crucifix—this book doesn't howl with
intelligence. Where the Pynchon is.
Homely. Honest dyslexic synthetic burst,
Margarita takes me by the telephone
of plenty hence. Horace declaimed
to a rapt audience
this contingency. This
cotton—this of hormonal
horse around the free market rioters.
Hostile. How about? And defecates. Sheep
shorn wins and polished three villages
aid diorama covering Giacometti—
how did they get there? How easy. How
man can Genet, no digital a fraught
chafe, the bit, not succumb its miracle.
How many forenoons—fatal habit of smoking
while singing. This freedom
gimme tlooth serum lickety
corrodes. This glass
of sherry swerves into
textualities. This is a boat
long writes tradition
aglow, Peter stanching f-verb
calisthenics. A blistering performance.

Gore presumed innocent
　　　　　　　until slightly guilty.

This is a cloud-in, feel Nietzschean!
　　　　　　　My mother would ardently nationalist,
　　　　but wavering the sequels suspending,
are in the shape of Elvis Presley.
　　　　　　　　This is a private
　　　　　　　　fasceme. This is a
　　　　　　　　torment. This joint practicing the way:
how to be in (Hsin).
　　　I'm entrusted
 to myself. I'm game, nothing compared
　　　　to the eyebags of wharf rats, are the
shrieks. Sign the live, Brasilia signs
　　　　of the elopement. Sills. Simply confine.
　　　　　　　　Simply punishing. Simultaneous way.
　　　Sin: paste here. This paragraph fell
from a dilettante. Sin the guidebook.
　　　　　　　This stroke is
　　　　　　　a privilege and don't
　　　　　　　you forget it. Property of cramps. Are
　　　for that—I've taxed full happenstance,
　　　　that.
This wallowing is merely tiring, but they poor.

I think polyphony
　　　　　　　metered fallacy's tits. Since they
　　　don't read. Sing. As organizers of change.
To this, a semi-colon

enhances a perception
    of this
    sink, in the decapitated dawn
        of nothing
        but one-sided exchange, I
    think to my benefit. I blackens the
teeth. As water. As. Asparagus. Emergence,
           Sister Montgomery with that Mark McGwire
           swing. Sue chew Providence,
    I think. I
    wouldn't say I cried, I'm
waving a glass
        of scotch. I: idea pets migrate. Tolls
    on the assay.

At a loss the television
whining. As to pay
    in earth of five
    colours, pheasant plumes from
        of mountains
into the ground of never-
reach-the-earth with
    comfort, the dominating
           teen spawns sox. Vitreous eyes the train
           entering the mute. Vocal in local a
    leveler's symptomatics. Some cessation.
Is all it finally from Algeria, can't
    instrumentation the geriatric speedometer
make sense
    of all those patterning pixel rot retire

a diet

porta-calls?

Whether

he cups two breasts with two hands or

merely critical conscience, that thrives

when it likes. But demonstrates,

which always begins the calisthenics

of relationships—but I'm free. But

I feel claustrophobic. Which are

—am dribbling on my skirt. But let's

continue with part of the

room. Streamline

the lemonade

till the gallon runs out. But my credit

—but my kiwi to become the

steps. Which

begins just when you need it. One of

Vernon's wives. Knees which is

convenient;

which one? Socks dripped

with sweat—but not the which should

fit like a leather jacket. Whistle.

Who approaches across the horizon, striking

thee ghostly? Who can shrink argued that being

the

Son of a God

attitude. But notify that pomp. But sincere. Aground.

Strip the landscape. Strip-search the

Speedo? Strongman in bullet-ridden

grave,

    him total control over the sex lives.

        Say this ain't a decent country.

My mind's not

    right. My mind is clear

as a rubber sunset

    for the stolen hat? Did you

fall my

privacy? My smiles are dependent

    on my lips. My song's night right, my

song's bright light. Narcissist. Narcoleptic

    cool Oz. Natural. Needy.

        Nerves burst in the eyes receiving.

As if stranded

        on a wind-swept promontory coke-addled

—is attractive. Is being held by a

    girl who's full of tyrannous adventure.

Is clear. Is soft and supple. Series

of sorority-Paleothic, admiring

    of the clowns, young teenagers.

        Some flew toward America: rings of division.

Something most of his

followers grew

to accept without question. Somewhere

        Pissarro wept in blindness, tethered.

        Is it the retention, that it? Is the

god ghosting the four corners of who

    kissed the carcinogenic sky with the

promiscuousness of chase, finding
the lines are even
in a poem, not sex?
    Is in couplets
    vision retracts its hand and the
    penis it creates, porcelain
    values? Are many Koreans at the zoo?
    Above my secret ladder, the field.
    No dialectic amenity
        could connect those dots: pride and penury.

Have been under-direct. Haven't been
    so chance. The royalty insistence of
a sky chugging champagne. The rude insistence:
    still with myself, for several years.
                Since achieving diabetes. Hazards
    are in rule
    that men bar. And a solid
addition. And after all enveloped. And
                on the soaps,
                hides the shy. The sanitary
                commitment to wiping out operas. And
    bed. And billowing reminders: the fake igloos with
sweat.

Celibacy tournaments. Celibacy.
    Chamomile. Chance ground down
toadstools, very offed: the detective
    levels
    a tremor valence.

Facilitating the nerves and their
    titillated
    room. The ice is delivered
coldly
of god—or this gallery wings a shout.
                Or. Orgones. Otherwise. Our stands can
    be so difficult, fanatically
pastiched
of rodent fashion. Lacks a dictionary.
              Fax me images of mittens. Feeling rather
              nasty in his roses, abed.
    Bleached out faces mix in gloom
presentiment, parade of hair
    —feint. Alternatively. The people's
    "If you wd/ grain the silos" were of the
ship to the matriculating dolphin
to
    torment content. Again struck. Again.

Alas party emptied 7 years of sterility
              der im baluba das Gewitter gemacht hat
    prayed on the mountain, good. Rather
avoided the attention.
    Hair-cut close
    to the skin, or a dancer
    enters, out of control. Speech. Rather
           nod, the recorder is on (is one). The
    refractory, long. Hampered by no
nunnery business, whims of its appliance. The
          responsible? The rhythm of

off. Rather

        grind it. Rather than comply with

    the purchase

    is

    furs. Hand

set his scholars to the stroke's gold.

        Inquire: and letters—and loss of promise.

    Saddling the pomegranate ecliptic with

    baroque masturbation.

Safire or was good

    for labor day. Rousseau? Said chin

women weren't given a proper weekend.

    The white walls of the

chapel. The whole

        list. The women of sox. Their drive-bys.

    Value in the Bible. He said. He shivers.

To the election. And sly melodic seductions.

        Their drive-bys. Their Vatheks their

      Vatheks, mustarding over the desert

    tray. Then disap… he taught that all

      the women in the world

    peered

    among the rain-drenched passengers.

Then he falls. I remember a dance

    outfit, and snares. And so as the butt

      of

      on

      the head of a skin? How

      sensational to hunger

jungle-disiac, Uma stands glu, storied
cuss. Since vacated by rabid Jesuits.
    As if she were strung out. A young Pyrrhic
            dangling, swift, Heracleitian fashion,
        Gary, though it may not persist.
Thoughtless in an encomium here-yes-here
                in new I-don't-claim-to-have-read-it.
                I don't claim, cableman, she has braid.
To
                have troubles strung around her
        shoulder, too cost owing to mescaline.
We're all in here, much or too, thus.
            Time... too dull for thumbs.

    Wrote an herbal fifteen,
                tigers made signs out of bird tracks
        contrived the making of bricks
and exaltation. Cannabis lector!
    tints return the landscape to its keepers
            of fratricide. Lured safely. M: certain
        salubriousness (salacity). That
was whispered from across,
            working the waters. That way one slumbers
                in hypertext burritos.
The silk worms
    mad as Ancient Greece on robes
            as like the sun and rain. You taught
    men
        to break a burnt donkey. Made some
wonderful. Magniloquent parses shelving

that which is derisive of laughing
        childish fables
        in corrupt stables
        in morse—card sharks.

Sturm bake heart strum,
        prayer gains in twilight's suspect
skeins, loose terminal infractions, a
        fickle agon
        that does not cut the
                air. Lager landscapes, a bolus
        of them. But the beauty who pales in
the gaslight.

Who would hum but knows
                the words? Who would,
        of this urban avenue, has the
        necessity one feels to have to make
                beneath drizzles of light, seek protected
        cellophane
        drop kick? Sublimity
takes on many moldy customs to forge
        the hack. Such a Rubrik pounced on westering
                borders. But above:
        my sister's largesse. Glockensmile clowning
is also a mastery. But
                lass. Last time.
                Lathers be around to
                play with the coda
                trails

off into singers. But the crush day
    fares. Such fear in the debutante heart.
  Such magnanimity. Up in fumigous, such
with its crutches, ghostly unvamped
  in the memorial drive. Such with its crutches
    ghostly unvamped in the memorial drive.
  Suffer invisible suggestive—and scream
of acrobatics. But forever
    sulk talents
    are promising for this. Summon a sort
    of the dull (from this perspective)
  the end of the religiosity in the communion
    sure-as-show. Sure. Take me! elaborate
  customs. Christian foam. Laughs unceremoniously
in the paradox of class,
  takes the foreign
  entrepreneur, takes watches
    from the eyes of coverlets—talks to his room.
  Who's Mae when you play
your game "The Three Stooges," who's Harry?
    Often I am returned
    to street
    facades
  are brighter for them. But are the teetering.

Tang not stinting of praise: taught
    the field where the dandelion
  roars. Fifties bound them to soporific
bleats. Of chords: taught men to
  the hand-wringing

no outline that is far-fetched, in the
history-sentence.
Leader of waters.
Leaks whom Oren tried to pick up in
Los Angeles—they know still where
the high, the vibrator
leather faced knee-jerks are on the
television. Leaving was not done easily.

Hole In One Sonnet
after Thomas Gray

Stigma 2001: "A New Hope"

2001 has seen th exaustion of everything. Most importnt: th exaustion of creativity.

We hav gotn too clevr. It's time to dum down a bit, relax and let th riting on th wal speak for US.

Th previus jenrations hav had ther chance to turn windo-dresng (th spectacl, th social) into revlatry moments, but hav faild. Th cause: th persnl signatur.

Th signatur has lead/led to th lording of specialized nolej ---- about politics, about filosofy, about poetic form ---- over th readr. This has stonewalled th posbility of a new readrship for poetry, and so must stop.

Today, a tecnlojicl storm is rajing, th result of wich wil be th ultmat democratization of poetry.

Therfor, we advocate/advocat th foloing radicl actions in th creation of poems:

1.1 Authr and publishr shal be th same persn, but wil not expend any cost in printng or distribution. Rathr, publishr shal oprate as parasite, and poems shal be created with a mind to extant forms of publishng that hav activ distribution processes in place ---- th internet, th bookstor, th mail ordr catlog. Specialty markets shal be avoidd, as wel as th negativ econmy of th poet/publisher.

2.2 As a corolry to principl 1.1, al poems shal be ritn with a mind to internet publication (even if they not apear ther), since it is th one cost-fre method of distribution availbl, and it is social. "Involvd" poems, not to mention "life works," ar unacceptbl. Al poems must take advantaj of th moment, and ar not constructd for posterity or th used book trade. Th plug may be puld any day on cultur; th poem must be prepared.

3.3 No text in a poem shal be "orijnl"; only th use of FOUND TEXTS shal be permitd. These texts can be editd----collaged, erased, reversd----but nothing stemng from th inr sanctm of th author's memry and sentmnts is acceptbl.

4.4 As a corolry to principl 3.3, only FOUND IMAGES shal be permitd. As for wethr orijnl imajs by th author's hand----childhood drawngs, doodls skechd out during half-concius moments at th ofice----qualify as "found" is a matr of particulr instnce. Certnly no drawngs intendd specificly for th work shal be permitd; only intentionl manipulations ((digitizations, filtrs, juxtapositions)).

5.5 In dijitl works, we disuade th use of "sound" unless it is directly linkd to th action of th poem. Loops ar to be avoidd at al costs, as ar clipngs from classicl symfnis and anything that detracts from concentration on th intrface. Of corse, only FOUND SOUND is permitd----ripd from CDs, mp3s, and th city streets----no orijnl "scors." (In print works, we disuade th use of special papers, special bindngs, and champion only those typs of materials that reflect th specificity of th production jenre----se next point.)

6.6 Litry jenres----th fable, th lyric, th epic----shal be replaced by th jenres of infrmation distribution----th newspaper, th e-comerce site, th chat room----or games----th puzl, th arcade game, role-playng games.

7.7 No abstractions ar permitd----"no ideas but in things," but also no incoate conceptul paradigms, no constructivist formalisms, no scolastic digressions or hairsplitting over termnolojy. Al words shal be in color.

8.8 As a corolry to principl 7.7 NO WORKS ABOUT "WRITING" and NO WORKS ABOUT DIGITAL TECHNOLOGY ar permitd. These typs of ritings ar realy translations, undr th gise of disclosur, of th ego into new forms. Th "esthetics of infrmation" is just a slik atemt to translate th sublimity of th cathedral to th computer screen; distnce between vewr and object must be abolishd.

9.9 [Put yr own dogma here. But use it, watevr it is. That's wy this is fun.]

10.10 Th author's name shal not apear on th work. Therfor, we advocate/advocat th use of made up names, especialy those that resembl corprations (such as "YOUNG-HAE CHANG HEAVY INDUSTRIES"), anmls ("Panda Ber"), or caractrs from works of sience fiction ("Roy Batty").

Th supreme goal is to force th truth out of my words and imajs----wich is to say, th INTERFACE. We swer to do so by al th means availbl and at th cost of any good taste and any esthetic considrations.

Synd,
"Curius" Jorj Wunsch
Dorothy Aschenback "Imagiste"
Jean "Democracy Bulevard" Hancoque

Atelos was founded in 1995 as a project of Hip's Road and is devoted to publishing, under the sign of poetry, writing that challenges the conventional definitions of poetry, since such definitions have tended to isolate poetry from intellectual life, arrest its development, and curtail its impact.

All the works published as part of the Atelos project are commissioned specifically for it, and each is involved in some way with crossing traditional genre boundaries, including for example, those that would separate theory from practice, poetry from prose, essay from drama, the visual image from the verbal, the literary from the non-literary, and so forth.

The Atelos project when complete will consist of 50 volumes.

The project directors and editors are Lyn Hejinian and Travis Ortiz. The director for text production and design is Travis Ortiz; the director for cover production and design is Ree Katrak.

Atelos (current volumes):

Distributed by:

Small Press Distribution
1341 Seventh Street
Berkeley, California
        94710-1403

Atelos
P. O. Box 5814
Berkeley, California
        94705-0814

to order from SPD call 510-524-1668 or toll-free 800-869-7553
fax orders to: 510-524-0852
order via e-mail: orders@spdbooks.org
order online: www.spdbooks.org

Fashionable Noise: On Digital Poetics
was printed in an edition of 1,000 copies
at Thomson-Shore, Inc.
The cover was printed at Southeastern Printing.
Text design and typesetting by Travis Ortiz.
Cover design by Ree Katrak.